Reading Their World

The Young Adult Novel in the Classroom

Second Edition

Edited by

Virginia R. Monseau and Gary M. Salvner

Boynton/Cook Publishers
HEINEMANN
Portsmouth, NH

Boynton/Cook Publishers, Inc.
A subsidiary of Reed Elsevier Inc.
361 Hanover Street
Portsmouth, NH 03801–3912
www.boyntoncook.com

Offices and agents throughout the world

Library of Congress Cataloging-in-Publication Data
Reading their world : the young adult novel in the classroom / edited by Virginia R.
Monseau and Gary M. Salvner.—2nd ed.
    p.   cm.
    Includes bibliographical references.
    ISBN 0-86709-473-7 (acid-free paper)
    1. Young adult fiction, American—Study and teaching (Secondary). 2. Young adult
fiction, English—Study and teaching (Secondary). 3. Young adult fiction—History and
criticism—Theory, etc. 4. Young adults—Books and reading. 5. Youth in literature.
    I. Monseau, Virginia R., 1941–   . II. Salvner, Gary M.

PS42 .R4 2000
813.009'00071'273—dc21
                                           00-033669

Editor: Lisa Luedeke
Production: Vicki Kasabian
Technology Project Manager: Dan Breslin and Eyeon Interactive
Cover design: Catherine Hawkes/Cat and Mouse
Manufacturing: Deanna Richardson

Printed in the United States of America on acid-free paper
05 04 03 02 01 00 RRD 1 2 3 4 5 6

Contents

Acknowledgments

We are grateful to the Youngstown State University Research Council for its support of this project and to the many students, teachers, and colleagues who have offered encouragement and valuable suggestions along the way. We also thank our research assistant, Mary Beth Bugno, for her diligent work and our editor, Lisa Luedeke, for her willingness to listen to our ideas and her efforts to make them a reality. Thanks, finally, to our contributors, whose hard work made this collection possible and whose enthusiasm made it a joy.

Preface to the Second Edition

In the years since publication of the first edition of *Reading Their World*, English teachers have been challenged by a multitude of new educational reform initiatives, including calls for state-mandated curricula, the institution of large-scale proficiency testing, the development of nationally normed tests to assess teacher competence, and the controversial call for standards in the teaching of English language arts. In one sense, these developments might be seen as threats to the use of young adult literature in secondary classrooms, suggesting as they do a minimalist view of English as a set of subskills best addressed in the classroom with "approved" reading lists and narrow views of reading and literature.

While these developments do, indeed, challenge English teachers' freedom to make professional decisions based upon a reasoned assessment of students and environment, we, as editors of this book, also choose to believe that they present teachers with new opportunities for teaching. In the matter of using young adult literature in secondary English classes, for example, which is the practice this text seeks to promote, teachers faced with accountability measures are aided by the well-established fact that adolescents connect with literature that addresses them directly by presenting them with characters and situations based on their own experience. What better rationale is there for giving students books they will read and delight in than the mandate that we make them into more skilled and insightful readers?

Fortunately, the field of young adult literature has continued to flourish since the initial publication of *Reading Their World*. As a result, in this second edition, readers will find revised essays alluding to exciting new works as well as wholly new ones that expand the discussion of our book's subtitle, *The Young Adult Novel in the Classroom*.

At the center of this second edition is our continuing belief that teachers who "read the world" of young adults—both by attending to their interests as readers and by exploring books that address the experiences of the young—will, indeed, teach their students well, according to both the narrow "accountability" standard of making them good readers and the more lasting goal of introducing them to the transforming power of literature.

Introduction

This book was born of our desire to provide students, teachers, and all interested readers with a collection of essays that address issues of selection, pedagogy, and worth of the young adult novel. Such a book is needed, we feel, not only because the genre is receiving increasing attention among both adolescents and publishers but also because young adult novels have come of age and proven themselves to be literature of quality.

While early novels for young readers tended to be excessively moralistic, rigidly formulaic, or both, today's books for and about young people, taken together, display the same elements of all masterfully crafted works of fiction: complex main characters who seek to resolve conflicts of tremendous consequence to themselves and the world; vividly drawn minor characters who not only create texture in the works they inhabit but also advance the action of those stories and serve as meaningful foils and allies for the protagonists; vivid settings, both real and imaginary; plots that hold the reader to the story through deft pacing, skillful use of suspense, and the use of flashbacks and other manipulations of time sequence; and, most recently, experimentation with various points of view from which the stories are told. Above all, as Ted Hipple notes in his essay in this book, young adult novels have come of age through their treatment of themes that matter not just to teens struggling with adolescence but to all of us—the quest for justice; the savagery of war and hatred; and the struggles for love, acceptance, and understanding, to name a few. Young adult novels have come of age because they have demonstrated the same skillful craftsmanship employed in all good literature and because they have translated to the world of the young adult the same conflicts and issues with which all humans struggle.

Unfortunately, despite the quality of many young adult books, their acceptance in classrooms has remained limited, partly because of misconceptions about the genre and partly because of uncertainty about how such works fit into the prescribed curriculum. How, for example, can young adult novels be incorporated into a historical survey course? What might be their role in a thematic approach to literature study? How can such novels be used to teach the literary elements? To answer these questions, teachers must come to know student readers better, as our title reminds us, by "reading their world," for only through entering the world of young adult readers will we know how to encourage and direct their reading, and only through reading those works that captivate and move young adults will we be fully able to understand and appreciate them as readers. A primary purpose of this book, then, is to enter the world of young adult readers through a literary form they know well, the modern young adult novel.

Another purpose of this book is to encourage the reading of young adult novels as a way of extending our own experiences with literature. Reading their world, after all, is also a means of reading our own, for we inhabit the same places, encounter similar struggles, and respond with similar emotions. As adult readers, we reencounter in young adult novels the baffling and oftentimes painful experiences of adolescence, and we become better readers as a result.

Our concern for the experiences of both adolescent and adult readers has led us to the work of Louise Rosenblatt, who has helped many readers understand better the nature of the literary transaction. Rosenblatt uses a musical metaphor for the act of reading literature: "The reader performs the poem or novel, as the violinist performs the sonata. But the instrument on which the reader plays, and from which he evokes the work, is—himself" (1988, 279). This metaphor reminds us that readers create the "music" of texts as they perform them and that the harmonies of reading come from placing the experience of a book alongside the experience of the reader. To adolescents, the advantage of young adult novels is that these books harmonize well with the experiences they have had in their young lives. As a result, instead of merely learning about the literature they read in school, as so often happens when they analyze literary classics, students become involved in the literature as a result of the connections they make between their experience and the text.

This book, then, invites us as readers and teachers of literature to take a closer look at the reading worlds of both our students and ourselves and at what we are doing in our classrooms when we read and study literature. Learning theory tells us that we best acquire new knowledge by relating it to what we already know. Do we give our students this opportunity in the literature class, or do we consistently present them with literary works to which they have no connection described in language that they find difficult to understand? Because young adult novels are written in straightforward language that reflects the adolescent world, they can become the means through which young adult readers gain new knowledge of themselves and others. But the best novels don't stop there. Through skillful writing and a keen awareness of the human condition, the authors of these works leave us with universal questions to ponder about our very existence.

To facilitate reading and to provide a logical structure, we have divided the book into three sections. In Part 1, "Reading the Young Adult Novel," Ted Hipple discusses the universality of young adult books, exploring the thematic significance of various young adult novels. In her discussion of young adult novels and the classics, Leila Christenbury demonstrates the important connection between the two, while John Moore gives teachers some valuable approaches to interpreting young adult fiction.

In Part II, "Writing the Young Adult Novel," Sue Ellen Bridgers, Will Hobbs, and M. E. Kerr, contemporary authors of young adult books, discuss young people and their literature, focusing on their own processes of writing and speculating on the needs and interests of young adult readers. Part III, "Teaching the Young Adult Novel," takes a look at various issues surrounding the genre and suggests innovative, provocative ways of incorporating this literature into the curriculum. Virginia Monseau illustrates ways in which the literature classroom can become a community of readers, encouraging student engagement and response, while Gary Salvner discusses the use of young adult novels in the traditionally structured literature curriculum. Lois Stover explores the world of diversity in young adult novels, providing sound reasons for their inclusion in the English curriculum, and Pam Cole and Patricia Kelly discuss the issue of gender in young adult books, focusing specifically on same-gender and cross-gender relationships. Chris Crowe gives us an informative look at the young adult sports novel, while Alan Teasley and Ann Wilder show us how to connect the YA novel with television in our curriculum. In the final essay, Gloria Pipkin examines censorship as it relates to young adult novels, providing a historical perspective while at the same time suggesting strategies for dealing with censorship problems.

We hope this book will demonstrate that reading the adolescent's world can result in an enriching and enlightening literary journey, whether we walk the path for the first time or retrace footprints made long ago.

Work Cited

Rosenblatt, Louise M. 1988. *Literature as Exploration*, 3d ed. New York: Modern Language Association.

1

With Themes for All
The Universality of the Young Adult Novel

TED HIPPLE

Literature captivates its readers in various ways. With many novels it is the story we remember. Our need to know what will happen next in the events Dickens weaves together in his *Tale of Two Cities* (1906) keeps us turning over the pages long after we should have been turning off the bed lamp. In other works characters loom significant and become as known to us as family and friends. Few readers of Twain's *Adventures of Huckleberry Finn* (1948) will forget central figures like Huck or Jim or even lesser ones like Pap or the duke and the king. Setting, too, can be an important element in our enjoyment of literature. Egdon Heath so clearly plays a role in Hardy's *Return of the Native* (1912) that it might well be listed in the dramatis personae of any staged version of that magnificent novel.

The foregoing paragraph could just as easily have contained young adult novels as illustrations of its points. Cynthia Grant's *Shadow Man* (1992) features a death on its opening pages, then explores that tragedy from a variety of viewpoints, all of them urging the reader onward, page after page. Authors of young adult novels also shape characters whom we love or hate or pity but absolutely never forget. In Robert Cormier's *Chocolate War* (1974) both Archie and Brother Leon lodge themselves in our memories, even though we squirm a bit in terror at the recollection of their seemingly innate evil. And what of the setting in Sue Ellen Bridgers' *All Together Now* (1979), the small North Carolina town that rises up as a single entity to protect the retarded Dwayne and prevent his being sent to a mental institution?

Yet possibly what most makes literature *literature*, what moves it from words on a page that we read to that which we return to again and again, is theme, the underlying philosophy embodied in the work, the view of the human condition it of-

1

fers. Even in classic novels like those just mentioned, the themes are as forceful as are their stories, characters, or settings. Dickens painted vivid portraits of class struggles on both sides of the English Channel between those with money and those without it. Twain's repeated explorations of good and evil, with Huck Finn usually astraddle them, give us pause for our own thoughts and make us rise out of our seats in triumphant joy when Huck refuses to turn Jim in. Though set in the most appropriate of places, the harsh and unforgiving Egdon Heath, Hardy's novel is really about humankind's minimal chances against a malevolent fate.

So also with young adult literature: it must be read with attention, not simply to its story lines, characters, or settings but also and very importantly to its themes. Those less familiar with young adult literature tend sometimes to believe that its thematic treatments are slight or superficial—"teenage," if you will. They are not. Like the best of literature written for adults, good novels written for adolescents possess themes that merit and reward examination and commentary. This chapter explores some of the more common themes found in young adult novels.

Alienation

"They murdered him." Cormier's *Chocolate War* (1974) begins with those three words. Though the murder described is not quite literal—it takes place during football practice—that sentence foreshadows the rest of the novel. "They"— Archie and the malevolent fraternity he manages, Brother Leon, fate maybe—do conspire to murder Jerry Renault or at least the spirit of this antihero of an out-standing novel about alienation and its complement, loneliness. The cards seem a bit stacked against Jerry: his mother is dead; his father is indifferent, not only to Jerry but to most of life; he has no siblings; his one close friend, Goober, succumbs easily to the power of the Vigils. Jerry is isolated. At first he obeys the Vigils' com-mand not to sell the school chocolates, but later, when told by the Vigils to sell them, he still refuses. Jerry asks the same question Eliot's Prufrock asks: "Do I dare disturb the universe?" He does dare, and he suffers for that presumption.

Like many adolescents, Jerry suffers alone, pressured by peers, unable to con-trol events, buffeted by life. In him many adolescent readers see themselves, more pawns than kings or queens or even knights. Yet Jerry resists; he fights. And in doing so he adds to the alienation, the separation, the loneliness. He is, through-out, on his own, and the message is clear: Life is tough.

Whether *The Catcher in the Rye* is a young adult novel may depend on one's definition, since J. D. Salinger clearly wrote it for an adult audience. Yet it has been and is being read each year by thousands of young people and is consistently found among the required readings in both high school and college literature classes. One of the reasons for its staying power—it was published in 1951—is its compelling portrait of an alienated adolescent. Holden Caulfield's troubles are many, including the very serious physical illness that removes him from New York City to the California sanitarium from which he tells his story of that "madman stuff that happened to me around last Christmas" (3), but chief among them and the cause of the others is his inability to relate to anyone else, save possibly his younger sister, Phoebe. He reveres innocence—his imagined former girlfriend Jane, who keeps her kings in the back row when they play checkers; the nuns he meets during his sojourn in Manhattan; his brother Allie, who has died—but finds it too seldom. More common is his revulsion to the hypocrisy he sees everywhere about him: the cool Stradlater at school; his theatre date, Sally Hayes, who always seems to be looking over his shoulder for someone more important; the three tourists from Seattle, who yearn to see a movie star. Holden's intolerance for people extends to an intolerance for society as a whole, and he withdraws, socially and physically. Like Jerry, he has been defeated by the universe.

Friendship

For many adolescents, however, the loneliness of a Jerry Renault seems remote; they have a good friend, maybe several. Perhaps more than most authors, Paul Zindel explores friendship as a theme, particularly in *The Pigman* (1968) and, a decade later, *The Pigman's Legacy* (1980), and also in such intervening novels as *Pardon Me, You're Stepping on My Eyeball* (1976), *The Undertaker's Gone Bananas* (1978), and the more recent *Harry and Hortense at Hormone High* (1984). Setting him apart from many of his fellow writers, Zindel crosses sex lines in his friendships— John and Lorraine in *The Pigman* books, "Marsh" Mellow and Edna Singlebox in *Pardon Me*, Bobby and Lauri in *Gone Bananas*, and Harry and Hortense. Friendship is significant in a Zindel novel just as it is in teenage and adult life. One has someone to talk to, to share with, to grow with. At a time when most adolescents are moving apart from family, especially parents, friends assume even more importance in their lives, so reading about friendships, even fictional ones, becomes telling.

Zindel's boy-girl couples do not have sex. Neither do Livvie and David in Jenny Davis' aptly titled *Sex Education* (1988). They are friends, though—fast friends, equal friends, true friends—and through learning their story, readers comprehend what friendship really is. No doubt, had the ending of this important and too often overlooked novel been different, their relationship would have included sex, but, unlike some of the novels of, say, Judy Blume or, more particularly, Norma Klein, it did not begin with sex.

Yet friendship, like alienation, is many-faceted. Take *Welcome to the Ark* by Stephanie Tolan (1996). Four Mensa-like, super-brilliant kids, loners for the most part, come together in a mental institution and soon develop significant friendships, born in part from having a common enemy, with a sort of "the enemy of my friend is my enemy too" philosophy. Their enemy is the head doctor. Ultimately they try to go beyond concerns about him and move to larger issues, to stem the rising tide of violence in the world. Not easy to do, of course, but given, first, their trusting friendship and, second, their considerable capability, they have a shot at it.

Still another explanation of friendship is that found in Bridgers' *All Together Now* (1979). It is 1951, and Casey, a twelve-year-old, comes to small-town North Carolina to spend a summer with her grandparents. Almost her first acquaintance is Dwayne, a retarded adult thirty-three years of age, who, thinking she is a boy, invites Casey to play baseball with him. Casey goes along with the deception, and soon she and Dwayne are good friends, fast friends, sufficiently so that when Dwayne finally learns the truth about Casey's gender, they remain friends. The two of them even discuss friendship, with Dwayne advising Casey, "You be nice to folks and they be nice to you right back. That's one thing for sure" (52).

In this same novel Bridgers examines friendship among adults, an unusual but needed study in young adult literature that is intended for teenagers who will, after all, very soon become adults. Casey's grandmother Jane and her lifelong neighbor, Pansy, "had been friends for so long, as long as either of them could remember, but there had never before this been any apprehension between them, no fear that what they said to each other could do irreparable damage to their affection, no inhibitions that kept them from speaking the truth" (71). Adolescents who read of friendships as strong as this one are, whether they know it or not, absorbing values about companionship and "otherness" that will inform their own ways of living, thus providing strong justification for the use of young adult fiction with teenagers.

Just these few examples of the way friendship is differently treated in different young adult novels offer a suitable paradigm to explain the universality of the themes found in this kind of literature and its appeal for not only adolescent readers but adult readers as well. What happens to teenagers happens to us all: the need, say, for friends is not limited to six-year-olds or sixteen-year-olds or sixty-year-olds; it is everyone's need. Hence, treatment of this important life concern, when well done as it is in these and numerous other young adult novels, supports the contention that young adult literature is thematically linked to all substantial literature, no matter the intended age of its readers. It is perhaps a critical overstatement to link Cormier with Conrad or Bridgers with Balzac, but their differences are more of degree than of kind; all of them take as their domain the study of the human condition.

The study of still other themes may reinforce the point.

Family

Tolstoy opened *Anna Karenina* with a sentence that has since become famous: "Happy families are all alike; every unhappy family is unhappy in its own way" (1965, 3). Unhappy families frequently make up the cast of characters in adolescent novels. In James Howe's incredible little novel *The Watcher* (1997), family life is studied obliquely rather than directly, but the initial uncertainty soon is replaced by increased awareness of Tolstoy's wisdom. Several families are summering at the beach. On the sand all seems well, save for one young girl who does not join the others but simply watches them each day, hence, the title of the novel. Yet young adult readers learn as the story unfolds that the watcher—as well as the watched—comes from a family we would nowadays label dysfunctional. And from this learning will perhaps come some greater understanding of their own families, a fuller awareness that what's right and what's wrong are complex issues viewed differently by different members of the family. To continue Howe's beach metaphor, we all occasionally stand on soft and shifting sands.

Life falls apart for a family in *Checkers*, by Australian John Marsden (1998). Here the protagonist, a young woman whom we readers soon learn is institutionalized, comes from a family newly made wealthy. Life suddenly is good. But then, through a picture of her dog, Checkers, we learn that the family's sudden wealth was obtained by fraudulent means. Their whole fabric comes unraveled; they become one of Tolstoy's unhappy families.

A variation on the theme occurs in novels like S. E. Hinton's *Outsiders* (1967) and Harry Mazer's *When the Phone Rang* (1985). In each novel the unhappiness occurs after the accidental death of loving and caring parents, leaving the three adolescent siblings in each book wondering what will come next for them. In both novels, they attempt to stay together.

Death

Adolescents die in real life. They die in young adult fiction. In fact, from a thematic point of view, death is one of the more common elements found in adolescent literature—just as it is in literature intended for adult audiences—mainly, of course, because of the powerful drama always associated with death. In *The Terrorist* (1997), a novel Caroline Cooney set in London, Laura's younger brother, eleven-year-old Billy, is innocently handed a package to hold and then suddenly realizes it may be a terrorist bomb—but too late. He can't throw it into a crowd of people, so he keeps it, it explodes, and he dies, all in the first chapter. From that point on, his death demands of Laura that she try to uncover the "why" of Billy's tragedy. In so doing she comes into grim contact with hatred in a variety of places, particularly her school for foreign students (Laura is American) and its mix of Arab, Israeli, Irish, and African students.

Death of a sibling plays a compelling role in Cormier's short but powerful novel *Tunes for Bears to Dance To* (1992). As in *The Terrorist*, hatred, too, is dominant. Henry's brother, Eddie, dies in a hit-and-run accident, and the family can barely recover. Henry's father becomes almost vegetative, unable to function. His mother tries to find employment, but, unskilled, she can't bring in much money. So Henry goes to work for an evil man, a grocer who will sell to but also hates "kikes, Polacks, and greaseballs." He makes Henry a deal: Do a maliciously evil thing to an old Jewish man and I will pay for a monument at the grave of your dead brother. Henry must decide, and as the story comes to a climax, it's as difficult to guess what Henry will do as it is to put down this book.

Suicide often appears in young adult literature, and rarely has its profound effect been better explored than in Chris Crutcher's *Chinese Handcuffs* (1989). Much of this fine novel, in fact, consists of letters that Dillon Hemingway writes to his dead brother, Preston, letters that go beyond the "Why did you do it?" kinds of questions to those that examine what Dillon is going through himself as a result of Preston's taking his own life in Dillon's presence.

Mental Illness

The most devastating result of mental illness among teenagers is, of course, suicide, but not all sufferers commit suicide; somehow they struggle on. Commonly the mental illness is that of a parent, as in A. E. Cannon's (1991) *Amazing Gracie* (a mother's almost suicidal depression) and Judith Caseley's (1992) *My Father, the Nutcase* (a father's depression), and it is the adolescent's reaction to the mental illness of an adult that becomes a central theme in novels.

A protagonist who is mentally ill, though readers are unsure about that, is found in Cormier's troubling *I Am the Cheese* (1977). Young Adam is on a bicycle trip, or so we readers are allowed to infer. In fact, we learn that he is imprisoned, not only in a home for the mentally unstable but in his own mind, the result of his seeing the murder of his parents, who were in a witness protection program.

But mental illness in young adult literature is not simply a problem of the young. Few authors have explored this theme more adroitly than Sue Ellen Bridgers, who makes such illness a major element in three different novels. Significantly, Bridgers' father was himself mentally ill while she was in junior and senior high school, and she invests in her adolescent characters many of the guilty feelings she experienced (was she in any way the cause of her father's illness?) and the fears she had (will the illness of the father be repeated in the life of the child?). In *All Together Now* (1979), Dwayne is a retarded adult who passes his days the way a twelve-year-old would: playing baseball, seeing movies, just "hanging out." Twelve-year-old Casey becomes his greatest friend, and it is she who galvanizes community reaction to keep Dwayne from being committed to a "home." More autobiographical in some ways among Bridgers' novels is *Notes for Another Life* (1981), in which father Tom is mentally ill and teenage son Kevin is filled with anger at Tom's inability to be the father Kevin wants and with doubts and fears about his own sanity. In *Permanent Connections* (1987), Bridgers explores agoraphobia, an illness she has hinted at through characterizations in her earlier novels. Here it is a central problem in the novel: Coralee Davis, the protagonist's middle-aged spinster aunt, will not leave her house. It takes the wise prodding of a sensitive neighbor, Ginny Collier, to help her overcome her fears and to move, first to the porch, then to the backyard, and then to the frightening world "out there." Coralee's, and Ginny's, triumph merits an accompaniment of *Ode to Joy*, but, beyond story, the significance lies in the novelistic exploration of this common and dreaded disease.

Sex

Few young adult novels examine sex quite so graphically or so commercially as Judy Blume's *Forever* (1976). It opens with "Sybil Davison has a genius IQ and has been laid by at least six different guys" and becomes even more specific thereafter. Kathy, a high school senior and a virgin, though not terribly hung up on remaining one, meets Michael, also a senior, not a virgin, and terribly hung up on Kathy's not remaining one much longer. In very explicit scenes, even to the point of naming Michael's penis Ralph, Blume presents first sex for Kathy in a way that gives one set of answers to the many questions all teens have about sex. Though "forever" isn't quite forever in their developing love, Kathy has no regrets about her sexual experiences with Michael and appears to regard them as one further stage in her maturation, a view Blume seems to share.

Not all readers take this tolerant perspective. While Blume's book is one of the most widely sold novels written for young adults, it is also one of the most widely censored, with most proponents of its abolition from school and public libraries arguing that the sexual content is one problem, the seeming amorality another and more serious one. Yet it cannot be denied that for many teenagers, Blume's book is their *Joy of Sex*.

Sex plays a very different kind of role in *The Toll Bridge* (1992) by Aidan Chambers, an outstanding British author too little read in the United States. In this you-won't-set-this-one-aside novel, seventeen-year-old Piers takes a bridge-tending job just to get away and find himself. He also finds Tess, who begins calling him "Jan," after the two-faced god of bridges, but also in light of Jan's looking forward and backward as he tries to make sense of his life. There's a girlfriend back home who yearns for sex with Jan. He yearns for sex with Tess—or he thinks he does. But then Adam enters their lives and Tess is drawn sexually to him. As it happens, Tess and Adam do have sex and are unaware that Jan is watching them and saying,

> I had not seen sex between two people before. I don't mean pretended sex between actors, not played at by gropers at parties or in public places, nor the clinical demonstrations in sex-education videos at school, but the all-out sweatlathered bodysquirming limbtangling skingreedy gutmelting mindlost neoviolent reality. So I didn't know by firsthand observation, much less direct experience about its animalness. The exclusive bodiliness of it. The utterly absorbed uninhibited unselfconsciousness of those involved as they writhed self-absorbed, lost to the world around them, lost, in fact, just like the cliché says, in each other. (128–29)

Not all the sex in young adult fiction is heterosexual. In Chambers' *Dance on My Grave* (1982), Barry and Hal are gay. Hal, the protagonist of this provocative novel, is also possessive, and when Barry has an affair—with a girl yet—Hal can barely handle his rage. Shortly thereafter Barry dies in a motorcycle accident, and Hal feels compelled to honor the pact the two of them had made that the survivor of the death of the other—decades from now they had assumed—would dance on the grave of the deceased. Hal does dance on Barry's grave and is arrested for doing so.

Michael Cart's *My Father's Scar* (1996) is an interestingly complex handling of time as readers are taken back and forth in the life of Andy Logan, from his current loneliness as a homosexual in college to his life as a child and young teen, when an abusive father berated him for not being athletic. When Andy finally does come to understand that he is gay, his father goes berserk and orders him out of the house, a directive Andy is pleased to follow.

Jack by A. M. Homes (1989) offers still another perspective on the theme of homosexuality. Jack's parents divorce when he is eleven, but it is not until he is fifteen that his father confesses about his gay life. Outraged and shattered by this revelation, Jack cannot keep to himself and soon is victimized by schoolmates who call him "faggot's son" or even "faggot" himself, a term that Jack had thought about only in connection with his father.

Chambers, Cart, and Homes present balanced books about homosexuality, just as Blume does about heterosexuality. Judgments are avoided, issues are thoughtfully explored, and both teens and adults act, albeit emotionally, with some ultimate intelligence. Again, these books provide examples of how seriously themes are treated in young adult literature. The long-held view that books written for teenagers rarely display affection beyond hand holding—or at least they ought not to—clearly is naïve, as unsophisticated about the literature of teenagers as it is about their lives.

Drugs and Alcohol

Sandra Scoppettone has written two significant novels about homosexuality, *Trying Hard to Hear You* (1974) and *Happy Endings Are All Alike* (1979), but her novel *The Late Great Me* (1984) has had greater staying power among teenage readers. It is about alcoholism, a kind of no-holds-barred, no-apology-given treatment of what happens when a high school junior, Geri Peters, goes off the deep end into whisky, gin, vodka, and whatever other liquor she can get her hands on. In Chapter 1, after establishing herself as a relatively normal high school junior, with a brother at Harvard, a mother and father who are themselves successful even if they may be on her back overmuch, the narrator ends with these lines: "I am, I have discovered, many things. I am a young woman, an artist, both considerate and inconsiderable, generous and selfish, funny and sulky, rigid and open, arrogant and humble, and absolutely, definitely, without any doubt a drunk. My name is Geri Peters and I'm an alcoholic and I think you should know about it" (5). Most readers take up Geri's challenge to "know about it" and, in the course of their education, learn a good bit about this increasing teenage scourge.

The sometimes deserved criticism that adolescent novels sugarcoat life's problems and solve them too easily, a point of view more readily exemplified a couple of decades ago than today, certainly does not apply to *Go Ask Alice* (1976). The anonymous diary of a hooked-on-drugs teenager, this compelling account of her victories and defeats in the adolescent drug culture perhaps has done more to deter other young people from a similar fate than all the "just say no" commercials and pious sermons ever delivered. Intense and devastating, *Go Ask Alice* pulls no punches in its message that drugs destroy.

The foregoing paragraphs barely skim the thematic surfaces of young adult literature; space does not permit a fuller treatment of the themes presented or of other themes found in fiction intended for teenage audiences: crime (see the novels of Lois Duncan or *Up Country* by Alden R. Carter [1989]); ethical dilemmas (Robert Newton Peck's *Justice Lion* [1981], another novel too often overlooked, places a boy squarely at odds with the father he had heretofore idolized); school life (*Harry and Hortense at Hormone High* by Paul Zindel [1984] implies in its title the less-than-positive picture of school life typically found in novels by that popular author, himself a former teacher for ten years); AIDS (see *Night Kites* by M. E. Kerr [1986] or Alice Hoffman's *At Risk* [1988], in which the victim is eleven-year-old Amanda, who five years earlier had an operation and was given a transfusion of contaminated blood); obesity (Robert Lipsyte has produced three books about overweight Bobby Marks: *One Fat Summer* [1977], *Summer Rules* [1981], and *The Summerboy* [1982]); sibling rivalry (in Lynn Hall's *Half the Battle* [1982] the reader's emotions are as torn as the relationship between two brothers, one of them blind); divorce (novelistic treatments as different as the optimistic *It's Not the End of the World* by Blume [1972], the thoughtful *Notes for Another Life* by Bridgers [1981], and the humorous *Divorce Express* by Paula Danziger [1982]); poverty (the deservedly Newbery-awarded *Out of the Dust* by Karen Hesse [1997] presents a picture of life in Oklahoma's Dust Bowl of the '30s and the poverty it created; set in a very different place, some unnamed urban area, *Make Lemonade* by Virginia Euwer Wolff [1993] examines the same depth of poverty with very different characters; both *Dust* and *Lemonade*, by the way, are written in effective blank verse); the uncertainty of the future (Lois Lowry's *Giver* [1993] presents a future society that makes Orwell's *1984* seem like a walk in the park); and on and on.

Racial intolerance plays a part in Bruce Brooks' *Moves Make the Man* (1984), religious intolerance in Arrick's *Chernowitz!* (1981). Cancer kills people in Carter's *Sheila's Dying* (1987). Walter Dean Myers' historical *Fallen Angels* (1988) portrays teenagers fighting the Vietnam War, and William Sleator's futuristic *House of Stairs* (1975) pits teens against a malevolent social psychologist. *Things Are Seldom What They Seem* by Sandy Asher (1983) provides a picture of sexual abuse by a teacher; *Abby, My Love* by Hadley Irwin (1987) offers a similar portrait, this time with the abuse perpetrated by an incestuous father. Handicapped teenagers are found in Robin F. Brancato's *Winning* (1977), Chris Crutcher's *Crazy Horse Electric Game* (1987), Emily Hanlon's *It's Too Late for Sorry* (1978), and Bridgers' *All We Know of Heaven* (1996).

And so it goes. The generalization that young adult literature, in some form or another, in some way or another, covers all of adolescent life and, for that matter, all of adult life, where the same themes are universal, can be defended, as these many examples make abundantly clear. The themes treated in novels written for young people cover the physical, social, and emotional waterfront so completely that many such novels are appropriate variations on themes, different treatments from different perspectives, writing "with a slant," as Emily Dickinson put it.

Which, of course, brings us directly to another element of adolescent fiction that adds to its staying power and its universal appeal, not always just among teenage readers: its literary quality. No matter what the subject treated—divorce, mental illness, or teenage sex—a bad book is a bad book and will garner few readers.

The books themselves offer, of course, the best argument about their quality, but other exemplars may be adduced. Writers as far different as Fran Arrick and Paul Zindel, and between them Brancato and Bridgers and Brooks and literally hundreds of others, are reviewed regularly in the pages of journals devoted to the study of seriously attempted and successfully written literature—the *New York Times Book Review*, for one example, *Booklist*, for another. And a whole host of journals focusing more specifically on adolescent literature has sprung up, most particularly *The ALAN Review*, *School Library Journal*, and *VOYA, the Voice of Youth Advocates*. These journals not only review new books for adolescents but also offer sound and scholarly critical analyses of the field and its significant authors. Young adult literature courses now are found in virtually every college and university and are among the fastest growing in the curriculum. Countless term papers and even many doctoral dissertations have been written on young adult literature.

Twayne Publishers has for years published single-volume critical biographies of the major canonical literary figures, writers like Shakespeare, Joyce, Twain, and Faulkner. In the late 1980s it added a new series imprint, *Twayne's United States Authors Series, Young Adult Authors*, and it has now published studies on, among others, S. E. Hinton, Robert Cormier, Phyllis Reynolds Naylor, Ouida Sebestyen, Gary Paulsen, Richard Peck, M. E. Kerr, and Sue Ellen Bridgers. Though Twayne no longer publishes these books more volumes are forthcoming from Scarecrow Press.

ALAN, the Assembly on Literature for Adolescents of the National Council of Teachers of English, has grown in its seventeen-year existence from a handful of founders to almost 2,500 members. Its convention each November tops out at the maximum number of three hundred registrants allowed within weeks of the opening of the registration period, but other folks crowd their way in to hear authors of young adult literature speak about their own writing and scholars speak about those authors. A field of lesser worth would not have this drawing power.

Thus, the broad appeal of young adult literature lies in part in its treatment of universal themes and in part in its high quality. Its writers write well. They tell good stories, inhabit them with memorable characters, place them in well-described settings, and do it all with prose that causes readers to linger now and again for a second reading, a moment of appreciation for the well-turned phrase or artistic metaphor. Three examples from three different authors may make the point and end the discussion:

1. Sue Ellen Bridgers lets Rob, the protagonist of *Permanent Connections*, provide his own autobiography in his thinking about an English assignment he has neglected:

     Right now, he should get up and write something. He would write about how it feels when you wake up in the night because your folks are arguing about you, about how lousy it is never to be left alone, about what a pain in the butt your twelve-year-old perfect sister is, about how you're already messed up. Already, at seventeen, boxed in with no way out. Not enough guts to scramble, never enough bucks to float. Sinking, always sinking. Holding tight and falling away at the same time. (1987, 6)

2. M. E. Kerr opens *Gentlehands*, a novel that explores both class and racial intolerances, with words that get directly into one of the key themes of the novel, status differences:

    > I wonder what the summer would have been like if I'd never met Sky Pennington. They always seem to have names like that, don't they? Rich, beautiful girls are never named Elsie Pip or Mary Smith. They have those special names and they say them in their particular tones and accents, and my mother was right, I was in over my head or out of my depth, or however she put it. My father said, "She's not in your class, Buddy." This conversation took place the first night I took her out. (1978, 1)

3. Their own hearts torn asunder with the doctor's report, her parents tenderly and lovingly break the news to eleven-year-old Amanda that she has AIDS and cope with her reaction in Alice Hoffman's *At Risk*:

    > She ran up to her room and locked herself in, and they let her. They let her sit in the dark and cry, they let her listen to one cassette tape after another, and when she came back downstairs at a little after nine that night, they nodded when she said her eyes might look funny because she was tired. They sat around the kitchen table, eating chocolate ice cream. But they didn't look at each other; they didn't dare speak above a whisper. They've become sleepwalkers, wandering through their own nightmares, each avoiding the others for fear that a word, a conversation, a kiss will make them realize they aren't dreaming. (1988, 57)

Yes, literature written for young adults is fine literature, about themes that are universal, with quality that is stunning. Such literature merits—and rewards—attention.

Works Cited

Arrick, Fran. 1981. *Chernowitz!* New York: Bradbury.

Asher, Sandy. 1983. *Things Are Seldom What They Seem*. New York: Delacorte.

Blume, Judy. 1972. *It's Not the End of the World*. New York: Bradbury.

———. 1976. *Forever*. New York: Pocket Books.

Brancato, Robin F. 1977. *Winning*. New York: Knopf.

Bridgers, Sue Ellen. 1979. *All Together Now*. New York: Knopf.

———. 1981. *Notes for Another Life*. New York: Knopf.

———. 1987. *Permanent Connections*. New York: Harper & Row.

————. 1996. *All We Know of Heaven*. Wilmington, NC: Banks Channel Books.

Brooks, Bruce. 1984. *The Moves Make the Man*. New York: Harper & Row.

Cannon, A. E. 1991. *Amazing Gracie*. New York: Laurel Leaf.

Cart, Michael. 1996. *My Father's Scar*. New York: Simon & Schuster.

Carter, Alden R. 1987. *Sheila's Dying*. New York: Putnam.

————. 1989. *Up Country*. New York: Putnam.

Caseley, Judith. 1992. *My Father, the Nutcase*. New York: Alfred A. Knopf.

Chambers, Aidan. 1982. *Dance on My Grave*. New York: Harper & Row.

————. 1992. *The Toll Bridge*. New York: HarperCollins.

Cooney, Caroline. 1997. *The Terrorist*. New York: Scholastic.

Cormier, Robert. 1974. *The Chocolate War*. New York: Pantheon.

————. 1977. *I Am the Cheese*. New York: Dell.

————. 1992. *Tunes for Bears to Dance To*. New York: Delacorte.

Crutcher, Chris. 1987. *The Crazy Horse Electric Game*. New York: Greenwillow.

————. 1989. *Chinese Handcuffs*. New York: Greenwillow.

Danziger, Paula. 1982. *The Divorce Express*. New York: Delacorte.

Davis, Jenny. 1988. *Sex Education*. New York: Laurel Leaf.

Dickens, Charles. 1906. *A Tale of Two Cities*. London: Dent.

Go Ask Alice. 1976. New York: Avon.

Grant, Cynthia. 1992. *Shadow Man*. New York: Simon & Schuster.

Hall, Lynn. 1982. *Half the Battle*. New York: Scribner.

Hanlon, Emily. 1978. *It's Too Late for Sorry*. New York: Bradbury.

Hardy, Thomas. 1912. *Return of the Native*. New York: Harper & Row.

Hesse, Karen. 1997. *Out of the Dust*. New York: Scholastic.

Hinton, S. E. 1967. *The Outsiders*. New York: Viking.

Hoffman, Alice. 1988. *At Risk*. New York: Putnam.

Homes, A. M. 1989. *Jack*. New York: Macmillan.

Howe, James. 1997. *The Watcher*. New York: Atheneum.

Irwin, Hadley. 1987. *Abby, My Love*. New York: New American Library.

Kerr, M. E. 1978. *Gentlehands*. New York: HarperCollins.

————. 1986. *Night Kites*. New York: Harper & Row.

Lipsyte, Robert. 1977. *One Fat Summer*. New York: Harper & Row.

————. 1981. *Summer Rules*. New York: Harper & Row.

————. 1982. *The Summerboy*. New York: Harper & Row.

Lowry, Lois. 1993. *The Giver*. New York: Laurel Leaf.

Marsden, John. 1998. *Checkers*. Boston: Houghton Mifflin.

Mazer, Harry. 1985. *When the Phone Rang*. New York: Scholastic.

Myers, Walter Dean. 1988. *Fallen Angels*. New York: Scholastic.

Peck, Robert Newton. 1981. *Justice Lion*. Boston: Little, Brown.

Salinger, J. D. 1951. *The Catcher in the Rye*. Boston: Little, Brown.

Scoppettone, Sandra. 1974. *Trying Hard to Hear You*. New York: Harper & Row.

———. 1979. *Happy Endings Are All Alike*. New York: Laurel Leaf.

———. 1984. *The Late Great Me*. New York: Bantam.

Sleator, William. 1975. *House of Stairs*. New York: Avon.

Tolan, Stephanie. 1996. *Welcome to the Ark*. New York: Morrow.

Tolstoy, Leo. 1965. *Anna Karenina*. New York: Modern Library.

Twain, Mark. 1948. *The Adventures of Huckleberry Finn*. New York: Holt, Rinehart, and Winston.

Wolff, Virginia Euwer. 1993. *Make Lemonade*. New York: Henry Holt.

Zindel, Paul. 1968. *The Pigman*. New York: Harper & Row.

———. 1969. *My Darling, My Hamburger*. New York: Harper & Row.

———. 1976. *Pardon Me, You're Stepping on My Eyeball*. New York: Harper & Row.

———. 1978. *The Undertaker's Gone Bananas*. New York: Bantam.

———. 1980. *The Pigman's Legacy*. New York: Harper & Row.

———. 1984. *Harry and Hortense at Hormone High*. New York: Harper & Row.

2

Natural, Necessary, and Workable
The Connection of Young Adult Novels to the Classics

LEILA CHRISTENBURY

For many English teachers, teaching literature means teaching the classics. These teachers know the classics often from their own college experience, and, in their classrooms, they believe in the value of all students reading traditional and demonstrably time-tested works of art. Further, many secondary school English teachers feel that familiarity with the classics will provide their students exposure to mainstream culture and the philosophical tenets and ethical values of Western civilization and will prepare them for college work. For these English teachers, doing their job well means teaching the canon of the classics.

And they are not alone in these beliefs. Many parents, school boards, and community members agree with them. To a number of individuals and constituencies, exposure to the classics is vital for a good English language arts experience and essential to a well-rounded education. In some quarters, teaching the classics is almost a political act and is seen as showing allegiance to traditional values and societal mores.

It is inviting to dismiss such arguments and to argue that an unrelieved diet of the canon provides nothing more than a curriculum that is an uncritical rehash of the traditional power culture: white, male, Christian, Anglophilic. Indeed, the classics most know and laud are surprisingly limited: in middle and secondary school curricula, the bulk of works considered classic consists of nineteenth- and early twentieth-century works of American and British fiction, nonfiction, drama, and poetry. It is also undeniable that many classics-loving teachers ignore the fact that such texts no longer hold the uncritical sway they once did in college and university English departments, rendering rather moot the argument that familiarity with the classics is an absolute prerequisite for a successful experience in higher education. Further, it is appealing to note that those who cling to the classics often ignore the rather idiosyncratic way a "classic" can arrive at such a designation: rarely, in fact, are the classics present in secondary curricula either the best work of an author or even work that has been consistently, over the decades, agreed upon as best.

Yet familiarity and tradition may be the central criteria for the continued use of the classics in secondary curricula. And, while it is not the most laudable aspect of the profession, it is undeniably true that many overworked English teachers do not continue to read widely beyond their own university education and find in the classics to which they were exposed as students comfort and an intellectual ease. As noted above, there are support and approval for teaching the classics. Many members of the school community and the public feel that reading and transmitting the time-honored values of the classics are precisely what good English teachers should be doing.

On the other hand, arguments for and against using the classics pale beside an important consideration that is rarely addressed. It is clear that many teachers who consistently use the classics ignore or dismiss student reaction. Teachers' dependence upon classic literature as the mainstay of English classroom reading can leave many students frustrated, disengaged, and desperately searching for *Cliffs-Notes*, which will, in some simpler form, unmask the mysteries of *The Scarlet Letter* (Hawthorne [1850] 1963) or *The Sun Also Rises* (Hemingway 1926) and render them comprehensible. Yet few schools and school districts are willing to take the classics out of their curriculum; few teachers who revere the classics are willing to replace them with either contemporary adult or young adult (YA) literature.

Clearly, the classics remain—and will probably continue to be—a staple of most school literature curricula.

In sharp distinction to the canon of the classics, young adult literature continues to struggle to find a permanent, respected place in mainstream school curriculum. Still relegated to students who are considered poor readers, shoved in the back of the classroom library, offered as a last resort for reading during those difficult times of school—before vacations, the prom, a snow alert—young adult literature has yet to take its rightful place as literature of quality that is respected, used, and recommended by teachers and librarians. Yet good young adult literature shares with the classics all the marks of literary excellence and, further, consistently inspires student reading response. While young adult literature often languishes in its place in the secondary curriculum, many young people identify with the stories of Jerry Renault in *The Chocolate War* (Cormier 1974) and Maniac Magee in the novel of the same name (Spinelli 1990) and not, to the dismay of many teachers, in the same degree as they identify with the predicaments of Lady Macbeth, Arthur Dimmesdale, and Tom Joad.

One possible approach to solving the classics dilemma is to link required classic texts to young adult texts and read them in tandem. Not only can this linkage provide students with exposure to the canon, but it can also give them a way to approach a classic through parallel literature that is contemporary, more than likely more appealing, and certainly more readily understandable. Connecting classic and young adult texts can help students and their teachers and can, as a powerful side benefit, keep students reading and expanding their interest in literature.

The Natural Connection of the Classics to Young Adult Literature

Good young adult literature is, simply put, good literature. Although it is geared specifically to the young adult reader and features young adult protagonists, readers find in contemporary YA literature the same literary features they find in adult literature. YA literature, in addition, spans the genres: while this chapter will focus on the novel, there are, as in classic literature, also YA short stories, poetry, plays, and nonfiction works.

Though stripped down in complexity regarding plot, number of characters, breadth of setting, and sheer length of prose, a good YA novel has all the basic characteristics of a good adult novel. In good YA literature, themes are multiple and identifiable; characters are well developed and experience change over the course of the novel. The protagonist in a YA novel confronts a challenge or test, and the plot moves logically through a succession of events. Dialogue is consistent with character, and setting serves a function beyond window dressing. In YA literature, genre also holds true. Good YA science fiction has the same marks as good adult science fiction; a YA mystery with a teenage central character has similar marks to those of a mystery geared to adult readers.

There is a natural connection between classic literature and young adult literature in their literary characteristics. And while, for instance, the hero-against-the-gang novel *Wringer* (Spinelli 1997) is not as weighty as the similarly themed *Lord of the Flies* (Golding 1954), and the magical realism of *Holes* (Sachar 1998) does not approach the complexity of *Beloved* (Morrison 1987), the novels share commonalities and, in their own right, an equivalent literary excellence. Thus in all good YA literature exist the same literary characteristics that classic literature contains; there is a natural connection between the two.

The implications for teachers are encouraging. In small group work, in large group discussion, in projects or papers or journal response, students do not have to consider character or plot or theme in ways that are markedly different in YA literature from classic literature. In both classic and young adult literature, for instance, motivation of character will drive plot development; use of dialogue will reveal character. When a YA novel and a classic novel are paired, the points of discussion can pertain to both pieces of literature, and students can look at literary characteristics and compare and contrast the two.

The Necessary Connection of the Classics to Young Adult Literature

As noted above, even the most fervent proponent of teaching the classics knows that many pieces are tough going for students. The syntax and vocabulary, the intricacies of plot and subplot, the use of multiple characters, geographical settings, and historical references may require more background and explanation—not to mention struggle—than most students are willing to attempt. In a defensive measure, often students will turn to commercial plot summaries and literary analyses, simplified versions of the original, or other similar sources so that they can do anything but actually read the work itself. And when it comes to research papers on classic texts, plagiarism is a real issue for many students and their teachers: if you cannot, for instance, understand *As I Lay Dying* (Faulkner [1930] 1964), it seems wholly logical to buy or borrow much of that required fifteen-page research paper on the text.

There is rarely this kind of struggle with young adult literature. The compressed plot, the limited number of characters, and the length of the works themselves distinguish YA lit from classic literature and make it more accessible and often more immediately understandable. In addition, the focus on a young adult protagonist with issues and concerns that engage and resonate with readers of that age ensures that many works of YA lit find a ready home with adolescents.

This picture is different from that of a steady diet of classical reading. When classics are the major required reading in school curricula—as they are in many schools in this country—consistently confronting complex, complicated texts whose main character is an older adult can turn students away from reading and intellectual engagement altogether. Thus using young adult literature as parallel reading, as a way *into* the classics cannot only keep our students reading (a wholly worthwhile, defensible end in itself), it can also help students make links to the classic novel, play, or poem. The connection is not a frill; for many students, it is truly necessary.

The implication for teachers is clear. When, for instance, students can see that the issues confronting a character in Thomas Hardy's nineteenth-century Wessex are essentially the same as those of someone who goes to the mall, struggles in biology lab, and dresses and talks like the readers, there is more possibility of understanding and connection. As will be explored later, seeing *Great Expectations'* Pip in the light of other contemporary heroes who must journey home, such as Russel in Gary Paulsen's *Dogsong* (1985), makes his story not only more comprehensible but more compelling. As another example, the unlikely but powerful adult friendship in *Of Mice and Men* (Steinbeck [1937] 1970) may seem more comprehensible after students have read Rodman Philbrick's *Freak the Mighty* (1993), which features a similarly mismatched pair of teenage friends. Linking classic to young adult literature is often, for student appreciation and understanding, highly necessary and can make a bridge between the two.

The Workable Connection of the Classics to Young Adult Literature

Putting dissimilar texts up against each other to illuminate both is a time-honored technique of the English language arts classroom. For years teachers have paired differing genres of literature (e.g., two novels; novels and poetry; short stories and poetry), have paired art with literature, and have paired film with literature. When confronted with two or even three differing texts, students often find that their difficulties with one are addressed by their understanding of the other and, further, that when asked to compare and contrast two dissimilar texts, new connections can emerge.

Thus the feud that rages in Verona's streets in *Romeo and Juliet* may be more understandable after reading *The Outsiders* with its similar, but perhaps more contemporary and compelling, gang tension and conflict. The Dust Bowl poverty of the Joads in *The Grapes of Wrath* may be more accessible after reading the nonfiction work, *Children of the Dust Bowl*, which tells the story of the 1930s school, Weedpatch Camp, and is written with younger readers in mind.

While students may be intimidated by a classic's number of characters, language, or even length, the paired texts may offer ways into understanding and appreciation. Students, through the use of multiple texts, can find avenues of approach, whether it be through theme, character, plot, genre, or even setting, whether it be through simplified language or characters who are more their age. Comparing and contrasting a classic with a contemporary YA work can be fruitful and help students read and keep reading. It is a workable connection.

The implications for teachers are that a unit of study will rarely be wholly lost; when students know that at least part of the literature will be accessible and appealing, it is more likely that they will read and attempt projects and responses and classroom activities. Further, understanding and appreciation can be greatly enhanced.

Making the Connection

Even with the best of intentions and acknowledging that linking classic and YA literature is natural, necessary, and workable, it is possible to present a young adult and a classic text and find that your students are not particularly engaged by the pairing. Obviously, just putting a young adult text and a classic text together is not sufficient; there needs to be a real and vibrant link between the two. A few common sense caveats are in order.

First, *select young adult literature that is of excellent quality*. Many classics have endured because, despite other drawbacks, they are generally considered the best of their kind. Choosing and using a relatively mediocre piece of YA literature for a pairing will doom the effectiveness of the linkage. Thus you need to consult award lists and ensure that the YA text you select is considered a strong piece of literature. The Newbery Award, the Orbis Pictus Award, the "best" lists from *English Journal*, *School Library Journal*, *Booklist*, or *Horn Book*, publications from the American Library Association and the National Council of Teachers of English book lists are all good sources for determining quality YA literature. Pairing a respected classic text with a weak piece of YA literature sends a confusing message to your students and clearly invites them to quickly dismiss the contemporary text.

Second, *try to use more than one piece of young adult literature as a link*. Often students will not warm to a single pairing but will find in multiple examples compelling links and commonalities. Putting all of the emphasis on one text "talking to" another is not always as successful as we might hope. For instance, following the protagonist-against-nature theme, *The Old Man and the Sea* (Hemingway 1952) is a classic text that could be paired well with *Hatchet* (Paulsen 1987), featuring a male stranded in the Canadian wilderness, as well as with *Julie of the Wolves* (George 1972), a Newbery Award–winning novel about a young girl trying to survive in the Arctic.

Finally, *choose companion texts that offer real connections*. Similarities in theme, plot, and character are obvious links; setting and genre can also provide useful avenues of exploration. Rarely is it possible to find a text that links to a classic work in all areas: Julius Lester's *Othello*, an imaginative reconstruction of William Shakespeare's play, is an unusual mirroring that is rarely equaled in the field.

Do not, however, despair: many classics feature the theme of growing up and facing a test, a theme that is present throughout most young adult literature. Characters who mature and change, characters who must overcome fears or faults are common to both classics and YA literature. Plots that feature a test, a decision between good and evil, are similarly common.

Do, however, be cautious and even skeptical: it is often only too easy to insist on a connection when there is none. While this may seem so obvious as to be insulting, it can be easy to assume that all novels that feature a female character will involve issues of love and self-image or novels that have African American characters will detail issues of poverty and crime. Such is not the case. Young adult literature is, in fact, as complicated and multifaceted as its older relatives, and assuming that certain topics, characters, or settings naturally lead to certain themes and connections can be dangerous. Be smart in your choices and look for real, not artificial, links.

The following section illustrates two sets of connections between classic texts and young adult texts and suggests ways that teachers and students can explore the two.

Connecting *Native Son* and *A Lesson Before Dying*

Published in 1940, Richard Wright's *Native Son* would appear to have little compelling to say to students and teachers in contemporary times. It is understandably dated in some of its details, it is long (around four hundred paperback pages), and, further, it is a profoundly disturbing, even depressing novel containing pointed and explicit discussions of race and racism. Yet *Native Son*, despite these drawbacks, is one of the great American novels. It is a true classic, written with literary art and skill and dealing with race issues that are, almost sixty years after its first appearance, still compelling, still unresolved, and still very much a part of the American social scene. *Native Son* is powerful, important, and memorable and, in many ways, still contemporary and fresh. It is a work of art and at the same time a political statement: for many young readers it may well also be a moral education.

Pairing *Native Son* with Ernest J. Gaines' *Lesson Before Dying* (1993) may help students in their reading. *A Lesson Before Dying*, originally written for adult readers, has found a home with young adults, and its author, Ernest J. Gaines, has a strong reputation as a young adult writer (*A Gathering of Old Men* and *The Autobiography of Miss Jane Pittman* are two of his most famous works). *A Lesson Before Dying* has similar themes and ideas to *Native Son*, though it focuses more on psychology and morality than on the realities of race. The two novels, however, make an excellent pair for reading and study, and some of their connections are strong and convincing.

To recap *Native Son*, the story of Bigger Thomas is not, on the face of it, an uplifting tale at all. Bigger is an angry young black man who lives in 1930s Chicago, where Jim Crow race separation reigns. He is not, on almost any level, an admirable character. A junior high school dropout with very little focus in his life and no clear ambition or industry, Bigger is at times a bully, a liar, a self-centered young man who has spent a brief period of time in reform school. Bigger's father is dead, and he and his family, who have come to Chicago from Mississippi, are eking out a living on the south side of the city.

Almost inevitably, Bigger comes to a bad end in *Native Son*. Virtually by accident, after taking a job as a chauffeur for the Daltons, a wealthy white family, Bigger murders two women, rapes one, and tries to extort ransom money. There is no neat, happy ending to *Native Son* as, predictably, Bigger is caught, tried, and condemned to death for his crimes. In prison, however, he meets the socially aware lawyer Max, who helps him understand the social and moral implications of race in America and also how in the world he came to this pass. In jail, facing execution, Bigger begins to articulate and understand himself as a human being and as a black man. To a certain extent, even on the brink of his own execution, Bigger makes sense of the senselessness of race oppression.

In Gaines' *Lesson Before Dying*, a barely twenty-one-year-old Jefferson is somewhat in the same situation as that of Bigger Thomas. Through a series of misadventures, Jefferson is involved in a robbery, during which the white proprietor and the other perpetrators are all killed. As the only survivor of the event, Jefferson is brought to trial and condemned to death. When Jefferson's lawyer makes a gratuitously insulting remark about Jefferson's ignorance and culpability, the black community is outraged.

As a response, Jefferson's grieving family invites—and then insists—Grant Wiggins, a young, university-educated black man currently teaching in a local school, visit Jefferson on a regular basis. During these visits, Grant is to try, before the execution date, to reach Jefferson and get him to understand in a more profound way what is happening and will happen to him. At the end of the novel Jefferson, much like Bigger, undergoes a "transformation" (254) and faces death bravely and with knowledge.

These two novels offer fruitful avenues of exploration in the areas of character, theme, and even setting. Students may want to look at the two in the following ways.

Character: Bigger and Jefferson

Looking at Bigger and Jefferson, comparing and contrasting who they are and how they react to their situations, can yield interesting points of entry for students. The following questions can help students look at these two dissimilar—and yet also similar—young men:

- What are the differences between Bigger and Jefferson as far as intelligence? Motivation? Awareness of the outside, white world?
- If somehow their verdicts could be reversed, who, Jefferson or Bigger, would you hope would be allowed to live? Why? What influences your choice?

In an essay accompanying *Native Son*, Richard Wright articulated some of his fears about writing the story of Bigger. Although we do not know, we can suppose that Ernest J. Gaines might have felt the same way about Jefferson. Wright observes:

Like Bigger himself, I felt a mental censor—product of the fears which a Negro feels from living in America—standing over me, draped in white, warning me not to write. This censor's warnings were translated into my own thought processes thus: "What will white people think if I draw the picture of such a Negro boy? Will they not at once say: 'See, didn't we tell you all along that niggers are like that? Now, look, one of their own kind has come along and drawn the picture for us!'" (xxi)

- How do you react to Wright's comment? Do you think that either Richard Wright or Ernest J. Gaines should have changed their portrayals of Bigger and Jefferson, respectively? Why or why not?

Character: Max, Grant, Bigger, and Jefferson

In both novels, the protagonists are balanced by outside figures who loom large. While Max in *Native Son* has a far different role than Grant in *A Lesson Before Dying*, both function as interpreters, witnesses, and even foils for the protagonists. Students may want to consider the following questions:

- To what extent is Bigger's socially aware lawyer, Max, like the teacher Grant Wiggins? To what extent are they different?
- Grant is coerced into helping Jefferson; Max, on the other hand, volunteers. How does or does not this make a difference in their roles regarding Jefferson and Bigger respectively?
- We know from *A Lesson Before Dying* what Jefferson learns because we have the evidence of his journal writing. We have, however, only Bigger's oral conversations with Max in *Native Son*. What lessons appear to be the same for Bigger and Jefferson? Which appear to be different?
- One of the points of *A Lesson Before Dying* is that Grant himself is changed by his conversations with Jefferson: the lesson learned before dying is learned by both Jefferson and Grant. Turning to *Native Son*, what do you think Max has learned, if anything, from Bigger? How do you know this?

Setting: The Role of Community and Family

In both of these novels, the familial setting of community and the blood ties of family are very important. Students may want to look at these settings, one in the South, one in a large urban area where many Southerners have emigrated, and compare and contrast them, possibly considering:

- Jefferson lives in the rural South and Bigger lives in Chicago. To what extent do these settings seem to affect the characters, their choices, and the reaction of their families to their crimes?

- The ministers who visit Bigger and Jefferson are very different in their approaches, and yet they both want essentially the same thing from the two young men. What is the difference in the function of religion for Bigger and Jefferson?
- Bigger's family is not as much of an obvious help to him as is Jefferson's. What could Bigger's family have done that might have been as beneficial as Jefferson's was to him? Why do you think that?
- We know some of the details of Jefferson's execution and some of the community reaction to the event. In Bigger's case, a race riot occurs during his flight from the police, but, beyond that, the last time we see Bigger is when he waves good-bye to Max from behind his cell-door bars. To the best of your judgment, what will be the reaction to Bigger's execution from Max? From Jan? From Bigger's mother? From Bigger's sister and brother? From the Daltons? Do you think a second riot might occur? Could such a riot be likely in Jefferson's community? Why or why not?

Theme: Morality and Culpability

Both of these novels deal with right and wrong; murder is a serious crime, and the main characters, though sympathetic to an extent, are both murderers. Students, then, will want to look at the following aspects of the two novels:

- Looking at both novels, how would you assess the crimes of Bigger and Jefferson? In your opinion, who is the more guilty? Why? Is it possible that, as both novels suggest, Bigger and Jefferson are on a certain level also innocent? How?
- In both Native Son and A Lesson Before Dying there is serious discussion of the possibility that no jury could judge either Bigger or Jefferson fairly. How do you react to this assertion in the novels? To what extent is it true for either Bigger or Jefferson? Who would be, for both Bigger and Jefferson, a jury of peers?

Other Connections of Native Son to Young Adult Literature

The character of Bigger can be effectively compared and contrasted to Walter Dean Myers' protagonists Slam in Slam! (1996) and Jimmy in Somewhere in the Darkness (1992) and to Robert Lipsyte's Alfred in The Contender (1967). While neither Slam, Jimmy, nor Alfred is in similar difficulty with the law, all are young urban men who feel the pressures of being young and black and trying to find their way in the world. Jimmy is dealing with the effects of a long-absent father and all that he represents, and Slam and Alfred are using their considerable athletic talent in basketball and boxing, respectively, to establish themselves as young adults, as well as dealing with other pressures. What Bigger faces and what he chooses is very different from what we know of Slam, Jimmy, and Alfred, and students may wish to look at the four young men with a critical, analytical eye.

Another young adult novel that may give some insight into Bigger's feelings about the white world is Julius Lester's *Othello* (1995), an imaginative adaptation of Shakespeare's play by the same name. In *Othello* the central character, an African American, must live and love in—and battle with—the white world. Like Bigger, Othello also commits a murder, and comparing and contrasting the two and their differing circumstances of the crimes may further illumine *Native Son*.

Connecting *Great Expectations* to Three Young Adult Novels

One of the most popular classic novels used in secondary English classes is Charles Dickens' *Great Expectations*, and the story of Pip and Estella and Miss Havisham has, for many, an enduring appeal. While contemporary film versions of this growing-up tale can help students understand the text, its relatively improbable plot, its daunting vocabulary and syntax, and its sheer length—four hundred pages in most editions—can make the Victorian *Great Expectations* less than every student's favorite classic reading experience. In addition, despite its omnipresence in the secondary curriculum, *Great Expectations* is neither the best of Dickens' works—that honor is usually reserved for *Bleak House*—nor, indeed, one of the most enlightened novels regarding gender issues.

Specifically, teachers and students with feminist sensibilities may be rather appalled at Dickens' women. From the crazed Miss Havisham, whose psychosis revolves around a faithless man, to the cruel Estella, who has been trained to enthrall and then punish men, to the loud and brutal Mrs. Joe, who routinely terrorizes both her brother and her husband, to the saintly Biddy, who loves Pip but demurely keeps to her place in the village, the main female characters in *Great Expectations* present fairly unpleasant extremes. Discussing stereotypes and archetypes may be helpful in class; it is also fair to say that the male characters in *Great Expectations* share some of the extremes the females exemplify only too vividly.

On the other hand, looking at *Great Expectations* through theme in particular and linking it to young adult literature can help students understand and more fully appreciate the journey and the challenge that Pip faces.

Theme and Great Expectations

While character, setting, and theme provide linking devices between *Native Son* and *A Lesson Before Dying*, theme and how the characters relate to the theme may be the best way to link *Great Expectations* to other young adult literature. There are many themes in the novel, among them the following:

money as a reflection of merit
the gentleman versus the working man
the purity of the country versus the corruption of the city
the quest for values
the search for self
the "great expectations" of any young person
roles of men and women
the importance of friendship

In addition, one of the most powerful and most archetypal of the themes (not listed above) is that of the hero leaving home in order to come home. The self-knowledge that Dickens' Pip earns is, additionally, similar to the self-knowledge earned by the main characters in three acclaimed young adult novels, and linking the four can be helpful to our students for their understanding and consideration.

To recap, *Great Expectations* first appeared as a serialization in 1860 and was written nine years before Charles Dickens' death. It is the story of young Philip Pirrip, known as Pip. An orphan living in the country with his violent sister and kindly blacksmith brother-in-law, Pip is sensitive and good-hearted. Both he and his brother-in-law, Joe, however, are rather brutalized by Mrs. Joe, who is prone to outbursts of temper and physical violence.

Pip's horizons are widened by his contact with the mad Miss Havisham, perhaps the most famous character in *Great Expectations*, who asks that Pip come to her house and serve as a playmate for her beautiful niece, Estella. Miss Havisham's claim to fame is her being deserted on her wedding day. In perpetual mourning, she dresses in her ancient and tattered wedding gown and, in general, centers her life upon the devastating event of her abandonment.

Pip, of course, is fascinated by the eccentric woman and, along the way, falls in love with the disdainful Estella. Estella has been schooled by Miss Havisham to scorn love and use her beauty as a weapon against faithless men. Pip's love for Estella gives him the desire to better himself, and when he becomes the recipient of money from a mysterious source, he goes to London—with great expectations—to become a gentleman.

Being a gentleman, of course, is not all it is advertised to be, and Pip not only loses his moral bearings, but he also becomes ashamed of his village origins. He eventually learns that the money that enabled him to go to London is not from Miss Havisham but from a grateful escaped convict, Magwitch, whom Pip encountered and helped many years ago. At any rate, Pip loses all of the money and, by the novel's end, a wiser and older Pip returns to the village to reconcile with Joe and reunite with Estella, who, widowed after an unhappy marriage and wholly changed in attitude, is now ready to marry him.

Essentially, Pip's leaving home to find himself—and to find that home far superior to what he left it for—is an archetypal theme. The mythic journey of leaving home to come home, of leaving the tribe on a quest that does nothing less than reaffirm the values of the tribe, is part of *Great Expectations* and a great deal of other literature. Pairing *Great Expectations* with a young adult novel such as Cynthia Rylant's *Fine White Dust* (1986), Gary Paulsen's *Dogsong* (1985), or Robert Lipsyte's *The Brave* (1991) can help students build a bridge from more contemporary work to Dickens and can provide illumination for the theme of leaving and returning, of leaving home to come home.

Great Expectations *and* A Fine White Dust, Dogsong, *and* The Brave

What Pete in Cynthia Rylant's *Fine White Dust*, Russel in Gary Paulsen's *Dogsong*, and Sonny Bear in Robert Lipsyte's *The Brave* learn is akin to what Pip learns in *Great Expectations:* home is not only the physical place one starts from and the place one necessarily leaves, it is also, essentially, a psychic destination.

In the case of Pete, the journey involves this middle schooler's interest in religion, which causes him to deeply admire and then try to run away with a religious preacher known as Preacher Man to work on a revival circuit tour. Although Pete is young and leaving would cause pain to his parents and friends, Pete decides to go. However, he is left behind, betrayed by Preacher Man, who, it turns out, is not who he appeared to be. In *Dogsong*, Russel, a fourteen-year-old Inuit boy, takes a more conventional journey and goes across the frozen Alaska tundra on a quest for self-knowledge. There he seeks to find himself and, during the journey, he not only has a vision of a warrior from another age but also helps a young pregnant girl who has fled from her town and who is stranded in the wilderness. In *The Brave*, Sonny Bear leaves the tribe literally: he is a Moscondaga Indian from a reservation in upstate New York. A seventeen-year-old boxer, Sonny ventures to New York City and finds danger, challenge, and a realization that home provides far more than he had anticipated or ever appreciated.

Theme: Points of Discussion

Once students have read all or a selected few of these novels, all of which pair well with *Great Expectations*, they may want to consider the following questions as they relate to the theme. The ten questions could be used as foci for large- or small-group discussions, journal entries, reflection papers, or even group projects. A teacher may want to use the recommended YA novels as a trio or, possibly, one at a time. At any rate, the links among the four are strong. Students may want to consider:

1. What is a *quest*? How is it different for Pip and for Pete? For Pip and for Russel? For Pip and for Sonny?

2. What is the specific journey Pip makes? Pete? Russel? Sonny? How is that journey part of the character's quest?

3. Make a list of what each character seems to want at the beginning of the novel. How is that list different at the end of the novel?

4. What truths have the characters in each novel discovered? To what extent do you think they expected to find those truths?

5. What is the home community like for each of the characters? What person or persons bother them? Don't understand or appreciate them? Support them? Why? When the character leaves and gets away from those persons, to what degree is the character's life easier? More pleasant? More difficult? Why?

6. What strengths of character or skills help Pip or Pete or Russel or Sonny find what he is seeking? What weaknesses block each of them?

7. Who helps the characters in their quest for self-knowledge? Who impedes them? How?

8. What would you say is the central "test" for each character? Why do you pick that one event or incident?

9. What is your definition of a *hero*? Could you call Pip a hero? Pete? Russel? Sonny? Why or why not?

10. "Leaving home to come home" is a paradox, something that, on the surface at least, does not seem to make sense. It is, however, what happens to all of the characters. Can you discuss why and how?

As a final note, while the three young adult novels used above are helpful, it must be mentioned that all three feature, as does *Great Expectations*, a sole male protagonist. In young adult literature, females also leave home to come home, and two novels that a teacher may want to consider are Cynthia Voigt's *Homecoming* (1981) and Jean Craighead George's *Julie of the Wolves* (1972). Asking similar questions about these characters who venture from the tribe may also be helpful to students in their consideration of *Great Expectations*.

Conclusion

If we honestly care about teaching good literature and, through that process, keeping our students reading long after they have left us and our class, we must provide for them effective ways into reading and understanding. It is not—and never has been—enough to insist that certain works are "good" for students. If we are honest, we know that such adult exhortations never appealed to us as young people, and their power has hardly been enhanced in the succeeding years. We must, therefore, connect those much revered, much treasured classics to something that our students can immediately understand. Natural, necessary, and workable, linking young adult literature to the classics can ensure understanding, enjoyment, and a continuation of lifelong reading.

Works Cited

Cormier, Robert. 1974. *The Chocolate War*. New York: Dell.

Dickens, Charles. *Bleak House*. [1852] 1971. New York: Thomas Y. Crowell.

———. *Great Expectations*. [1861] 1962. New York: Macmillan.

Faulkner, William. *As I Lay Dying*. [1930] 1964. New York: Random House.

Gaines, Ernest J. 1971. *The Autobiography of Miss Jane Pittman*. New York: Bantam.

———. 1984. *A Gathering of Old Men*. New York: Random House.

———. 1993. *A Lesson Before Dying*. New York: Alfred A. Knopf.

George, Jean Craighead. 1972. *Julie of the Wolves*. New York: Harper & Row.

Golding, William. 1954. *Lord of the Flies*. New York: G. P. Putnam.

Hawthorne, Nathaniel. [1850] 1963. *The Scarlet Letter*. New York: Bobbs-Merrill.

Hemingway, Ernest. 1926. *The Sun Also Rises*. New York: Scribner.

———. 1952. *The Old Man and the Sea*. New York: Scribner.

Hinton, S. E. 1967. *The Outsiders*. New York: Dell.

Lester, Julius. 1995. *Othello*. New York: Scholastic.

Lipsyte, Robert. 1967. *The Contender*. New York: Harper & Row.

———. 1991. *The Brave*. New York: HarperCollins.

Morrison, Toni. 1987. *Beloved*. New York: Alfred A. Knopf.

Myers, Walter Dean. 1992. *Somewhere in the Darkness*. New York: Scholastic.

———. 1996. *Slam!* New York: Scholastic.

Paulsen, Gary. 1985. *Dogsong*. New York: Bradbury Press.

———. 1987. *Hatchet*. New York: Bradbury Press.

Philbrick, Rodman. 1993. *Freak the Mighty*. New York: Scholastic.

Rylant, Cynthia. 1986. *A Fine White Dust*. New York: Bradbury Press.

Sachar, Louis. 1998. *Holes*. New York: Farrar, Straus & Giroux.

Shakespeare, William. 1942. *Macbeth. Othello: The Moor of Venice. Romeo and Juliet.* In *The Complete Plays and Poems of William Shakespeare*, edited by W. A. Neilson and C. J. Hill. New York: Houghton Mifflin.

Spinelli, Jerry. 1990. *Maniac Magee*. Boston: Little, Brown.

———. 1997. *Wringer*. New York: HarperCollins.

Stanley, Jerry. 1992. *Children of the Dust Bowl: The True Story of the School at Weedpatch Camp*. New York: Crown.

Steinbeck, John. [1937] 1970. *Of Mice and Men*. New York: Bantam.

Voigt, Cynthia. 1981. *Homecoming*. New York: Atheneum.

Wright, Richard. 1940. *Native Son*. New York: Harper & Row.

3

Interpreting the Young Adult Novel
Reading the World of Spite Fences

JOHN NOELL MOORE

All photographs are memento mori. *To take a photograph is to participate in another person's (or thing's) mortality, vulnerability, mutability. Precisely by slicing out this moment and freezing it, all photographs testify to time's relentless melt.*

Susan Sontag, On Photography

In recent years no young adult novel has affected me more immediately and profoundly than Trudy Krisher's *Spite Fences* (1994). Why is this? Is it because I have such vivid mental pictures of 1960, the year in which the novel is set? Because that year Maggie Pugh and I were both thirteen? Or is it because I, like Maggie, grew up in a deeply religious rural South where I felt constantly the weight of my "Baptist sin" (Krisher 1994, 12)? A South where people in my small Baptist church warned that if John F. Kennedy got elected president, the pope would run the country? Or is it because that year, my first in high school, I became more aware of the national unrest, things falling apart, a fragmentation I was as yet unable to articulate? Is it because some white people I knew seemed so comfortable with the word *nigger* that they spoke casually about taking a shortcut through "Niggertown" to reach the small country store where we all bought our groceries? Is it because when we took that shortcut, we passed the "colored" school, where, surrounded by a hard-packed dirt yard, the dilapidated and peeling white-frame building stood in the shadow of a grove, frozen as in a black-and-white photograph? Was it because I was secretly glad when we passed that ghost of a school that I did not go there?

Perhaps it is because I remember vividly a day in the school library when the librarian asked some eighth graders about Negroes, a moment when a tall blond girl confidently remarked, "Niggers are alright in their place," and I quickly responded, "But, what *is* their place?" I did not know then that I was developing a social consciousness; such language was far removed from my world. I knew, though, how I felt at that time in my life, the child of a "broken" home, always aware of what it meant to be different, to be an outsider.

Perhaps Krisher's novel affected me so much because my reading was visceral: I crawled into the skin of budding photographer Maggie Pugh. In my thirteenth year I had no camera to help me see, but I fought bravely behind the celebrated shield of Achilles, enjoyed the warm companionship of David Copperfield and Aunt Peggoty, rode like the wind on the Black Stallion. I chased butterflies with my homemade net (a coat hanger and scrap cloth); I ensnared them, and with great care, I pinned them down, preserving them, meticulously classifying them in my adolescent love affair with biological classification systems. I enjoyed the symmetry of their burnished wings displayed in my homemade cases, cellophane-covered boxes, the best of those saved from the last Christmas. Though I did not understand it then, my collection of *Danaeus plexippus* (monarchs), *Papilio* (swallowtails), and *Lepidoptera* (moths) symbolized freedom and flight. Reading my adolescent world in retrospect, those butterflies were signs of the hope I held that one day I would fly away from my hamlet at the foot of the Blue Ridge Mountains. Ironically, I had to freeze my vision of freedom as Maggie freezes history in her photographs before I could take flight on the wings of my destiny: delicate and powerful words.

Ways of Reading: Ways of Knowing

> *How (by what codes) is the audience inscribed within the system of*
> *the text?*
> Susan Sulieman

The series of questions and answers that open this chapter reflect a reader-response approach to *Spite Fences*, weaving me into Krisher's text, negotiating a transaction between me and its language, its characters and their stories, and the culture the novel represents. An excellent way to begin the study of a text, reader-response theory opens up the world of the text and leads naturally to other, multiple readings.

Teachers who want to engage adolescents in the study of literature will see the value in guiding them to give multiple readings. Learning to approach texts from multiple perspectives expands students' interpretive powers; encouraging them to create and compare alternative interpretations leads naturally to the development of their abilities to evaluate a wide range of readings. Young adult literature provides an excellent vehicle for this intellectual process because it offers students texts that are immediately accessible; from students' first reader responses to young adult texts, teachers can guide them to multiple readings of both young adult literature and the standard works in the secondary school canon.

To visualize the processes of multiple readings, imagine reading development as a "series of concentric circles leading out from the text to its cultural and literary contexts" (Suleiman 1980, 12). Three key questions guide readers' interpretive performances: (1) "How (by what codes) is the audience inscribed within the system" of the text? (2) What other formal and thematic aspects of the text "determine readability or intelligibility?" and (3) "What are the codes and conventions—whether aesthetic or cultural—to which actual readers refer in making sense of texts and to which actual authors refer in facilitating or complicating, or perhaps even frustrating, the reader's sense-making activity" (12)?

Responding to these questions, I plan here to generate multiple readings of *Spite Fences* to illustrate how such a task might be accomplished with a young adult novel. I'll read Maggie's world as a language system (semiotics) of historically recurring narrative patterns, characters, symbols, and themes (archetypes), and in the largest circumference, as the intersection of cultural codes inscribing gender, race, and class (feminism, black theory, cultural studies). Finally, because it dominates the teaching of interpretation in American secondary schools today, I'll address the limitations of the close reading strategies of New Critical formalism.

Reading the Worlds of *Spite Fences*

Krisher weaves an intricate text of multiple narratives to create Maggie Pugh's adolescence in a world defined by gender, race, and class. Maggie compares the geography of her town, Kinship, to a baseball diamond. Railroad tracks cut through it from east to west (first base to third). The rich live in Clifton Hill, north of the tracks (second base), and coloreds live to the south (home plate); the middle class lives to the west (third base), and poor whites live to the east (first base). Krisher's main characters are the Pughs (poor whites); their neighbors, the Boggses (poor white trash); Elmer Byer, owner of the local drug store, and other whites (middle class); and Zeke Freeman and the Reverend Potter (coloreds). Two major black characters from Atlanta, mathematics professor and political activist George Hardy, and Ida Mae Thatcher, a lawyer, come to Kinship; their influence both educates Maggie and brings the civil rights movement to her small Georgia town.

In this fictional topography we live through character relationships and the issues and themes that emerge from them: (1) Maggie, Gardenia, and Izabelle (child abuse and child exploitation); (2) Maggie, Zeke, and Pert (cameras, photography, coming of age, and learning to see); (3) Maggie, Zeke, and George Hardy (racial discrimination); and (4) the Pughs and the Boggses (class hatred). Krisher frames the novel in two historical events one hundred years apart: the Civil War and the

Civil Rights movement. The past haunts Kinship. Henry Pugh, Maggie's father, refuses to acknowledge present problems by constantly telling Civil War stories. Her mother, Izabelle Pugh, applies to the United Daughters of the Confederacy to legitimize her personal history in a connection with the Confederate past. Most important, powerful whites in Kinship refuse to grant its black residents the freedoms accorded to them by the Emancipation Proclamation.

One narrative thread ties the novel together: Maggie's secret, an experience so horrible that she has repressed its memory. As the unfolding events of her daily life at age thirteen accumulate, Maggie remembers what she witnessed a year ago. When she remembers, she can read her world, and her way of reading gives her the power to change it.

Maggie's memory returns gradually in a series of flashbacks, each signaled textually by a shift from standard type to italics. In the first memory (52–53), five-year-old Maggie drinks from a water fountain marked "COLORED" in Byer's Drug and incurs her mother's wrath: "Don't you know what color you is yet?" (53). When she is twelve (65–70), Zeke Freeman is arrested at Byer's for going into the restroom marked "WHITE," and Elmer Byer threatens him: "We got laws in this state to keep things separate, and you and your friends here better learn to respect them" (67). Subsequently, Zeke files a lawsuit that precipitates the horrific event (183–88) Maggie represses for a year. Angered at the lawsuit, white men beat Zeke, who protests, "Just wantin' my rights, is all. My rights and my people's." "Niggers ain't got no rights," Virgil Boggs retorts. After the men beat Zeke in the eyes, ears, and mouth in a brutal incantation of "See no evil, Hear no evil, Speak no evil," Virgil urinates and then ejaculates on the black man's swollen face (184). One year later, in the present of the novel, Maggie reads her world through the lens of her camera. Her prize-winning photographs in *Life* magazine expose the racial violence in Kinship to the whole country and perhaps portend a bright future for her in photojournalism.

Semiotics: Reading the World as Sign

We can read Maggie's world using the strategies of semiotics, a linguistic theory based on the idea that human beings use language systems to construct social reality. Whites construct racial reality in Kinship, empowering themselves and oppressing blacks by perpetuating the use of the word *nigger*, a corruption of the Latin word *niger* (black) and its subsequent linguistic transformations in Portuguese, *negro*, and Middle French, *negre*. Throughout its etymological history, *niger* and its transformations signified "dark-skinned," but in the early eighteenth century the offensive word *nigger* appeared in English (*Webster's Ninth New Collegiate*). In the United States it came to signify the low socioeconomic underclass perpetuated when whites refused blacks access to education and other avenues to power. In the 1930s the less offensive *colored* (*Webster's*) came into polite use, although its ugly predecessor did not disappear. Both words encode class status in Kinship. The Black Power and Black Arts movements of the 1960s popularized the word *black* to signify racial pride. Confused when George Hardy refers to himself as a black man, Maggie wonders if he does not know that folks in Kinship say "colored." She is unable to read the changing language of the world beyond Kinship.

The language of George Hardy's notes to Maggie when she begins cleaning for him introduces her to the power of education and experience. When he compliments her for "*splendid work*" (79) on his fancy letterhead, she rhapsodizes, imagining her own letterhead: "*Magnolia April Pugh, Housekeeper, Splendid Work, Kinship*" (80). Hardy's compliments heighten her self-esteem. When she hears the word *respect* in reference to her, she feels that something has suddenly taken off inside her, "like a tiny jackrabbit" (110).

Sign systems extend beyond linguistic codes. Although Zeke is illiterate, he reads Maggie's body language, studying her face, she notices, as if there is "something written that he wanted to read" (97). In her eyes he reads worry and fear, in her shoulders, heavy burdens. In her bruises and welts he reads hurt, but he cannot read "the truth behind it" (101). Zeke's illiteracy affirms the power of nonverbal sign systems in the construction of meaning.

Linguistic sign systems that function through binary oppositions (good/bad; white/black) privilege one idea over another. George Hardy's Independence Day speech in Negro Park illustrates how such systems represent cultural power in Kinship. Blacks are all too familiar with the words *shame, ignorance,* and *injustice,* he tells the crowd, but he advises them to study the words *equality, mercy,* and *justice,* "fit to read" words (188). Hardy constructs the binary opposition *not fit to read/fit to read* as he encodes the black/white power structure of Kinship.

The sit-in illustrates the cultural power of sign systems. Blacks signal peaceful protest in the language of their two-rule system: (1) Quiet dignity. (2) No violence. Zeke's Bible, the ancient code, lies open to Romans 12, from which Maggie remembers the verse "Recompense to no man for evil." The language of hate explodes in racial epithets: "Blue gum," "Jungle bunny," and "Coconut head" (270).

As violence erupts, Maggie's visual attempts to read the world fail as everything around her melts together "like a watercolor gone wild" (271). She begins taking pictures, tripping the shutter to frame and freeze the awful moments, writing a text in darkness and light, a text of history and hurt, of hate and horror. When Virgil smashes his fist into George Hardy's face, everything fuses in a single image that swims red and fills up the lens of Maggie's camera. In this bloody image she reads geography and personal history: standing on the red earth, living through a summer colored by bloody violence, everything suddenly comes together in "the color of Kinship" (272). Confident in what she sees, she feels empowered "to tell the world" (274). Writing in darkness and light, she photographs Kinship at its worst, constructing history through the eye of her lens, constructing a cultural text for the world outside.

Archetypes: Reading the World as Narrative

> *What other formal and thematic aspects of the text determine readibility or intelligibility?*
> Susan Suleiman

Moving farther out on our interpretive circumference, we can read *Spite Fences* from the perspective of archetypal theory, according to which a narrative is a historical and cultural continuation and accumulation of earlier plots, characters, symbols, images, and themes. Archetypal theory echoes the familiar notion that there are no new stories, just new ways of telling the old stories. As the Preacher of Ecclesiastes proclaims: "What has been is what will be, and what has been done is what will be done; and there is nothing new under the sun" (Ecclesiastes 1:9). In this context, *Spite Fences* rewards an archetypal reading in its familiar elements of fairy tale, myth, and epic.

Reading the Novel as Fairy Tale

The story of Izabelle, Maggie, and Gardenia is a version of *Cinderella* with a twist: both daughters are Cinderellas. Izabelle is both mother and wicked (step)mother. Like the mother of Cinderella's stepsisters, who wants one of her daughters to marry the prince at all costs, in her selfish pride Izabelle exploits seven-year-old Gardenia's innocence by entering her in a series of beauty contests. Like Cinderella's wicked stepmother, she verbally abuses Maggie; in a departure from the fairy tale, she also physically abuses her daughter in her violent fits of anger. With the help of her "fairy godfather," George Hardy, Maggie triumphs over her mother's abuse. Henry Pugh, out of touch and benign throughout most of the novel, serves metaphorically as Cinderella's dead father, powerless to protect his daughters from their mother.

Other Cinderella elements appear in the novel. Gardenia's name, Maggie tells George Hardy, "fits like a glass slipper." Izabelle's efforts to get Gardenia a dress for the first pageant parody the fairy godmother's magic in creating Cinderella's gown. To get the dress she wants, Izabelle battles another contestant's mother at a rummage sale, unchivalrously brandishing her umbrella as if it were a sword. Like Cinderella, Gardenia faces adversity before she goes to the state pageant (her

Cinderella ball) when Virgil Boggs spitefully shears off her golden curls. Maggie assumes the role of fairy godmother, cleaning at George Hardy's to earn the five dollars that will buy Gardenia a wig. In a fusion of *Cinderella* and *Gone with the Wind*, Gardenia wins the state pageant in Savannah, where the stage looks like a shabby Tara with columns of white cardboard attached to a frame of chicken wire. Gardenia's win assures her of a place in the national pageant.

As Cinderella, Maggie is abandoned by her mother in favor of her sister and relegated to domestic drudgery. Maggie is beautiful, though, and she takes pride in her maturing body. Standing seminude before the mirror in her room, she admires herself: "I saw how tall and strong I was. How splendid" (86). She describes her physical beauty in similes from nature: her thick hair rushes down her shoulder "like a waterfall"; her neck slopes into her shoulders "curving like a river into a gentle bend"; and her breasts are "tender as new-laid eggs" (87). In a Cinderella reversal, Virgil Boggs as the Peeping Tom anti-prince destroys Maggie's reverie with a mocking laugh "like a whinny" (87). Later, when he attempts to rape Maggie, she hears the sound again, "a whinny, a rough, full-throated snort. Like a horse tossing back its head" (127). This horse imagery reverses the traditional role of horses in fairy tales, where they often appear as "prophetic creatures with magical powers, speaking with human voices and providing advice for those who are entrusted to their care." Virgil Boggs' equine voice reflects another attitude toward the animal: early church fathers considered the horse "haughty and lascivious (it was said to neigh longingly when it saw a woman)" (Biedermann 1989, 178).

Fairy tales often include an amulet, a magic object that protects a character and wards off evil; Maggie's amulet, which she wears around her neck, is the gold key to George Hardy's door. When Virgil attacks her and chokes her with the chain, he touches the charm and vulgarizes it: "Use it to unlock your pretty secrets" (Krisher 131), but the key empowers Maggie. Virgil's touch "unlocked something inside of me, something strong" (132). Kneeing him in the crotch, she escapes.

Back at home she suffers her mother's wrath and her vow to avenge Virgil's defilement of her daughter. Izabelle directs the construction of a fence between the Pughs and the Boggses. This is the "spite fence" of the novel's title, and it symbolizes all the fences in Kinship: the railroad tracks that signal class structure, the public signs that privilege whites over blacks, and the historical and cultural fences of the mind and heart that separate love and hate.

When Maggie's wins the *Life* magazine photography contest, Krisher weaves together the two Cinderella stories. Pert tries to explain to Izabelle that Maggie "had won a contest and that [she] was something like Gardenia" (279). Too ashamed at Maggie's connection to black people, Izabelle refuses to acknowledge this sibling link. Maggie's Cinderella story continues, however, as she and Pert travel to Atlanta, where she is the official photographer at the marriage of George Hardy and Ida Mae Thatcher. Though Maggie is not the prince's bride and the novel's final scene does not ensure a happy-ever-after ending, the wedding offers promise and hope, and it situates Maggie in a brave new world.

From the perspective of feminist theory's basic principle that gender is the fundamental category for reading the world, the double Cinderella story invites several interpretations. Gardenia's story as a critique of "beauty" pageants and their exploitation of female bodies recalls the videotapes of JonBenet Ramsey, a beautiful child in adult makeup and extravagant costumes, mimicking adult sensuality in poses and dance routines. An innocent constructed by adults as a little princess, JonBenet had embarked on a decade-long quest to become a queen, Miss America. In contrast, Maggie's Cinderella critiques the patriarchy that denies women respect for their substantial abilities and contributions, for their vision, and for their power to effect cultural transformation.

Reading the Novel as Myth

Circling outward once more, we read *Spite Fences* in a larger cultural and historical context as the archetypal story of the struggle between good and evil. Several narratives support this interpretation: the American frontier Western, and the myth of the Garden of Eden.

Images of the Western recur throughout the novel. When Virgil Boggs destroys Gardenia's doll—a foreshadowing of his later physical abuse of both sisters—Izabelle, irate that Maggie has failed to protect her sister, whips Maggie with a rosebush stem that Maggie compares to a whip in a scene "of cowboys breaking horses." The whipping draws blood in "thin red trails, the color of Kinship dirt" (51), and these trails, both literal and metaphoric, locate Maggie in the archetypal struggle between good and evil that defines the American Western. When Pert hears about the whipping, she vows to avenge her best friend with an imaginary pistol in an imaginary holster. As they ride out of town on their Roadmaster bikes, Maggie refers to herself as the "sidekick" to Pert's "outlaw" (60).

Maggie describes racial conflict in Western images. When Zeke is arrested at Byer's Drug, she thinks he is treated like an "outlaw on a TV western" (68). Later, George Hardy reveals his reasons for coming to Kinship, and his eyes remind Maggie of cowboys in TV Westerns, "aiming through their rifle sights" (256). Her image fits George perfectly: he comes to Kinship to right a wrong, to teach blacks how to demonstrate for their rights, how to aim for a future of freedom and peace.

Other recurring imagery in *Spite Fences* suggests the ancient myth of Eden, a story of the fate of innocence in the primordial garden. Edenic imagery enters the novel in a dream. After Izabelle whips her, Maggie drifts into a "dream. Of a garden. In a land far from Kinship," a "land of green and freedom" (53). Krisher counters the freedom of this paradisiacal garden with a nightmare of imprisonment. After Izabelle determines to build a spite fence, Maggie dreams "about being holed up in a place surrounded by high wood fencing like a stockade" (145). Like the Alamo, it is located in the deep South, and Maggie feels doomed there. In an ironic contrast, her mother imagines a fairy tale fence "high as a castle wall" (143), surrounding the property "like a fortress" (144). Her fence seems medieval, designed to protect the privileged and to keep out the undesirable and the vulgar— the Boggses.

Maggie's dream garden corresponds to her experiences in Negro Park before she witnessed Zeke's beating there. Remembered as a place of "laughter and music," "invitation, entertainment, [and] shelter" (61), it remains Edenic in the natural beauty of spring's pink flower spikes, summer's orange honeysuckle splashes, and fall's flaming pimento blossoms. In contrast, its facilities are shabby. Ironically, Kinship's whites give the park to blacks as a gift after Zeke drops his lawsuit against Elmer Byer.

Archetypally, Negro Park is the garden where Maggie falls from innocence into experience at the Negro Independence Day celebration. Two events precipitate her fortunate fall: George Hardy's passionate speech provokes a fully developed memory of Zeke's beating, and her Kodak Retina I, a birthday gift from Pert, becomes a photographic eye as she records images that later threaten to destroy her world. When George Hardy lifts Maggie to his shoulders so she can pick a flower from the Ghost Tree, Pert takes the last picture on the roll; developed, it symbolizes Maggie's emergence into a brave new world. Rising above the merriment into the night sky exploding with brilliant fireworks, she feels "for the first time in [her] whole life, like [she'd] finally been born" (195). Maggie's metaphoric (re)birth situates her in a complex matrix of human experiences, of literature, history, religious allegory, science, psychology, and anthropology. In the intersection of archetypal gardens, fairy tales, Westerns, and weddings, we approach the novel from the most current development in literary theory: cultural studies.

Cultural Studies: Reading the Novel's Intertextualities

> *What are the codes and conventions—whether aesthetic or cultural—to which readers refer in making sense of a text and to which authors refer in facilitating or complicating, or perhaps even frustrating, the reader's sense-making activity?*
>
> Susan Suleiman

As the intersection of literary and formerly nonliterary disciplines, cultural studies moves us outward again; as a way of reading, it implicates many of the literary theories that preceded it. To illustrate: Consider the progression of my readings of *Spite Fences*. I began with a reader-response strategy, locating myself in the 1960 historical and cultural milieu of my adolescence. Without explicitly identifying the theory, my response implicated black literary theory, in which race is the fundamental category of literary investigation. Extending and amplifying my initial reading, I examined the novel's archetypes, story patterns posited in the Jungian collective unconscious. Now I complicate and enlarge these previous readings as I interpret the local history of Kinship in its broadest historical and cultural context as epic, a narrative about the fate of a race or nation, centered on the actions of a hero, and occurring in a vast setting. Zeke's story links Kinship to the biblical epic of loss, suffering, redemption, and apocalypse. *Spite Fences* serves as a metaphor for the vast panorama of the Old and New Testaments. It echoes familiar themes: the epic journey of the Israelites from bondage in Egypt to the Promised Land; the story of the heroic Messiah, whose persecution and sacrifice will prepare the way for the post-Armageddon paradise, a new Eden, the New Jerusalem.

As a source of the town's cultural knowledge, Zeke has been "in the center of things" (20) in Kinship for as long as Maggie can remember. His name, Ezekiel Jeremiah Freeman, links him to two Old Testament contemporaries, the prophets Ezekiel and Jeremiah. Zeke feels the connection in remembering his mother's advice to live his name, "to be a prophet," and to offer hope to others (95). The biblical Ezekiel, taken into Babylonian captivity by King Nebuchadnezzar, has a vision of dry bones that come to life, a vision that prophesies freedom from slavery and the restoration of the Jewish nation. In its imagery Zeke reads the history of his people: "Ezekiel's speakin' 'bout my people, Maggie. About the black folks here in Kinship, here in Georgia, here all over these United States" (97). When God spoke to the valley of dry bones, Zeke explains, a great wind breathed life into the bones and clothed them in flesh. He interprets the story as a metaphor: His people have found hope for a new life in places like Montgomery, Alabama, Nashville, Tennessee, and Atlanta, Georgia. Can Kinship offer them the same hope? Zeke aims "to find out the truth about" that (98). A cultural studies perspective invites close study of blacks' long journey to freedom from their oppressors. Maggie identifies Zeke with the New Testament hero who promised eternal peace: when he tells her that he got arrested in Byer's intentionally, she thinks, "Zeke Freeman and Jesus Christ were about the two bravest people in this world" (92). Zeke's last name symbolizes the Holy Grail of his quest: He wants to live his last name, to become a free man, and to guide his people to freedom.

The image of the biblical prophet recurs near the end of the novel and ties together many of its themes. George Hardy shows Maggie a little bridge he has built near his house. His symbol of hope for Kinship, it is a countersymbol for the fences, literal and figurative, that separate the races. At that moment, Maggie looks up to "the dome of the sky" and sees "the sun spinning way up in the middle of the air like a wheel" (262). In a complicated intertextuality, her vision of the spinning sun echoes the theophany in Ezekiel 1; the biblical prophet receives his call to prophecy from God, who is seated on a sapphire throne surrounded by sparkling and spiraling wheels within wheels. Her vision echoes the language of the African American spiritual "Ezekiel Saw the Wheel." As a way of reading, cultural study invites a closer examination of spirituals as historically coded language. In his Independence Day speech, George Hardy encodes another spiritual, "Ain't Gonna Study War No More," as he talks about *ignorance, injustice,* and *shame* as words black people "are not going to study anymore" (188). His speech and the crowd's vigorous reaction (178–90) represent another site for cultural studies exploration, the call and response through which slaves communicated with each other.

In these biblical intertexts Krisher seems to envision peace in Kinship. Weaving together the Hebrew's journey to the Promised Land and black Americans' epic journey to freedom, she suggests that the nation will be restored. How? The principal metaphor of the novel implies that this restoration can take place when people pass through the red seas of bloody violence to tear down fences, real and imagined, and to build bridges in their place.

New Critical Formalism: Reading the World as Image

New Criticism or New Critical formalism is the theory that dominates the teaching of literature in American secondary schools today. Educated almost exclusively in the principles of this theory, I found it immensely comforting as a way of reading. Learning to interpret texts without authorial or historical contexts, I grew confident in my ability to use the golden key of New Criticism to unlock literary treasure chests and discover the single dazzling jewel, the one "correct" reading of the work of art. Over the last decade my life in theory has taught me how privileged and small the New Critical world is, how its one way of reading constrains me and my students.

Were I to offer a New Critical reading of *Spite Fences*, I would focus on the image of the camera as metaphor, linking photography and theme throughout the novel. The novel opens with Maggie remembering Zeke's beating as if it were a picture that she has tried to keep out of her mind (2). Snapping back to reality from one of her memory sequences, she compares her mind to the camera's eye gone black as the light vanishes (70). In an elaboration of this image, she becomes the camera, her body a tripod topped with the camera's eye (86). When she discovers that George Hardy is black, she compares her eyes opening wide in surprise to a camera lens (108). After Izabelle destroys the camera Zeke gave Maggie, the camera becomes a metaphor for the world of Kinship: both are smashed and broken (171). After she takes pictures of the sit-in, she understands how photography reads her world, and she declares that she will share with the whole world the story that her pictures tell (274). As official photographer at George and Ida Mae's wedding, Maggie realizes that, through the lens of her camera, she reads the world as "a curious place, full of change and wonder." She also learns that it doesn't matter what side you are, "Somehow, we're all kin" (283). A complementary series of images link Zeke Freeman to an African king in a picture in *National Geographic*. Maggie is arrested by the similarity in the way that Zeke holds his head as compared to the African king, towering above his villagers, resplendent in a flowing robe ablaze in purples and golds (32, 68, 182).

Aesthetically these beautifully interwoven images of cameras and kings appear at one level to unify the novel, but what value are they to me as an interpreter once I have traced their weave in the text? Certainly I have demonstrated my close reading ability, but in the broader context of cultural studies, this reading seems too tidy, too easily achieved, little more than an academic exercise. Such a reading often destroys the reading experience for students in classrooms that privilege treasure hunts for symbols, images, metaphors, poetic devices, and other elements of literature.

What can be done to breathe new life into the dry bones of this overused interpretive pedagogy? We do not wish to abandon close reading skills; however, if we enfold them into other ways of reading, we can amplify our textual experiences, both literary and lived. Consider, for example, the effect of reading Krisher's fictional world against the world described in my epigraph from Susan Sontag's *On Photography*, a nonfiction text in which she discusses the cultural power of photographs. In traditional ways of reading, photography is a nonliterary phenomenon. Sontag's text invites me to construct a cultural studies reading of *Spite Fences*, perhaps as a photographic essay on the Civil Rights movement in 1960, with quotations from the novel juxtaposed against black-and-white photographs of the movement. Situating Krisher's fictional world against the backdrop of American cultural history clothes the dry bones of the metaphor as a literary device. For adolescents learning to read their world, this way of reading enables them to see what has been, to read what is, and to construct the text of what can be.

What I have demonstrated here is a pluralistic approach to reading the world of young adult fiction. For teachers and students wishing to learn more about literary theory and interpretation, I offer a bit of advice gleaned from my life as a reader and teacher: do not be intimidated by literary theory; though the theoretical conversations seem overwhelming, we have to begin somewhere. Begin where you are: consider your education, your reading, your teaching, then start with some questions that intrigue you. Be guided by your intellect, enthusiasm, and love of language and remember that you are a scholar teacher.

This brief list of texts may assist you in getting started: *Literary Theory: An Introduction* (Eagleton 1983); *Reorientations: Critical Theories and Pedagogies* (Hendrickson and Morgan 1990); *Text Book: An Introduction to Literary Language* (Scholes, Comley, and Ulmer 1995); *Conversations: Contemporary Critical Theory and the Teaching of Literature* (Moran and Penfield 1990); *Reading Texts: Reading, Responding, Writing* (McCormick, Waller, and Flower 1987); *A Reader's Guide to Contemporary Literary Theory* (Selden, Widdowson, and Brooker 1997); *Textual Power: Literary Theory and the Teaching of English* (Scholes 1985); *Literary Criticism: An Introduction to Theory and Practice* (Bressler 1999). My own *Interpreting Young Adult Literature: Literary Theory in the Secondary Classroom* (1997) offers practical introductions to literary theories and demonstrates detailed readings of young adult novels. The theories and texts that I explore are New Critical formalism in *M.C. Higgins, the Great* (Hamilton 1974), archetypal theory in *Dogsong* (Paulsen 1985), structuralism and semiotics in *The Moves Make the Man* (Brooks 1984), deconstruction/post-structuralism in *The Giver* (Lowry 1993), reader response in *Fallen Angels* (Myers 1988), feminism in *The Leaving and Other Stories* (Wilson 1992), black aesthetics in *A Lesson Before Dying* (Gaines 1993), cultural studies in *Night Kites* (Kerr 1986), and multiple perspectives in *Jacob Have I Loved* (Paterson 1980).

As encouragement to engage and enjoy literary theories and new interpretive strategies, I offer a personal story. For years I worried about my expertise as a classroom teacher: Did I know enough? Did I read enough? Was I up on the latest pedagogical trends? Did I demand, encourage, stimulate, provoke, and model enough? The list of verbs echoed down the years, but one day I had an epiphany: being a teacher means *becoming* a teacher, dreaming and doing, teaching and learning, constructing, deconstructing, and reconstructing myself. In "First Letter: Reading the World/Reading the Word," Paulo Freire articulates the lesson of my enlightened moment: "Teachers first learn how to teach, but they learn how to teach as they teach something that is relearned as it is being taught" (1998, 17). My readings of *Spite Fences* demonstrate what I believe is the recursivity of the teaching life: in learning new ways of reading, we learn new ways of teaching, and in our teaching, we and our students learn new ways of reading our world.

Works Cited

Biedermann, Hans. 1989. *Dictionary of Symbolism*. Trans. James Hulbert. New York: Facts on File.

Bressler, Charles. 1999. *Literary Criticism: An Introduction to Theory and Practice*. Upper Saddle River, NJ: Prentice Hall.

Brooks, Bruce. 1984. *The Moves Make the Man*. New York: HarperCollins.

Eagleton, Terry. 1983. *Literary Theory: An Introduction*. Minneapolis: University of Minnesota Press.

Freire, Paulo. 1998. *Teachers as Cultural Workers: Letters to Those Who Dare to Teach*, trans. Donald Maledo, Dale Koike, and Alexandra Oliveira. Boulder, CO: Westview Press.

Gaines, Ernest. 1993. *A Lesson Before Dying*. New York: Knopf.

Hamilton, Virginia. 1974. M.C. *Higgins, the Great*. New York: Macmillan.

Hendrickson, Bruce, and Thais E. Morgan, eds. 1990. *Reorientations: Critical Theories and Pedagogies*. Champaign IL: University of Illinois Press.

Kerr, M. E. 1986. *Night Kites*. New York: Harper.

Krisher, Trudy. 1994. *Spite Fences*. New York: Bantam Doubleday Dell.

Lowry, Lois. 1993. *The Giver*. New York: Bantam Doubleday Dell.

McCormick, Kathleen, Gary Waller, and Linda Flower. 1987. *Reading, Responding, Writing*. Lexington, MA: DC Heath.

Moore, John Noell. 1997. *Interpreting Young Adult Literature: Literary Theory in the Secondary Classroom*. Portsmouth, NH: Heinemann–Boynton/Cook.

Moran, Charles, and Elizabeth P. Penfield. 1990. *Conversations: Contemporary Critical Theory and the Teaching of Literature*. Urbana, IL: National Council of Teachers of English.

Myers, Walter Dean. 1988. *Fallen Angels*. New York: Scholastic.

Paterson, Katherine. 1980. *Jacob Have I Loved*. New York: HarperTrophy.

Paulsen, Gary. 1985. *Dogsong*. New York: Puffin.

Scholes, Robert. 1985. *Textual Power: Literary Theory and the Teaching of English*. New Haven: Yale University Press.

Scholes, Robert, Nancy R. Comley, and Gregory L. Ulmer. 1995. *Text Book: An Introduction to Literary Language*. 2nd ed. New York: St. Martin's.

Selden, Roman, Peter Widdowson, and Peter Brooker. 1997. *A Reader's Guide to Contemporary Literary Theory*. 4th ed. London: Prentice Hall.

Suleiman, Susan. 1980. Introduction to *The Reader* in *The Text: Essays on Audience and Interpretation*, edited by Susan Suleiman and Inge Crossman. Princeton: Princeton University Press.

Wilson, Budge. 1992. *The Leaving and Other Stories*. New York: Philomel.

4

Creating a Bond Between Writer and Reader

Sue Ellen Bridgers

I came to write books of interest to young people quite inadvertently, having spent part of 1974 and 1975 writing a story about a migrant girl living in the South who wanted a place to call her own. It was a story set in a Southern farming community, and the landscape and the home place were as important to me as the characters were, perhaps more so. Once the manuscript was finished, I thought *Home Before Dark* was a good story, but I had no idea who might want to read it. It didn't seem to fit anywhere.

An editor at *Redbook* magazine suggested I send the manuscript to Pat Ross at Alfred A. Knopf, where the readership issue eventually became the publisher's decision. I didn't know there was such a thing as a young adult novel until Ross asked me how I felt about *Home Before Dark* being designated as such.

I was so delighted to be published by Knopf, to have an editor who understood my intention and celebrated my attempt, to have readers of any age, that I certainly wasn't compelled to question the publisher's judgment. Although the book was marketed as a young adult novel, the mail I received about *Home Before Dark* (a condensed form also appeared in *Redbook* and the *Reader's Digest Condensed Books* series) indicated a broad readership. Letters came from elderly readers, nostalgic for the rural life the story evoked, as well as from young people who were curious about Stella's family and intrigued by her determination to have the life she'd envisioned.

When I began thinking about my second book, I knew I wanted to keep the rural Southern setting, but I hoped to find a more lighthearted story to tell. A person out of my husband's past, a retarded man who was loved and protected by his community, provided the impetus, but I immediately felt the need for a companion for Dwayne Pickens, someone whose mind would be more accessible to me than his could be. At first I envisioned another man, then a boy in his late teens, and eventually a young girl who could pretend to be a boy. This deception on Casey's part added a dimension to their friendship that I knew would hold my interest. So by a process of selectivity, I found myself with a protagonist even younger than Stella Willis, a flat-chested twelve-year-old tomboy who met the needs of the story I wanted to tell.

During the struggle to find my story, I wasn't thinking about the reader at all. In fact, although I now feel some pressure to write for the teenage audience, I still try to write to please myself, to write the story I want to read. This is especially true during the first stage of the process, while I am getting to know my character. The reader I imagine, if I imagine one at all, is hidden behind the book.

The fact remains that since all my books have young people in them, teenagers have turned out to be my sustaining audience. And what a wonderful audience to have! They read with enthusiasm. They are impatient and forthright. When they like a book, they pass it around. When they love one, they hold the memory of it close. They let it affect them.

Young people energize me. I like the intensity with which many of them live. Their lives seem more exciting, more on the edge than those of adults. But many middle-class young people seem sad to me, too. If they are aware of world events, they have reason to be concerned, and I am appreciative of the positive outlets many have found to let their voices be heard about social and political issues, such as students who, in the early nineties, succeeded in having tuna banned in their school cafeteria. Surely they have used that experience to tackle other environmental issues since then. I also admire students here in North Carolina who formed an organization in their community to help other at-risk students to stay in school.

But frequently teenagers' worries are turned inward, and they grapple with their problems alone. Too many of them don't seem to have appropriate skills or information to cope successfully. They become enmeshed in thought patterns that lead them to racial and hate crimes. With no regard for life, they kill others. Often they kill themselves. Then there are the kids on drugs, truant or failing at school; there are children having children or suffering abuses many of us didn't know existed a few years ago. Kids who are too hungry to think, who sleep in abandoned automobiles, vacant buildings, boxes. Then there are the students who seem to be sleepwalking through school, their major interest the jobs that provide car payments and gas. Their most urgent cause is getting an "open campus" lunch policy. Even those students intrigue me. What is going on behind their sleepy eyes? What motivates the teenage athlete? What kind of home life does the perfect student have? How will the decisions they make today affect their adult lives? What are they thinking, feeling, longing for?

In fiction I can ask: "Who are you?" And over a period of months, the answers come. Once I described this process as one of having a room inside myself that gradually fills, the clutter of a life haphazardly pushed into corners and against the walls. A life collects itself within my own life—a separate identity I am always questioning: "What do you think? How do you feel? What will you do next?"

But how does this process begin? Usually it starts with a visual experience. I see a person in my mind's eye. In the case of *Sara Will*, I saw this woman coming down the road in the twilight. She had work gloves tucked in her belt and carried a rake over her shoulder. I knew what her name was. I went to my typewriter and wrote exactly what I had seen. Then I started questioning her. "Where are you going?" "Where have you been?" "What was your life like before this moment?" What Sara Will told me was intriguing—I discovered she had a closed-up life and very limited experience. I learned she was frequently frustrated and sharp-tongued; what others may have considered composure was actually rigidity. Sara Will rarely took a deep breath. Her determination and forcefulness was a cover-up for an emptiness she didn't know how to fill. Not an especially pleasant person, this middle-aged Sara of firm lip and flashing eyes! So why did I spend three years with her? The main reason is that I am a lot like Sara. My exterior life may not be—it is, in fact, very different from hers—and yet we had similar interior lives: fear of failure, a protective rigidity in our thinking, an unwillingness to change. A friend called while reading *Sara Will* to report tearfully that she was just like Sara. "Oh," I said to comfort her, "we all are."

By the time I had this visual experience of Sara Will coming down the road, I had learned to be accepting of these experiences. The first one, however, was somewhat startling in its immediacy. It occurred while I was traveling toward my hometown with my family. Suddenly I saw this girl there in the car with us, and I knew she wanted the home we were going to. But why did she want it, and how would she go about getting it? She didn't have a name; she didn't have a past. She was just present with her scruffy family. We made quite a crowd in the car, although my family seemed unaware of the extra passengers. All weekend at my mother's, I thought about these people. In fact, they were on my mind for several months, and I wrote fifty pages about them before putting the manuscript away as a failed short story. After a couple of years of what must have been much subconscious ruminating, I began working on Stella's story again. By then she had a new name, a history, and identifiable people in her life. Suddenly and inexplicably, I had a great deal of faith in her.

My first recognition of the characters in *Notes for Another Life* also occurred in an automobile; perhaps it is the movement of the car, the sense of not being completely grounded anywhere that causes these experiences. At any rate, these characters were singing, and I didn't have my radio on! On the edge of a pocket calendar I wrote, "They would start out singing," and listed the songs I heard. When I reached my destination, I quickly wrote down what these people looked like and what their names were.

Now that I understand my process, those early experiences with a new character before the story begins to take shape are the most exciting time for me as a writer. In my enthusiasm for these people I am about to know, I don't think about which genre they will fit into. I am too busy just getting to know them because it is through their past and present that I discern their future—the story I will tell. More often than not, the character that interests me most is a young person.

The most obvious reason for my interest in young people is that I was once one myself. Of course, in the seventies and eighties, I had teenagers in the house who kept me knowledgeable about what young people were up to, although, while my children were living at home, I never used them or their situations for subject matter. It seemed too much an infringement on their privacy; besides, I was too involved in their ups and downs to see literary merit in their stories. Whatever the reason, it was not until *Permanent Connections* that I used my children in any way, and by then they were grown. There is a brief argument between the mother and daughter in that book that is similar to an argument I had with one of my daughters. When I asked permission to use it, she couldn't recall the incident, although I remember thinking at the time that what she was saying was book-worthy. I also asked my son, who had played high school football, to write a conversation about an upcoming game, which I was able to use, except for necessary expurgations.

Memories of my own teenage years are probably the true catalyst for discovering these young characters. I remember my teenage years much better than I do more recent times, but I find it isn't the events I need to remember so much as the feel of things. The gamut of teenage emotions I experienced is somehow always at my disposal. Envision a character, give him or her an internal life and a problem, and I'm on a journey full of all the emotional turmoil I knew forty years ago.

I have always written about people and places I love. I can't imagine spending three years living with characters who bore me. I'd like to avoid the sinister in my fiction, but that seems less and less possible. When bad things happen to my characters, I want to take the time to understand the circumstances and to find whatever good might be in the event. I want to give the reader reason to hope.

In *Home Before Dark*, Mae's death, although painful to write, turned out to be the impetus for the family's liberation from a life of instability and poverty. Dwayne's brother's attempt to have him institutionalized in *All Together Now* gave his community a chance to act and gave Casey a growth experience that would help shape her life. In *Notes for Another Life*, the father's emotional illness and the difficult relationship between mother and children gave the young characters the conflict required for a successful story. *Permanent Connections* gave me a chance to write about the mountains of western North Carolina where I now live and to deal with issues affecting young people here. Christina in *Keeping Christina* provided Annie with understanding about the nature of caregiving, which young women embrace so readily, sometimes to their own detriment. Joel in *All We Know of Heaven* darkened Bethany's world, but she survived with the help of her family and her own youthful hopefulness.

The basis for fiction is always conflict, and the most prevalent form conflict takes in my work is the character who wants something worthwhile but difficult to achieve. The ensuing struggle provides the plot. Stella Willis wants a place to call her own. Casey wants to feel close to her extended family, to have Dwayne for a friend, and ultimately, to protect him. Kevin and Wren, the teenage siblings in *Notes for Another Life*, want a functional family—their father well, their mother with them. Rob and Ellery in *Permanent Connections* want to feel connected. Annie in *Keeping Christina* wants to keep her friendships intact. Bethany in *All We Know of Heaven* wants the family she had missed when her mother died. None of these goals is perfectly achieved—easy goals make for lightweight fiction—but there is always growth and personal achievement. For the characters, there is always the beginning of acceptance of themselves as they are.

I wish I could say I have some finely honed method of plotting the action. It would relieve my mind considerably to have an outline for reference, index cards in order, a plan. While I don't have a plot, I don't exactly fly by the seat of my pants either. The year in which I think about my characters, without writing more than the opening few pages and notes on bits of paper, provides me with time to get to know them fairly well. I start writing when I sense the characters are ready to tell their story. This process is not as hit-and-miss as you might think. By having a comfortable setting and a basic conflict, which has been provided by the main character, I begin with a situation that is bound to develop into action. Occasionally a young reader complains that my characters think too much. I never worry that they are thinking too much, but I do worry that there's not enough action.

"Nothing is happening," I moan to my family when I stumble out of my study at the end of an unproductive morning. Eventually my husband reads the uneventful pages and jots down a list of all that happens, giving me temporary solace. It is good that I worry about the action. Ever conscious of the necessity of movement in the work, I keep it moving as best I can.

I don't know of any writer who claims to have been born with a style; certainly I wasn't. I remember well my struggle to find one. In my youth, this process involved several months of trying to write like a favorite author and then moving on to another writer whose style had attracted me. Periodically I tried to write like Charlotte Brontë, Ernest Hemingway, Thomas Wolfe, John Steinbeck, Boris Pasternak, Jane Austen, Eudora Welty, and a host of others. They were wonderful teachers but frustrating, too. Their material was so different from mine.

I envy the young writer of today who can find writers to emulate closer to home, writers dealing with issues that affect him or her directly, that are in his or her personal realm of reality. Studying young adult novels can show students a wide variety of writing styles and subjects from which to draw inspiration. Reading stories to find your own stories is a perfectly valid way to approach writing, and all writers do it. Reading and writing go absolutely hand in hand. Writers love books, they love words, they love stories more than they love the idea of being writers.

Any book that holds a young person's interest, that portrays the human condition with care and is well crafted, could and should be a young adult novel. The categories of books are more a marketing device than a limit to the appeal a book might have. If the characters and situations in a novel are relevant and meaningful to the teenager, that's the book he or she will read. The book without the reader has no life; it is static without the imagination and experience of another mind, the hand eagerly turning the page, the receiving heart.

I hope teenagers have good young adult books to read for many years to come. There are many already available that will be enjoyed by future generations looking for a "good read," and I expect more quality young adult books will be written if they continue to be taught in the classrooms, suggested for book reports, and made available in the libraries and class sets—in other words, if there continues to be a market. I don't think there'll be *CliffsNotes* for them, though, and that's a blessing in itself.

Having been discovered by a teenage audience, I have come to treasure the bond between us. I expect the bulk of my future writing will be relevant to teenage readers, since their experiences continue to interest me. It is a young voice that I most often hear in my head.

I hope my books reflect the hopefulness I feel for young people as well as my seriousness about my work, because I believe young adult books not only help young people grow emotionally but also contribute enormously to their becoming better readers and writers. These books make reading a recreational activity, setting the stage for years of adult enjoyment. At their finest, young adult books provide reading experiences kids never forget, moments they make their own. Imagine that.

Books by Sue Ellen Bridgers

All Together Now. 1979. New York: Bantam Starfire.

All We Know of Heaven. 1999. Wilmington, NC: Banks Channel Books.

Home Before Dark. 2000. Wilmington, NC: Banks Channel Books.

Keeping Christina. 1998. Bridgewater, NJ: Replica Books.

Notes for Another Life. 1998. Bridgewater, NJ: Replica Books.

Permanent Connections. 1999. Wilmington, NJ: Banks Channel Books.

Sarah Will. 1985. New York: Harper & Row.

5

Navigating by the Stars
A Writer's Journey

WILL HOBBS

"Your novels always seem to involve a journey," a teacher pointed out to me recently, and I was pleased. Like Joseph Campbell, I've long been a student of the journey as one of the major themes in literature.

"Homer was on to something," I replied, thinking fondly about my newest novel, *Jason's Gold*, in which my young protagonist travels five thousand miles to the Klondike gold fields.

"There's the physical journey that your characters take," she continued, "but what interests me more is the moral journey that your books involve, the moral truths they offer young readers."

I must have squirmed noticeably.

"Really," she said. "Think about it."

Almost at once, I was doing just that. What came immediately to mind was the disclaimer Mark Twain posted at the outset of *Huckleberry Finn*: "Persons attempting to find a motive in this narrative will be prosecuted; persons attempting to find a moral in it will be banished; persons attempting to find a plot in it will be shot" (1958).

But of course, Twain *had* written a moral journey and arrived at great moral truths. Even so, he seems to be insisting "That wasn't my intention." It's an *entertainment* first and foremost. It's a *story*, not a morality play. I'd bet that Twain would say about his book that *theme* didn't come first. Theme was a by-product. I'd hazard that guess because that's the way it has been with my own writing. I've come to realize that I write *subconsciously*, by imagining being the character. I don't worry about theme; it's embedded in the story. One of my writing heroes,

A. B. Guthrie Jr., author of *The Big Sky* and *The Way West*, went so far as to say, "It seems to me that every good story has a theme, recognized or not. Tell your story and don't worry. The theme lies in it, maybe to be discovered by critics, not by you" (1991, 77).

A fiction writer is always working with the particulars, the details of setting and character and so on, and shrinks from abstractions, even abstract nouns like *love* and *hatred* and *anger* and *courage* whenever they can be avoided. The readers want to figure those things out for themselves. As the story unfolds, the reader intuits the writer's moral sensibilities, and that's part of what makes the book interesting. As readers ourselves, writers know that preaching is the last thing we want to do. The reader will quickly suspect that the characters and situations are being manipulated, and the reader in turn will feel manipulated.

Having posted my own disclaimer, I'd like to take a look at my books and see what sort of moral sensibility I might find there. Could there indeed be moral journeys, moral truths?

In all of my novels, I notice that my stage is the outdoors. Readers often comment that, in my books, the landscape is as important as one of the main characters. I enjoy hearing how entranced they were with red rock canyons or the alpine tundra or the Grand Canyon. Although I was a classroom teacher for seventeen years, I haven't yet written a novel with a school setting. It's a setting I know well, but my heart is really in the outdoors, the world of mountains and rivers, as it has been since I was a kid.

One of my earliest memories is of the woods behind our home in Falls Church, Virginia, when I was four and five years old. That was where the box turtles lived. I loved the woods; I loved the turtles. Those woods are all gone now, and the turtles, too. Kids living on that street now don't have the woods to go to anymore. And that's a loss for the human spirit as well as for the flora and fauna itself, wherever it happens. It's a loss of primary experience and it's a loss for the imagination. If I hadn't fallen in love with turtles when I was four, I never would have written *Changes in Latitudes* one day, a novel that has a lot to do with a boy falling in love with sea turtles and the idea that these sea turtles might navigate by the stars.

The older I get the more I understand Thoreau's phrase "In wildness is the preservation of the world" and the more deeply that sentiment informs my writing. In my books, I'm taking readers out into the wild on an adventure in their imaginations in hopes they'll be inspired to also get out and do the real thing. But whether or not they do, many will experience a lot of feeling, a lot of affection, for those wild places. In turn, that's what wild places need to survive: human affection. For this reason, "Man *versus* Nature," a common thematic tag historically attached to outdoor books, hasn't made a very good fit with my writing—until the sixty-below-zero temperatures in *Far North* came along, that is.

But what does all this have to do with moral journeys and moral truths? Wouldn't moral concerns be limited to the characters in the story, their ethical growth as individuals and members of a community? What does the setting, the environment, the landscape have to do with it?

Everything, I would reply. Ethics applies to *land* as well as to people. A few years ago I finally sat down and read *A Sand County Almanac* (1989) by Aldo Leopold, originally published in 1949. I was already familiar with many quotations from it; I'd even used one at the beginning of *The Big Wander*: "I'm glad I shall never be young without wild country to be young in. Of what avail are forty freedoms without a blank spot on the map?" (1989, 149).

In the foreword to the book, Leopold writes:

> We abuse land because we regard it as a commodity belonging to us. When we see land as a community to which we belong, we may begin to use it with love and respect. There is no other way for land to survive the impact of mechanized man, nor for us to reap from it the esthetic harvest it is capable, under science, of contributing to culture. That land is a community is a basic concept of ecology, but that land is to be loved and respected is an extension of *ethics*. That land yields a cultural harvest is a fact long known, but lately often forgotten. (viii–ix)

In his last, philosophical section of the book, Leopold makes the case for a "land ethic" by describing it as the third and necessary step in the evolution of ethics. I'd like to paraphrase this "ethical sequence." The first stage was ethics that dealt with relations between *individuals*. He cites the Ten Commandments as an example. The second stage was ethics that dealt with the relationships between the *individual and society*. To illustrate this, he cites the Golden Rule. The third stage must deal with humankind's relation to *land* and to the plants and animals. "The land relation," he writes, "is still strictly economic, entailing privileges but not obligations. The extension of ethics to this third element of human environment is, if I read the evidence correctly, an evolutionary possibility and an ecological necessity . . . A land ethic changes the role of *Homo sapiens* from conqueror of the land-community to plain member and citizen of it. It implies respect for his fellow-members, and also respect for the community as such" (203–204).

Certainly, my stories involve the first level, ethical relations of the protagonist with other individuals. For example, Cloyd's growth in *Bearstone* and *Beardance* comes when he overcomes his anger and resentment and forges a relationship with the old rancher, Walter Landis. Jessie's relationships with the other seven kids in *Downriver* is of paramount interest to readers of *Downriver* and *River Thunder*. Relationships with other individuals is the day-to-day business of kids; it's what being a teenager continues to be about.

In my novels, I also see the second step in Leopold's ethical sequence: the relation of the individual and society, with the Golden Rule unstated yet pervasive and kindness being the basic yardstick of character. "You'd have done the same for me," says the stranger who helped Cloyd in *Bearstone*. What underlies a good villain, like Kane in the mystery *Ghost Canoe*, or even a good miscreant, like Troy in *Downriver*, is the refusal to evolve to this extent of social cooperation.

As I look at my novels, I also see the third in Leopold's sequence of ethics: people as members of a community, including land, water, plants, and animals. As I look at my stories, I see realistic fiction, fantasy, mystery, historical novels, first-person books and third-person books, books in which the main character's greatest problem is internal and books in which it is external, yet here's the common thread—they all reach to include in their sense of ethics what Leopold has called "the land ethic."

At this juncture I'd like to follow my instincts as a fiction writer and *show* rather than *tell* you how I've been trying to get at some basic moral truths in my books, to enable my characters to go on moral journeys without being heavy-handed about it. My intent is that my readers, through my characters, will find themselves falling in love with the wonders of the natural world.

In *Changes in Latitudes*, my narrator is Travis, a rather self-absorbed teenager at the beginning of the story. He gradually comes to care a lot more about his family and even about endangered sea turtles through the influence of his little brother, Teddy:

It seemed like Teddy wanted to say something more. "What is it?" I asked.

"I had a dream I was swimming with thousands of turtles far out at sea."

"Tell me about it."

"It wasn't that I was *like* one of them—I *was* one of them. I could feel my flippers and everything. I didn't even have to come up and breathe hardly. There were turtles all around me, and we were swimming together on a long journey. It was what flying must feel like for birds, only the air was water."

"That's really great," I mumbled.

He had that faraway look on his face, yet at the same time he was talking to me. "No one knows how they navigate over thousands of miles, always back to the same beach. There's a theory that they navigate by the stars. The funny thing about my dream, Travis—I was navigating by the stars." (95–96)

In *Bearstone*, my main character is Cloyd, a Ute boy in a group home who goes to work for an old rancher and ends up helping him reopen his gold mine up in the Colorado mountains. Here's the moment when Cloyd is realizing his dream of climbing to the top of the Rio Grande Pyramid:

Cloyd was sure he'd make the top as he'd ever been of anything. He seemed to float up the last little bit and stepped to the very tip of the Pyramid.

Peaks on all sides were riding in the blue sky. Peaks everywhere, dancing, jutting up, all in motion. He had to sit down and grip the rock. Peaks, as far as he could see, peaks, rock and green tundra, snow banks, spruce forests, river canyons.

Cloyd thought about how Walter liked to be deep in the cold darkness of his gold mine. He wished the old man could have stood here with him. He wanted to tell him *this* is the heart of the mountains, up here in the light where you can see forever. Where you feel like you're part of it all, like the beating heart of the mountains is your own heart. He'd never felt this way before, free and peaceful at the same time. If only there was a way to show the old man how thankful he was, for this, for Blue-boy, for everything. He could show he cared for Walter like a son for a father. (111–12)

Jessie, my narrator in *Downriver*, is a troubled girl who's on an illegal rafting trip through the Grand Canyon with a group of kids who call themselves "The Hoods in the Woods":

The current swept us around a little bend in the river, and the bridge was lost from view. It may as well have been hundreds of miles behind us.

From somewhere along the shore came the most delightful bird song I'd ever heard in my life, a series of lyrical whistles cascading in pitch and slowing as they fell. Star and I looked at each other. It was one of those moments you share with some-body, moments you never forget. She was so happy. Those green eyes were singing their own song.

There the song came again and again. "I wish I knew its name," I said.

"Canyon wren," Freddy volunteered.

"How do you know?" Pug asked.

Freddy didn't bother to answer, just paddled on, with his eyes on the cliffs high above. It was almost as if he were reading lines in a book, his concentration was so focused. A mile or so later, he cocked one ear downstream, and then the other. I couldn't tell what he was hearing. Just then Troy yelled over from his boat. "What's that sound?"

Troy seemed kind of spooked; I still couldn't hear anything.

"Listen," he said. "Listen."

There was a background hum, or a vibration or something, coming from down-stream.

"An airplane," Pug guessed.

I glanced at Freddy and saw a quiet smile on his face.

"Tape hiss," Adam declared. "Canyon tape hiss."

Then it dawned on everybody at once. First rapid, of course. This was a white water river, after all.

We rounded a bend, and the sound wasn't so subtle. "Tape *roar* is more like it," I said.

"River Thunder," Adam named it. "Prepare to die, funhogs." (64–65)

River Thunder, of course, becomes the title of the sequel. As action-packed as *River Thunder* is, I like to think of it as a love story. It's the story of Jessie falling in love with the magic of moving water, with rowing the Grand Canyon, with being in what she comes to think of as "the *real* world."

My first fantasy story, *Kokopelli's Flute*, is told by a boy named Tepary Jones— Tep for short—who is growing up on a seed farm in northern New Mexico:

The sunrise that morning was the finest I'd ever seen at the Seed Farm, the finest I may ever see again. I walked down from the rimrock and joined my parents as they watched from the cabin step, hugging each other. A cloud bearing all the colors of the rainbow was advancing on our valley. Out of the cloud, broad shafts of light spoking from the sun lit our world with color from horizon to horizon. My parents reached out and hugged me too.

The breeze was out of the south, and it felt all different from the air we were used to, the skin-cracking dry air of New Mexico.

My parents and I were just looking at each other, looking back to the sunrise, feeling about as good as we'd ever felt or were ever going to in this life, I guess. We didn't even try to find words. When a tear left my father's eye, my mother and I couldn't help it either, and then all three of us were sniffling and laughing and shaking our heads. There was more to it than anticipating our crops getting a good soaking, more than words can tell. I guess rain on its way will do that to you if you're dry-farming in dry country, but this one wrung out our hearts but good. (81–82)

In my hang-gliding story, *The Maze*, which has its roots in the Icarus myth, we see the natural world offered as a model. Lon Perigrino, a bird biologist who has named himself after peregrine falcons, is talking with Rick Walker, a troubled kid who has inadvertently landed in Lon's remote condor reintroduction camp out in Utah's Canyonlands:

Lon got up, stretched, then pointed at the chest-high gnarled juniper next to him, growing out of a crack in the slickrock. "See this tree, Rick? It might be two hundred, three hundred years old. Never had much of a chance to flourish because it was born on such a rough spot. We've got it a heck of a lot easier. Just like this old juniper here, we might have been born in a rough spot, but at a certain point we realize we can help ourselves. We can pick up and move to better ground."

"I like your way of looking at it," Rick said.

"We'll never turn out cookie cutter normal, my friend, but we've got character. We're survivors, like those condors. Tough as condors, too." (116–17)

A great personal favorite among my characters is Johnny Raven, the Dene elder in *Far North*. Johnny made it possible for two teenage boys, Gabe and Raymond, to survive through November and December in the backcountry of Canada's Northwest Territories, and now they're going to have to try and go on without him. Here Johnny is speaking after he's dead, through the letter that the boys discovered on his body:

> There is so much unhappiness among the young people now. Anger . . . drinking . . . fighting . . . They say they are bored, and I believe they are. If I didn't stay busy, always making something, I would be bored, too. We Dene used to roam over the land; there was always something new. The land is all around us, the land has the answers, but many of us don't even go there anymore.
>
> In the old times, when the elders passed on what they had learned to the next generation, it wasn't so we could go back to the past. It was to ensure that the people would know what they needed to continue to survive. That's the way the elders still feel today. We want to help our young people face the future. If they lose their knowledge of the land and the knowledge of their own language, the real Dene will disappear forever.
>
> I hope the old stories will not die. They are beautiful. They help us to pass the wisdom down from all the elders who are gone. The elders had strong medicine that was gained from the land and the spirits of the land, and it could be passed down. Myself, I have always had strong raven medicine. I wish I had someone to give it to.
>
> The nurse asks how it's been in the hospital. I say, I miss the taste of moose tongue and beaver tail. I don't know if I will ever taste them again. The doctor wants me to stay here, but as I told him, it's time to go back to Nahanni now.
>
> And so I say to you: Take care of the land, take care of yourself, take care of each other. (134–35)

I recently visited four junior high schools in Lawrence, Kansas. The seventh graders there had read *Downriver* and the eighth graders *Far North*. I was touched by all the art I saw on the walls of the schools, by my readers' own images of crucial moments in the stories. Some of them had even figured out how to make rose hip tea and bannock. In one of the schools, right across from the library, was a banner that declared, "TAKE CARE OF THE LAND, TAKE CARE OF YOURSELF, TAKE CARE OF EACH OTHER." I realized at that moment that Johnny Raven's message and mine are the same, that if there is a theme running through all of my novels, that is what it would be.

I want my books to be read first and foremost for enjoyment. It's essential that they have a page-turning quality. I keep my audience very much in mind as I'm writing—kids across *all* ability levels, boys and girls both. If they're turning the pages, now's my chance to write about something important, something with content and depth.

My own experiences lead me to believe that today's kids still have a deep well of idealism. They want to believe in their futures, they want to find meaningful ways to contribute. This innate idealism needs to be nourished and given the encouragement to grow. They need *us* to offer some kind of a vision of hope, of basic goodness. More than ever, they're in need of inspiration. I hope I'm offering some of that in my books. And who knows? Some of my stories might even turn out to *be* moral journeys.

Works Cited

Guthrie, A. B. 1991. *A Field Guide to Writing Fiction*. New York: HarperCollins.
Leopold, Aldo. 1989. *A Sand County Almanac*. Cambridge: Oxford University Press.
Twain, Mark. *The Adventures of Huckleberry Finn*. Cambridge, MA: Riverside Press.

Books by Will Hobbs

Beardance. 1993. New York: Simon & Schuster.
Beardream. 1997. New York: Simon & Schuster.
Bearstone. 1989. New York: Simon & Schuster.
The Big Wander. 1992. New York: Simon & Schuster.
Changes in Latitudes. 1988. New York: Simon & Schuster.
Downriver. 1991. New York: Simon & Schuster.
Down the Yukon. 2001. New York: HarperCollins.
Far North. 1996. New York: HarperCollins.
Ghost Canoe. 1997. New York: HarperCollins.
Howling Hill. 1998. New York: HarperCollins.
Jason's Gold. 1999. New York: HarperCollins.
Kokopelli's Flute. 1995. New York: Simon & Schuster.
The Maze. 1998. New York: HarperCollins.
River Thunder. 1997. New York: HarperCollins.

6

Choices and Challenges
Writing for Young Adults

M. E. KERR

Some of my colleagues say they don't think about the audience when they write; they just tell their stories.

My longtime friend Louise Fitzhugh, author of *Harriet the Spy*, was outraged that her books were classified as children's literature. She'd say, "How dare they decide who my books are for?"

And there was a time, early in my career, when I never took aim, but wrote whatever came out, rarely rewrote, and, although I was well aware my audience was teenagers, I liked to brag that I didn't stoop. Let them rise to my level; why should I sink to theirs?

Some of the time I was lucky that my method worked, but there were other times when there were so many subplots in a book that even today I cannot keep track of the characters. A book I wrote called *The Son of Someone Famous* (1974) is like that. It stars Brenda Belle Blossom, the fictional character most like me when I was young . . . and in her sassy ways not unlike Dinky Hocker.

Occasionally I'll reread an old book of mine to compare what I was doing then with what I'm doing now and to check on some of the sayings, ever since a reader wrote that in two of my books I'd had someone say, "An ass who goes traveling doesn't come back as a horse." One of my father's favorite quips.

So when recently I reread *The Son of Someone Famous* I was a little confused by all the activity, particularly the things that happened back in the past to the parents of the story—was all that necessary, and more important, did all that complicate the novel?

I had never really believed there was such a thing as a reading problem before I went into the schools. I'd heard that was why the YA field was created in the first

60

place: to try to seduce today's kids with stories about characters their age. A brave, optimistic belief that if kids could identify with the kids in books, they'd want to read.

And kids did read more, for awhile . . . until the computer came along, and the VCR, and MTV, and magazines like *Rolling Stone* and *Spin* and all the ones that know a cover with Leonardo di Caprio on it will sell in the millions.

On one of my early school visits I'd just finished a book about teenage dwarfs called *Little Little*. During the question period a student raised his hand and asked, "Miss Kerr? How long were you a dwarf?" He was booed and hooted at by the other kids and sat down red-faced, but he got me thinking: he had either read very little of the book, or he'd read it too fast; and if this was the problem, and I was the book's writer, I was part of the problem.

I began to think about what I might have done to keep him interested in the book, without in any way jeopardizing the story's strength. For one thing, I decided, I could have weeded. All my books had too many characters and subplots. I was brought up on Charles Dickens, so that isn't surprising, but in Dickens' day there were almost no other media competing for the reader's attention. If readers had to work a little—or concentrate a lot—to grasp brilliant stories like *A Tale of Two Cities* and *Hard Times*, they would do it. Today if one has to read a difficult book, there are always *CliffsNotes* and its imitators, some provided by publishers.

I became interested in how to tell a story aimed at kids.

I became interested in what kind of story a kid might like and what kind of story I might like to tell him. For that is part of the equation: wanting to be as excited by your story as you hope your reader will be.

One summer in East Hampton, where I live, a young man who was gay was renting down the street with pals, waiting tables and doing odd jobs. He'd cut my grass, and I'd invite him up on the porch for a Coke. That was when he told me that he thought he was falling in love with one of the Irish waitresses at the restaurant where he worked. Over the summer I'd hear more from time to time. His boyfriend was part of a band on tour. His boyfriend knew nothing about the girl. "I'm not even sure I'm in love with her," Kyle told me. "Maybe it's just that I like walking down the street hand in hand with her and everyone smiles at us. Wow! Approval! Maybe that's what it's about! I mean, one night in North Carolina, Larry and I were asked to leave a restaurant because we were showing affection. We hadn't even kissed. He'd just reached over and held my wrist a moment."

At the end of the summer the romance was over. The young woman went home to Dublin, and Kyle went back to his boyfriend. He said he guessed he'd always remember the summer he loved a girl.

The same summer I met Kyle, a young man his age joined my writing workshop. He was working as a caretaker, with his mother, a cook, on the estate of a very famous rock star—one who was retired, and reclusive. Lenny always had some stories to tell about life on that estate. So I listened on the one hand to Kyle, and on the other to Lenny, and finally I had dreamed up Lang Penner, a young gay man who spends a summer in East Hampton on a rock star's estate with his mother, who is the cook there.

My title, *"Hello," I Lied*, came from something Penner says:

> Alex used to say that in that closet we all tried so hard to come out of were all the letters you wrote home changing he to she; all the memories of saying "Hi, there!" brightly to someone getting off a train you haven't seen in ages and want to hug to death; all the secret long looks across the crowded room; all the times you didn't say who you were with last night while others did say; all the artifice, evasion, sub-terfuge, and hiding that goes into being gay . . . from your first hello. (1997, 75)

Here's how I began *"Hello," I Lied*.

> Some people said I'd never see him. Very few had seen him in ten years. That was when he quit playing, writing, performing—quit everything. Retired at thirty-two. Not burned out like some rockers. Just finished.
>
> Ben Nevada was a star like Elvis, John Lennon, Dylan or Mick Jagger. Even if he wasn't around anymore, the name would be. The fame would be. (1)

It is Ben Nevada's idea that this seventeen-year-old gay man would be a per-fect escort for a young visitor of his from France. She would be safe with him.

What I liked about telling this story was its provocative nature: It posed the idea that you are not necessarily, indelibly, without exception, either gay or straight. You may be, but you also may surprise yourself one day, as Kyle did that summer. Everything about our lives isn't written in blood. People are far more in-teresting and varied than that.

I like to ask kids if they can guess what the one subject is I shouldn't write about. After they've mentioned everything from religion to sex, I tell them it's rock music. If I were to mention 98 Degrees or Tom Petty & the Heartbreakers five years from now, kids might say, "Who're they?" Unlike most adult books, our books can have a ten-year life span, or longer. . . . We don't want to date our books; we don't want kids to think they're reading yesterday's news.

Because I love rock music and lore about rock stars, I often slip in things I know about the performers and composers. In *"Hello," I Lied*, it was fitting to do so, I felt, for our rock stars were the first entertainers who dramatized androgyny to kids and acted out the varieties of male/female posturing.

I tell kids how so many of our big stars were yesterday's losers—it's there in their music—and I tell them to think twice about putting down those outsiders no one wants to eat with in the cafeteria. Years from now their own kids might be in the autograph line of one of these ex-dorks, nerds, whatever.

It's important, when you write for kids, to enjoy your material. It'll show when you do.

I am always pleased when a book of mine makes the Reluctant Readers list . . . but more and more I think a good majority of today's kids *are* reluctant readers, not ones who have trouble with words—with the actual reading of them—but kids who are okay, can read, yet don't choose to. Kids who never got into that habit.

They are on my mind, not just when I'm writing something for them but also when I'm between books.

Then I always enjoy a few months off. The hours between 3 P.M. and 8 or 9 P.M., when I usually write—every day but Sunday—are free. I read, walk, swim, cook for friends—all without watching a clock as I do when I'm on schedule.

But ultimately the thought comes into my head that I'd better start thinking about my next idea.

When it comes—Paul Zindel sometimes makes a firecracker go off when he speaks to kids to demonstrate how some ideas just explode into your consciousness—when it *does* come, I'll give a lot of thought to things like interesting names, just the right ones for my characters. Can you imagine *The Catcher in the Rye* if the starring preppy had been called Jim Sears instead of Holden Caulfield?

I will think hard about how to begin my story. I will remember an afternoon in Flint, Michigan, sitting on stage as three hundred teenage kids trudged into the school auditorium to hear me—last period, doors open on a perfect sunny May day—and I thought to myself, *I'll never hold their attention.*

I didn't, either. It was a disaster. But I hadn't set the time, made the weather that beautiful, or opened the doors of the auditorium. And I didn't have any Paul Zindel firecrackers with me.

When I begin a novel, however, I have control. I have the opportunity to invite the reader to listen. I have a fair chance to hold my audience, if I remember all the rules from the days when I was writing mystery and suspense.

Begin with an interesting sentence. Remember the first sentence of *Charlotte's Web* by E. B. White? It was like something Stephen King would have opened with: "'Where's Papa going with that axe?' said Fern to her mother as they were setting the table for breakfast" (1952, 1).

It doesn't hurt to end a chapter with a cliff-hanger.

In *Fell*, at the end of the first chapter, my hero meets his nemesis, someone who will change his life. Fell has just been stood up by a girl he had hoped to take to her senior prom. He is in tears as he drives away from her house:

The car I didn't see coming was a dark blue Mitsubishi I'd seen going in and out of there before. But I'd never come as close to it as I did that night—I rammed right into its back end. Then I sat there with my horn stuck, waiting for doom to descend.

That was how I met Woodrow Pingree. (1987, 10)

I don't worry a lot about subject matter. It's the story, for me, whether it's about a young butch lesbian on a farm in Missouri in *Deliver Us from Evie* or about a young man who joined the Marines to learn a trade and ended up fighting in the Gulf War in *Linger*.

That, to my mind, is the beauty of being a writer.

You can tell any story. Some will be more popular than others with teachers and librarians, but you know that before you begin. The challenge lies in how well you can tell it, how fascinating you can make it.

When I was a young writer, there was a rich woman living up in Sneden's Landing, New York, near where I lived. Here's how I describe her in my latest book, *What Became of Her* (a young boy is telling the story):

Rosalind Slaymaster sat at the head of the table that night. I was seated at the other end, facing her.

She was said to be the richest woman in Bucks County, Pennsylvania. She didn't look rich, not then and not when I'd see her around town. But it didn't take very long after talking with her to realize that she wasn't just like anyone else, either. It wasn't only because she had piles of money. It was the toughness of her, the hard twang in her voice, and this walk she had like she was Boss of Everywhere.

She looked and acted more Texan than Eastern. But she'd been born here, the last one anyone ever thought would come back to lord it over everybody.

Next to me my mother perched excitedly on the edge of her cushioned chair. On the other side of me Mrs. Slaymaster's niece, Julie, age fifteen, a year younger than I was. Red Brillo hair. Thick glasses. Beside Julie was the real star of the evening. Named for a preacher who'd baptized Mrs. Slaymaster's late husband, he was called Peale.

Peale was not a person, not an animal, but a large leather doll, dressed that evening in a black suit with a bolo tie, a black silk vest with silver threads, and black suede boots. (2000, 2–3)

Now the real Mrs. Slaymaster had a small man doll, as well. He was dubbed Lord Tod Wadley. She spoke of him as her dearest friend; had expensive outfits made for him on Saville Row; ordered tiny leather shoes for him from Italy; had golf clubs made for him, and cuff links, tiepins, and several tiny ticking wristwatches; and placed his name along with her own on a plaque over her front door. When she ate dinner out with friends, Wadley always went along, and in the restaurants they frequented, a high chair was always brought out for him.

64

I know I described myself as a young writer, but even more important, I think, was the fact that I was a very poor writer back then. I would watch this woman and Wadley cruise through town in a grand black Rolls Royce, and I would think to myself, "What about dollnapping? Could that be considered a crime?" This woman would pay a fortune for Wadley, for she couldn't go anywhere or do anything without him.

Once, when I arrived early for a dental appointment, there sat Wadley while his owner was inside having her teeth cleaned. "Be quick about it!" I told myself. "Just walk out with him now. No one has seen you enter." Well, I resisted kidnapping Wadley—for over forty years. In my newest novel, *What Became of Her*, I finally take him . . . quick about it, making my own dream come true. Of course, in this book, I am not an old woman named M. E. Kerr. I am a young man named Edgar.

When I write for young people, I often write from the male viewpoint. I think I started doing it when an editor told me that boys didn't like stories from a girl's viewpoint, but girls liked stories from a boy's viewpoint—I always look for the larger audience.

Sometimes kids ask me about this. How can I write from a male point of view? I answer that it's my job. Before I wrote for young people, I wrote mystery and suspense books. In them, sometimes, I wrote in the voice of a murderer.

I always liked something Robertson Davies said in a 1989 *Paris Review* interview:

> Sometimes I'm asked to talk to groups of students about writing, and the poor souls are filled to the brim with all the complex business about theories and types of narratives, and this that and the other. What I say to them is, "If you're a writer, a real writer, you're a descendent of those medieval storytellers who used to go into the square of a town and spread a little mat on the ground and sit on it and beat on a bowl and say, "If you give me a copper coin, I will tell you a golden tale." If the storyteller had what it took, he collected a little group and told them a golden tale until it got to the most exciting point and then he passed the bowl again. That was the way he made his living and if he failed to hold his audience, he was through and he had to take up some other line of work. Now this is what a writer must do. (51)

I agree wholeheartedly with Mr. Davies, but our situation today with kids is a little different.

Picture this: Here comes one of those medieval storytellers into the square of a town. He spreads a little mat on the ground, sits on it, and beats on a bowl for attention. Across from him there is a snake charmer with the deadliest trio of jungle reptiles, their necks stretching to the sounds of a tantalizing tune on a recorder, as a woman dances seductively around them. Down the way a small crowd is gathering as a cart arrives with assorted felons who are about to be beheaded. Near them there is a gambling game in the dirt played with sticks of ivory, golden bowls, and spoons for prizes. A small troop of traveling actors arrive on foot, pitch a tent, and build a stage.

You see what I'm getting at?

Would the fellow on the mat banging on his bowl have an assured audience with all the competition from other entertainers around him?

There has never been a generation with so many media options.

I have written a book called *Blood on the Forehead: What I Know About Writing* (1998). I have told the story behind many of my books, and I have described some of the tricks in my bag, when I bang on my bowl.

More than ever now, I believe in aiming at the audience.

More than ever I perceive my audience as entirely different from me when I was a kid and entirely different from kids in the '60s, '70s, and '80s. I don't think their problems are that different, or their feelings, but I think they are on information overload. I think they are slightly impatient with ideas that take too much time and effort.

These kids are graphically oriented, from the time they learn numbers watching *Sesame Street* to the time they watch their mass fantasies on MTV. When I was a kid, if a song played, I had my own little fantasy about it. These kids are fed the fantasy and when they hear the song again, they see the same thing in their minds.

The teenagers I know are incredibly knowledgeable when it comes to computers, cameras, music, health, sports, even business, many of them, but that old reading thing—a habit of curling up with a good book—it's not there for so many.

I hope the day won't come when kids will be downloading parts of books, or inserting disks into small frames with green lights, or finding other ways to "read" that haven't yet been perfected.

That is why I aim at my audience when I write, and it's why I try everything in the book to keep the book alive.

Works Cited

"The Art of Fiction." 1989. Interview with Robertson Davies. *Paris Review* 110:90.

Kerr, M. E. 1974. *The Son of Someone Famous*. New York: Harper & Row.

———. 1987. *Fell*. New York: HarperCollins.

———. 1997. *"Hello," I Lied*. New York: HarperCollins.

———. 1998. *Blood on the Forehead: What I Know About Writing*. New York: Harper-Collins.

———. 2000. *What Became of Her*. New York: Harper.

White, E. B. 1952. *Charlotte's Web*. New York: Harper & Row.

Books by M. E. Kerr

Blood on the Forehead: What I Know About Writing. 1998. New York: HarperCollins.

Deliver Us from Evie. 1995. New York: HarperCollins Children's Books.

Dinky Hocker Shoots Smack. 1999. New York: HarperCollins.

Fell. 1989. New York: HarperCollins.

Fell Back. 1989. New York: Harper & Row.

Fell Down. 1991. New York: HarperCollins Children's Books.

Gentlehands. 1990. New York: HarperCollins Children's Books.

"Hello," I Lied. 1998. New York: HarperCollins.

Him She Loves. 1984. New York: HarperCollins Children's Books.

I Stay Near You. 1999. New York: Harcourt Brace.

If I Love You Am I Trapped Forever? 1973. New York: HarperCollins.

I'll Love You When You're More Like Me. 1989. New York: HarperCollins Children's Books.

Is That You Miss Blue? 1975. New York: HarperCollins Children's Books.

Linger. 1999. New York: HarperCollins.

Little Little. 1991. New York: HarperCollins Children's Books.

Love Is a Missing Person. 1975. New York: HarperCollins Children's Books.

Me, Me, Me, Me, Me: Not a Novel. 1983. New York: HarperCollins.

Night Kites. 1999. New York: HarperCollins Children's Books.

The Son Of Someone Famous. 1974. New York: HarperCollins Children's Books.

What Became of Her. 2000. New York: HarperCollins Children's Books.

What I Really Think of You. 1982. New York: HarperCollins Children's Books.

7

Seeing Ourselves in the Mirror
Students and Teachers as a Community of Readers

VIRGINIA R. MONSEAU

SALLY (TEACHER): I was so disappointed in this book. I just kept getting more angry. The more I read it, the more angry I became. I grew up on Pearl Buck, and when you grow up on Pearl Buck you expect . . . "Oh, I can't wait to get into a Chinese book!"

TIM: Well, I *liked* this book because I like history. I like reading about old China . . . their customs and things.

SALLY: I like history, too. But, as I said, if you've ever read any Pearl Buck . . . she wrote about China back in the days of the dynasties . . . when they were put out of their homes, and the women were sold into slavery . . .

CHET: Are you saying she had more detail in her books?

SALLY: More detail, right. I cried and laughed with those people, but with *this* book . . .

TIM: Yes, but you already know all that. You read about it before. Do you know what I mean? You already knew what was going on back then in China, so this book doesn't measure up. But this is all new to us.

CHET: You were spoiled, in other words.

SALLY: Yes. Yes, I was spoiled for this book. I expected great things of it. (Monseau 1986, 131–33)

This dialogue took place in a student-teacher discussion of Katherine Paterson's *Rebels of the Heavenly Kingdom* (1983), a novel that depicts the struggle of a secret group of rebels to overthrow the Manchu Dynasty in China in the 1850s. Both the ninth graders and their teacher were reading the book for the first time. Though this was an informal after-school discussion rather than a classroom situation, it clearly indicates the value of student-teacher dialogue about literature—dialogue that encourages critical thinking and promotes examination of individual response to a work. That the examination here was prompted by the students rather than the teacher is significant, for it reveals a source of knowledge that is often ignored in a literature class.

Because literature classrooms are largely teacher-centered, students rarely have the opportunity for an exchange such as this; even if they did, most would be reluctant to disagree with a teacher's opinion about a book, let alone try to show that teacher where he or she went wrong. Yet the classroom is a perfect place for this kind of community building, and the young adult novel is an excellent vehicle for learning how to construct meaning together through student-teacher reaction to literature.

The idea of classroom as community is not new. It has been discussed frequently in relation to the writing class, where students read and respond to each other's work and collaborate on writing tasks. But this idea can just as effectively be applied to the study of literature, which ideally would be integrated with the teaching of writing.

Central to such a literature class is honest discussion—not one-sided, teacher-directed questioning, but true explorations of student and teacher response to a work. James Moffett emphasizes the importance of dialogue as cognitive collaboration:

> One of the unique qualities of dialogue is that the interlocutors build on each other's constructions. A conversation is verbal collaboration. Each party borrows words and phrases and structures from the other, recombines them, adds to them, and elaborates them . . . Inseparable from this verbal collaboration is the accompanying cognitive collaboration. A conversation is dia-logical—a meeting and fusion of minds even if speakers disagree. (1968, 73)

Another look at the earlier conversation among students and teacher reveals the truth of Moffett's words. Because of the teacher's negative reaction to a book they liked, the students were prompted to speculate on the reason for that reaction. The teacher, in return, picked up on the students' use of words like *details* and *spoiled*, using them as part of her own explanation of her response. In essence the students were helping her understand why she reacted as she did to this particular novel. As an adult who brought years of reading experience to the book, she was disappointed that it didn't meet her expectations. As adolescents whose reading experience with historical novels was fairly limited, they found the book exciting and informative. The teacher-student hierarchy was put aside for a while as they interacted as readers.

Emphasizing the role of language in the development of community, David Bloome tells us:

> Since reading and writing are inherently social processes, one way to think about literacy is in terms of community building. As people use language they signal their membership and participation in a community. Regardless of whether the community is a professional community, a neighborhood, a religious group, a children's peer group, or a classroom, people are expected to use language, including reading and writing, in ways consistent with that community. To do otherwise would signal that one was not a member of that community. (1986, 71–72)

Alan Purves goes further by connecting the idea of classroom community with the study of literature:

> Communities are in part held together by shared experiences, shared perceptions, and shared language . . . Literature provides a major vehicle for creating communities, as witness the power of religious literature to hold together millions over time and space and language. (1984, 18)

The word *shared* is the key to connecting the concept of literature class as community to the response approach that is necessary to its success. In her classic text *Literature as Exploration*, Louise Rosenblatt repeatedly reminds us that reading is an active process that aids in the development of social understanding as students and teacher work together to construct meaning in a text. Discussing the role of the teacher, she says:

> A much more wholesome educational situation is created when the teacher is a really live person who has examined his own attitudes and assumptions and who, when appropriate, states them frankly and honestly. He does not have to seem to possess "all the answers," which the students then need only passively absorb . . . The teacher needs to see his own philosophy as only one of the possible approaches to life . . . Tolerance of other points of view is extremely important for the teacher—an attitude those who are insecure and fearful of challenges to their authority find most difficult to maintain. (1988, 130–31)

The sharing that is essential in a literature classroom community is inherent in a teaching approach that values all responses to a work, invites examination of those responses, and helps students find meaning in the literature they read. Teachers must become listeners and learners, refraining, as Rosenblatt says, from imposing their own ideas, beliefs, and interpretations on their students. This does not mean that teachers must relinquish classroom authority, only that they must share that authority with their students where literature study is concerned.

Robert Probst suggests that in designing a literature course teachers ask themselves this question: "What do we want the literature students to experience and learn in our classes?" If we don't do this, he says, "we assume that the goals of the professional literature student are also the goals of the secondary school literature student, though instinct, common sense, and brief experience in the classroom all tell us that this is not a safe assumption" (1988, 6). Most high school students will not become literary scholars, yet literature courses are commonly designed around objective analysis of classic texts. As Rosenblatt says, "In our zeal to give students the proper literary training, we constantly set them tasks a step beyond their powers, or plunge them into reading that requires the learning of a new language" (1988, 215). She goes on to say that intensive analysis of the classics often forces students to work so hard to understand the language that the work loses its power to affect them. This kind of classroom encourages students to indulge in what Bloome calls "mock participation," where students employ deceitful behavior (1986, 72–73). In the literature class this may mean copying the answers to the study questions from a classmate, extracting an "interpretation" from *CliffsNotes* and presenting it as one's own, or simply parroting information from lecture notes. None of these activities requires a true understanding of a literary work—or even a reading of it.

Contrast this with a classroom where engagement with literature is the primary concern and where students are not only encouraged but expected to help each other find meaning in what they read. Listen as the same group of students quoted at the beginning of this chapter discusses an Arthurian fantasy, Susan Cooper's *The Grey King* (1985), asking each other questions, trying to clarify mysteries of plot and character, helping one another understand the story. This particular discussion began with the villain, Caradog Prichard, and eventually led to questions about the identity of Guinevere:

DARIA: I hated him! [Prichard]

SCOTT: He was the dark . . . The Grey King's servant.

CHET: But he didn't know it. He didn't know it until the end.

SCOTT: When he went mad, yeah, at the end.

DARIA: I was hoping Bran's mother would come back.

SCOTT: She was . . . she was Guinevere, wasn't she? [Will] was told twice about Guinevere, wasn't he? Once by John Rowlands and once by somebody else? Who was the somebody else? One of the lords?

CHET: What was he told?

SCOTT: He was told . . . about . . . how Bran was brought into the future by Guinevere when he was a baby.

DARIA: It was Aunt Jen, wasn't it?

SCOTT: I don't know.

CHET: Owen Davies?

DARIA: No. Aunt Jen was telling Will, right?

SCOTT: Yeah.

DARIA: And then . . . they had flashbacks while he [Will] was lying there with the dog.

SCOTT: Yeah, and towards the end John Rowlands told Will again. (Monseau 1986, 61–62)

This verbal-cognitive collaboration is not just apparent among students. In the following discussion, two teachers try to help each other make sense of the setting and cycle of events in *The Grey King*. At one point, the first teacher is confused about Guinevere's reasons for bringing her child Bran into the future:

CRAIG: Bran was Arthur's son? Did they send him back because of her little affair with Lancelot?

JENNA: She thought that the son was in danger.

CRAIG: Did she feel that Arthur thought maybe it was Lancelot's son and not his, and that's why she came back with him?

JENNA [reading from book]: "She betrayed her king, her lord and was afraid that he'd cast out his own son as a result." But even so, why would Prichard cause her to rush back [to the past]? Did I miss so much of that scene that I didn't know if that was enough motivation for her to flit back? I couldn't decide if that is just Davies' interpretation, or if that's the reason she went back.

CRAIG: I was thinking all the way through that she went back because she just brought the boy [into the future], and she intended to go back all along.

JENNA: OK, so that's just Davies' interpretation?

CRAIG: That's what I think. I don't know if that's right or not. (122–23)

Just as dialogue worked in these after-school discussions, it can also work in the literature classroom. Essential to success, however, is the establishment of an atmosphere of trust where readers can take chances without fear of being ridiculed for giving a "wrong answer." And teacher attitude is crucial to the building of this trust. Reading a young adult novel together with students for the first time is a positive step in this direction. Instead of preparing a list of study questions for the students, why not invite them to bring a list of their own questions to class to be used as the basis for small-group discussion? Representative questions from each group could then be shared with the entire class. When given the chance, students often come up with questions that relate to the very same material a teacher would cover in discussion. And since the questions emerge from their own curiosity about a work, the answers become more meaningful to them. Another alternative is to divide the class into pairs of students and assign each pair to "teach" a particular novel to the rest of the class. This is where teacher modeling can really become apparent, as students will often borrow teaching techniques that they feel are effective. This approach not only invites students to become responsible for each other's learning but also requires them to become well acquainted with the text as they prepare for discussion, group work, writing assignments, and so on. The atmosphere of sharing and trust created in such a classroom puts the students at the center, making them responsible for their own learning. The teacher's role is to create conditions conducive to this learning—to guide, encourage, and learn along with students.

Because the successful classroom community is dependent upon a response approach to literature, we teachers must realize the importance of engagement to the development of literary appreciation in students. Reader-response theorists have long believed that what a reader brings to a work of literature is at least as important as the work itself. In his book *Readings and Feelings*, David Bleich says that readers can only view literature objectively by beginning with their subjective response. He points out, "Critical judgments are implicit in emotional reactions . . . however, the process of making intellectual judgments is always conscious . . . There is a discoverable causal relationship between the conscious judgment and the earlier subjective reaction" (1975, 49).

The comments of participants in the earlier dialogue show that teachers become as fully engaged with a work of literature as do their students, even when that literature is categorized as a young adult novel. In the classroom, however, teacher engagement seems to become buried in an avalanche of objective analysis, which threatens to bury student engagement as well. Yet, as these conversations have shown, engagement is an element that is natural and necessary to the understanding of literature. That such an important factor is often overlooked in the literature classroom may be a major cause of student boredom and lack of interest. Perhaps it is a cause of teacher boredom as well.

A group of ninth graders in an urban school illustrates the effects of boredom and the significance of engagement in understanding a work. Having read Walter Dean Myers' *Somewhere in the Darkness* (1992), they sat in a circle in preparation for our discussion of the book. The story focuses on Jimmy Little, whose father, Crab, has just been released from jail and comes to take Jimmy away from the only caretaker he has known, Mama Jean. Jimmy is reluctant to leave, but Mama Jean feels he belongs with his father and encourages him to go. Jimmy and Crab set off on a road trip that eventually results in Crab's death.

The students were uneasy, never having participated in face-to-face discussion in their classroom, and they were unsure what I was expecting of them. Accustomed to taking objective tests on what they read, they were a little suspicious of suddenly being asked for their reactions to a novel. I had asked the students to write on index cards a question about the book that they would like us to discuss as a class. A portion of our discussion follows.

VM: Who would like to ask the first question?

(No one answers. Some students look at each other and giggle.)

VM: Do you wonder about anything that happened in the story? Is there anything that made you particularly sad, angry, or happy?

(No answer. We wait a while. Still nothing.)

VM: OK. Then I'll ask a question. Why didn't Crab show more love for Jimmy? This is something that bothered me throughout the book.

ANTONIO: That's how Crab's dad treated him.

TUFFY: Because he's been away from him so long.

VM: Does anybody think that Crab did show love for Jimmy?

KELLY: When he came back for him.

TUFFY: When he tried to start over a new life with him.

(Students are silent again, reluctant to talk. They stare at the floor. All of a sudden Antonio raises his head.)

ANTONIO: Hey, when did this story take place?

VM: Hmm. That's a good question.

KELLY: Early 1990s 'cause of his hairstyle.

(Several argue at once.)

ANTONIO: The 1980s because of the hairstyle.

KELLY: They had that hairstyle in the 1990s, too.

TUFFY: It could be the '80s, though. Look at the car that he had.

KELLY: Did they have cars like that back then?

ANTONIO: Those hairstyles, they're bringin' 'em back. They bringin' the curls back, they bringin' the perms back, they bringin' the Afro back . . . (laughter)

TUFFY: You gettin' points here! (laughter)

VM: Yes, but, you know, you're paying attention to details here. Maybe it was the '80s. We don't really know for sure, but we know it was fairly recent times. (To Antonio) Is the time the story takes place important to you?

ANTONIO: Yeah, a little bit . . . (There's laughter and kidding; Antonio looks down and stops talking. Silence again.)

VM: Here's another question someone wrote. What was wrong with Crab? We know he's sick, but Walter Dean Myers never tells us exactly what's wrong with him. How did he die?

ANTONIO: He didn't take his aspirin.

VM: But what do you think it was that killed him?

KELLY: The police shot him.

ANTONIO (disgusted): He didn't get shot.

KELLY (animated): Yes he did! They really did shoot him!

ANTONIO (interrupting): No, no, no. He didn't get shot.

KANDIA: He had emphysema.

ANITA: His kidneys . . . he was tired and worn out.

VM: Why do you think it was his kidneys? I thought the same thing at one point.

ANITA: Earlier in the story, they said that he had a disease of the kidneys.

VM: Yes, he was always complaining about his back hurting. That's one of the symptoms of kidney disease, isn't it?

KELLY: Didn't he have yellow eyes, too?

TUFFY: This was a sad book. You ain't got nothin' to laugh about. I think the best book we read was *Gilly Hopkins*. You could be mad or somethin', and you start readin' that book, and you start laughin', and you feel a little bit better. (laughter)

KELLY: That book sends a strong message 'cause she thought her mom was nice at the beginning of the story, and loved her and everything, then she found out that her mom really didn't love her at the end. She wanted to go back to that lady, what's her name?

VM: Mrs. Trotter.

KELLY: Yeah, she had to go live with her grandma, and she didn't want to live with her grandma.

VM: It's really like Jimmy's situation, if you think about it. Jimmy wanted to go back to Mama Jean, and Gilly wanted to go back to Trotter. Difference is that Jimmy got to go back and Gilly didn't.

KELLY: Could she go back when she's grown up?

VM: You could write a sequel to the story and make her go back.

KELLY: Um-hum. She could have run away.

VM: That's true. Sometimes you find that you're happier with people who aren't your relatives. Trotter wasn't a relative; she was a foster mother. Mama Jean wasn't Jimmy's real mother, either, but she treated him like a son.

KELLY: You can be close to people that are not related to you. They can be like your real family.

TUFFY: That's how people in gangs feel. They feel they don't get no love at home, they gonna go out and get it in the street.

It's not surprising that these students were reluctant to take part in this face-to-face group discussion. They were used to sitting theatre-style in class and having questions directed at them by their teacher, who was concerned she'd have discipline problems if she gave them too much latitude. Unlike the students whom we heard discussing *Rebels of the Heavenly Kingdom* and *The Grey King*, these students were uncomfortable at first, but they gradually took charge of the discussion when Antonio asked his question about time and place. They forgot about me at that point and began arguing among themselves about the time period in which the novel was set: Was it the '80s or the '90s? Can we tell by paying attention to the characters' hairstyles and the cars they drove? Of course we can, and these students discovered for themselves just how much attention they paid to the details that helped them make sense of the story. Later, when Kelly was convinced that the police killed Crab, Antonio was adamant that they did not. He was positive and confident: "No, no, no," he said. "He didn't get shot." Several of the students tried to figure out just what killed Crab until Anita, who hadn't said much until then, explained why she thought he had kidney disease.

After class ended and the students left the room, their teacher expressed amazement at the level of participation they showed and at the fact that they sustained a discussion for thirty minutes. She observed them closely the entire time, noticing that they were watching me and listening to each other. She marveled that even two young men who had behavioral disorders sat quietly, participating in the discussion briefly once or twice.

When I expressed surprise to her about the fact that the students wanted to talk about *The Great Gilly Hopkins*, she said, "*Somewhere in the Darkness* hits too close to home. That's the life they live. They want to escape that life and read something that will make them laugh." I thought back to their comments about family and about how important it was to them that Gilly go back to Mrs. Trotter, who loved her more than anyone. Tuffy's comment about gangs was especially touching. These ninth graders, who were in the lower English track, had significant things to say once they formed a reading community. As Brown and Stephens point out in *Teaching Young Adult Literature*, "The ongoing process we identify in the Young Adult Reader Involvement Model is that of sharing. As students and teachers share their experiences with literature, they clarify and articulate their reactions, their ideas, and their beliefs about what they have read" (1995, 195).

Boredom need not reign in the literature class, but to create a student-centered environment in which the students are fully engaged with what they read requires carefully chosen selections, and this is where the young adult novel can play an important role. Bleich points out that adolescents are intensely preoccupied with themselves—physically, psychologically, and socially—and that teachers can make conscious use of this preoccupation (1975, 17–18). In creating an analogy between reading and playing a musical instrument, Rosenblatt observes that "in the literary reading, even the keyboard on which the performer plays is himself" (1978, 14). These two statements make a powerful connection among transactional reading theory, young adult literature, and teaching. If adolescent readers are so preoccupied with themselves, and if they are both player and instrument, as Rosenblatt suggests, how much more intense is their reading experience with a work of young adult literature? How much more potential exists for a meaningful learning experience? The reading of young adult novels can help students become equals—if not experts—in the literature class, making the idea of community possible. Yet the overall reaction of teachers to using young adult novels has been dubious at best. Some feel that these works are too simple and that high school students should read mature works of adult fiction. Others think that such novels should be used only in developmental classes. Still others believe that these novels speak only to the adolescent and do not address universal literary themes. (See Hipple's chapter in this volume for an extended discussion of universality in young adult novels.)

G. Melvin Hipps makes an important point about teachers who have been willing to use young adult literature in their slow or average classes but have steadfastly rejected it for advanced students:

> What we often forget is that bright students are not necessarily more advanced socially or emotionally than other students their age . . . We also forget sometimes that conflicts that seem trivial or inconsequential to us are of earth-shaking importance to young people. Bright students, who may have more capacity for enjoying subtle vicarious experiences than slow ones do, may still have great difficulty becoming involved with the aging, impotent, cynical characters of Hemingway or Fitzgerald. (1973, 46–47)

G. Robert Carlsen makes a similar point: "Adults do not seem to realize that teenagers are still growing and changing in their literary tastes just as in their physical bodies," he says. "They assume that the teenager is ready to move into *great* literature. Nothing is further from the truth" (1980, 33).

In all fairness to teachers, however, skepticism about the literary value of young adult books may not be the only reason for their reluctance to incorporate them into the curriculum. Censorship fears are also very real. In discussing the young adult novel, we must remember that many of the so-called classics have suffered the slings and arrows of the censors over the years. One of the most notable examples is Salinger's *Catcher in the Rye*, but history shows innumerable instances of attempts to remove Shakespeare and other literary masters from library shelves. Censorship concerns will always be a factor in book selection, but they must not turn well-meaning teachers away from young adult literature. It's important that we teachers come out from behind the protective wall of the classics and risk making some literary judgments of our own about the books we will use in the classroom, keeping the needs and interests of our students in mind. Since engagement is the first step toward literary appreciation, it's essential that we give our students literature in which they can become involved, if we hope to create an active literature classroom community.

In selecting books for our students to read as part of their literary community, it might be useful to give some thought to adolescent readers and what they expect of a literary work. Walker Gibson contends that there are two different readers distinguishable in every literary experience:

> First, there is the "real" individual upon whose crossed knee rests the open volume, and whose personality is as complex as any dead poet's. Second, there is the fictitious reader—I shall call him the "mock reader"—whose mask and costume the individual takes on in order to experience the language. (1980, 2)

Gibson feels that the term *mock reader* may be useful in recognizing reader discrimination and in providing a way to explain what we mean by a good or bad book. "A bad book," he says, "is a book in whose mock reader we discover a person we refuse to become, a mask we refuse to put on, a role we will not play" (5).

Keeping Gibson's idea in mind, we might ask ourselves some questions: How seriously do we take our students' evaluations of the literature they read in school? If they judge a book as "boring," can we assume that they are intellectually inferior or unable to appreciate good literature? If their opinion of a work differs sharply from our own, can we simply dismiss their views as immature or lacking in knowledge? If we accept Gibson's concept of the mock reader, then it's natural to expect and accept reader discrimination, regardless of that reader's age or literary sophistication. The problem arises when a teacher must decide what to do about this discrimination, and this is where the classroom community works nicely. Instead of viewing student disagreement as hostile response, teachers must begin by looking at the reader's tendency to evaluate literature as a natural inclination that should be respected and capitalized upon. If a teacher feels that a book is worthwhile, but a student considers it boring, the next step might be to examine the criteria each is using and the personal experience on which these criteria are based. This kind of examination might be done first in writing, as in a journal response, then in discussion, promoting both private and public exploration of how and why readers find meaning in a text. In this way, examining evaluative criteria can become an important part of literature study, as both students and teachers learn to trust each other and discover the mock reader in themselves.

Discussion of teaching approach in the communal literature class might also include the potential of the student reader as critic. Literature teachers work so hard to impart their literary knowledge to their students, yet it seldom occurs to them to capitalize on the knowledge those students may already possess. As one teacher pointed out, "We teach criticism of works we were taught to criticize in college, we say the same things our professors said, and we don't respond on our own level, nor do we allow our students to respond" (Monseau 1986, 184). Perhaps part of the reason we don't allow our students to respond on their own level is because we don't attach much importance to what they have to say. They don't usually talk directly about allusion, imagery, or symbolism; they want to discuss the plot, the characters' actions, and what it all means to them. Yet this kind of personal response is seldom valued in the classroom, where the focus is objective analysis. But if subjective response is the root of the objectivity teachers seek, as Bleich and others say it is, then student readers do have a built-in critical resource that needs to be tapped and used, not stifled and ignored. Again we can listen as two students talk about the criteria they use to evaluate books:

JEFF: I generally base it on what I think of the characters, basically, and how they're built up. If you can tie yourself in with one character and relate to that person, it helps you become involved in the book.

LYNDA: Then again, it can be just the opposite. If it's someone that you have nothing in common with, you feel like you're learning something.

JEFF: It's like a magnet—opposite ends pulling in the same direction.

LYNDA: Yeah, telling you about something you don't know. Just like . . . teen books about girls. They're all the same . . . because you relate with them so much that you know what's going on, and most of them just tell you things you already know. Just . . . a girl falls in love with a guy who's in a different crowd, and at the end she gets him, and that's all it is. (Monseau 1986, 42–43)

The students we met at the beginning of this chapter further discussed their reaction to Paterson's *Rebels of the Heavenly Kingdom*, revealing a sense of point of view, characterization, and irony:

CHET: I learned something from this book. I learned that Chinese women have to get their arches broken. That made my feet hurt every time I read about it. It was a good book. I liked the idea of the whole thing—the Rebels being crusaders and all.

TIM: It reminded me of . . . cults.

CHET: I thought they were brainwashing—doing something they shouldn't do.

DARIA: This was like a book my brother would read. It's just . . . I don't get into this war stuff . . . this fighting with the Rebels. This book didn't invite you in too well. I thought it kept you . . . like an outsider. You were only seeing what was going on. You weren't really there.

CHET: In other words, it wasn't first-person narrative.

DARIA: I don't think she [Paterson] gave them much personality, as far as each character. I just don't think you got a chance to really know them.

TIM: I thought that Wang Lee was a good character. He was a peasant before, like his dad, and in the end he became a peasant again. What he was before, he ended up being the same thing, even though he fought with the Rebels.

CHET: They reminded me of unmilitary geniuses.

TIM: The leaders of the Heavenly Kingdom were corrupt. Everybody wants more power. It's like in the eleven and twelve hundreds . . . even the Church. They were fighting to see who had more power.

CHET: What really bothered me was those people are supposed to be heavenly, and they're all yelling "Destroy" "Destroy!" People use God's name . . . they abuse religion so that they have an excuse for killing.

TIM: History has been shaped by war.

DARIA: I have to reread this book. I can see that I missed a lot of things. From what I read, it's not my type, but you guys said a lot of things I didn't realize were in the book. (Monseau 1986, 49–50)

As these discussions illustrate, student readers do have a built-in critical resource—their subjective response. Though they approach elements like plot, theme, characterization, and irony indirectly, it's apparent that they have developed a certain critical judgment in themselves over the years as readers—and they don't even realize it's there. What a wonderful opportunity the communal literature class affords to help students discover this ability in themselves.

The benefits of creating a literature classroom community are apparent. Perhaps the most significant of these is the dialogue that takes place among students and teachers, making teaching and learning an interactive process. Here we can go back to Moffett's idea of dialogue as verbal and cognitive collaboration. Moffett contends that thinking is "soliloquizing" and claims that "conversational dialogue exerts the most powerful and direct influence on the content and forms of soliloquy" (1968, 70, 72).

In relation to students, teachers, and literature, we can look at this dialogic interaction in two ways, using James Britton's concept of participant/spectator. According to Britton, the language of participation is language to get things done—informing, instructing, persuading, explaining. The language of spectatorship, on the other hand, is language from which we derive pleasure and enjoyment—storytelling, gossiping, daydreaming aloud, reading fiction (1970, 122).

Student-teacher dialogue about literature is a participatory activity, establishing communication and fostering thinking on both sides. It is language to get things done. Students realize that they are being taken seriously by their teachers and that their input is welcome. Teachers realize that they can learn from students and possibly improve their teaching as a result. The thinking of both students and teachers can be altered by what each has to say.

Seeing the benefits of this kind of student-teacher interaction, then, we can go a step further and speculate on its value for the study of the young adult novel. Wolfgang Iser has said that "the manner in which the reader experiences the text will reflect his own disposition, and in this respect the literary text acts as a kind of mirror" (1980, 56). In a small group of student readers the same mirror can reflect five or six different images, creating a potentially powerful learning situation, especially when that mirror is the young adult novel. Dialogue about this literature allows students and teachers to be both participants and spectators. On the one hand, they are taking an active part in a teaching/learning situation; on the other hand, they are contemplating their experiences with the literature, enjoying them, and perhaps reconstructing them as well.

The evidence indicates that a combination of responsive dialogue and young adult literature is essential to the successful creation of a classroom community in the secondary school; but curricular constraints, censorship worries, grading concerns, and accountability are real obstacles to the ideal. Though these obstacles can be dealt with and overcome, it takes unwavering conviction and commitment on the part of everyone involved. But if the discussions presented here are any indication, there is great potential for the use of responsive dialogue and the young adult novel in the classroom. While the dialogue exerts a powerful influence on thinking, the literature gives students an opportunity to exercise and develop their critical judgment through subjective response. All of these factors, combined with a view of teaching and learning as a back-and-forth process among students and teachers, lend even more significance to Moffett's statement that "interaction is a more important learning process than imitation, whatever the age of the learner" (1968, 72).

It seems appropriate to end the way we began, with the voices of students and teachers. This particular discussion focused on possible ways of changing content and method in the high school literature course.

TIM: I like to talk to other people about what I read. Sometimes I pick up things I missed before. Then I go back and read over that part.

CHET: Yeah, you can find out what other people think about it. And like he said, if you missed anything, they might have spotted it.

JIM (TEACHER): Wouldn't it be nice if you could do this and not be graded by tests?

TIM AND CHET: Yeah!

JIM: I suppose you could find a half dozen or eight adolescent novels to cover the course of the year . . . and get writing assignments out of them, do some composition along the way . . . and find some research work to do . . .

SALLY: But I have to spend eighteen weeks on grammar. I don't have any choice. My curriculum says I spend eighteen weeks on grammar.

JIM: But we can *change* the curriculum. We can change whatever we want. We've done it periodically over the last few years anyhow. Wouldn't it be great to say, "All right, we've got nine months of school. We're going to read . . . fourteen books. Go! Get done. Come back and discuss them, write about them, or whatever." Wouldn't that be ideal? Wouldn't that be great?

TIM: Yeah. Some people do. I think some people do that. Why couldn't we? (Monseau 1986, 138–39)

Works Cited

Bleich, David. 1975. *Readings and Feelings: An Introduction to Subjective Criticism*. Urbana, IL: NCTE.

Bloome, David. 1986. "Building Literacy in the Classroom Community." *Theory into Practice* 25.2 (Spring): 71–76.

Britton, James. 1970. *Language and Learning*. Middlesex, England: Penguin.

Brown, Jean E., and Elaine C. Stephens. 1995. *Teaching Young Adult Literature: Sharing the Connection*. Belmont, CA: Wadsworth.

Carlsen, G. Robert. 1980. *Books and the Teenage Reader*. 2d rev. ed. New York: Bantam.

Cooper, Susan. 1975. *The Grey King*. New York: Macmillan.

Gibson, Walker. 1980. "Authors, Speakers, Readers, and Mock Readers." In *Reader-Response Criticism: From Formalism to Post-Structuralism*, ed. Jane P. Tompkins, 1–6. Baltimore: Johns Hopkins University Press.

Hipps, G. Melvin. 1973. "Adolescent Literature: Once More to the Defense." *Virginia English Bulletin* 23 (Spring): 44–50.

Iser, Wolfgang. 1980. "The Reading Process: A Phenomenological Approach." In *Reader-Response Criticism: From Formalism to Post-Structuralism*, ed. Jane P. Tompkins, 50–69. Baltimore: Johns Hopkins University Press.

Moffett, James. 1968. *Teaching the Universe of Discourse*. Boston: Houghton Mifflin.

Monseau, Virginia Ricci. 1986. Young Adult Literature and Reader Response: A Descriptive Study of Students and Teachers. Diss., University of Michigan, Ann Arbor.

Myers, Walter Dean. 1992. *Somewhere in the Darkness*. New York: Scholastic.

Paterson, Katherine. 1983. *Rebels of the Heavenly Kingdom*. New York: Avon.

Probst, Robert E. 1988. *Response and Analysis: Teaching Literature in Junior and Senior High School*. Portsmouth, NH: Boynton/Cook.

Purves, Alan C. 1984. "Teaching Literature as an Intellectual Activity." *ADE Bulletin* 78 (Summer): 17–19.

Rosenblatt, Louise M. 1978. *The Reader, the Text, the Poem: The Transactional Theory of the Literary Work*. Carbondale, IL: Southern Illinois University Press.

———. 1988. *Literature as Exploration*. New York: Modern Language Association.

8

Time and Tradition
Transforming the Secondary English Class with Young Adult Novels

GARY M. SALVNER

We teachers have lots of explanations for what we do in our classrooms. We also have explanations for what we don't do. Given the bureaucracy of American public education and the long-established rituals through which education is practiced, it is not hard to find explanations, even though they are more often based on our observations about schools themselves than on our understanding of how learning occurs.

What explanations do we offer for not using more young adult novels in our classrooms? Perhaps some of them do reflect reasoned thought. After all, young adult literature is still, as Robert Carlsen has observed, in its own adolescence as a genre (1984, 28). Since Dora V. Smith first split young adult from children's literature nearly sixty years ago, we have been watching the growth of YA literature in the same way that parents observe a child's growth—curious about each new development, hopeful as a result of certain marked accomplishments, yet suspicious about whether this youngster will ever fully grow up and become something. Maybe we don't use young adult novels because we are still not sure that they are worthy of our students' attention.

Yet some of our explanations have little to do with a reasoned consideration of the issue. Many teachers, for example, have been convinced for at least a decade of the quality of young adult novels and of the appeal they have among adolescents, and yet those teachers still don't find ways to incorporate such works into their literature classes. Arthur Applebee's recent study of high school literature programs confirms what we all suspect—what we have students read in our literature classes is what we have always had them read: a curiously formed but exceedingly durable "canon" of great works that contains very little minority or women's literature and relatively little of anything written in the twentieth century. The ten most frequently taught literary works in our classrooms today, notes Applebee, are nearly identical to the ten listed more than thirty years ago in another study of literature classroom practices (cited in "Teaching Literature in High School" 1989, 4–5). The more the world changes, the more our literature classes remain the same. And reasoned thought, in the end, has very little to do with it.

Why, then, are so few young adult novels found in English classrooms? Why, if we know and believe adolescents will read young adult novels and if we recognize that examples of such works can be found that have substantial literary merit and quality, do we not make greater use of them? I know why. You know why, too: time.

Curious quantity, time. Einstein taught us about its relativity, and our schools teach us about its preciousness. We all know that the customary schedules under which our secondary schools operate leave little time for actual teaching. Our usual 180-plus school days, carved down into forty-five- or fifty-minute sessions with each group of students—minus interruptions for such priorities as office announcements, pep assemblies, and competency testing—come to look like mere moments when we teach. Parcel out those moments to address the conscientious English teacher's various responsibilities for composition instruction, language study, media, speech, and literature course work, and they shrink further. Ask any English teacher why he or she doesn't do more. You'll most likely hear the answer "Time."

Time harasses most English teachers, keeping us from all we know we should be doing and all we want to do. From September to June we all bustle about like Alice's White Rabbit, checking our watches and muttering, "I'm late!"

If limited time is our curse, then surely the most vivid reminders of that curse are those curious and altogether maddening school documents we call curriculum guides. "I might be able to elicit more and better student response to their reading if only the curriculum guide allowed more time for it." "There might be time for a young adult novel or two if only the literature course of study didn't contain all those objectives that seem to almost demand that we teach the classics."

The irony in all of this is that, in most school districts, it is the teachers who create curricula—create them badly, perhaps, but still create them. Few district school boards dictate what will be taught and when. Teachers do that, usually by a process of cumulative compromise in curriculum meetings: you go along with *Romeo and Juliet*, which I really love to teach, and I'll agree to your *Scarlet Letter*, even thought I'm as uninspired by Hawthorne as my students are. You'd think we were pork barrel politicians. Look at the curriculum guides sometime. Most are doorstop size, almost arbitrary, and filled with our own biases and compromises. The time that we don't have enough of is so precious because we have filled it—

or allowed it to be filled—with matters that may have limited connection to what we know to be our students' best interests.

If we can make overweight and out-of-balance curriculum guides, then certainly we can remake them. All of us need to become more insistent about our professional judgments; and if they include teaching Cormier's *The Chocolate War* (1974) instead of *Lord of the Flies* as an examination of humans' capacity to do evil, or Cynthia Voigt's *Homecoming* (1981) as a study of the journey motif in literature rather than Twain's *Huckleberry Finn*, we must see that decisions to include these books get made. We are often reminded by our students that they will read if we work with them to find literature to which they can easily relate. We can no longer neglect those students by shaping our curricula around outmoded assumptions. Demands for stressing basic skills, along with testing pressures and state mandates, may be increasingly restricting our ability to make professional judgments, but we have not yet reached the point of mandated curricula. If young adult novels make sense to you, then find a way during the next curriculum revision to see that they become included in those guides.

In the meantime, of course, there is still much we can do to make better use of YA literature in our classes, which returns us to a consideration of time and how we use it. Perhaps time is preciously short in schools, but nearly all of us know from our own days in school—and, if we are honest, from our own teaching experiences—that time is also wasted. Time isn't only a fixed, quantitatively measured commodity; like teaching itself, it is qualitative as well.

As teachers of literature, then, our question might be "How can we improve the quality of our classroom time?" The answer might not be in changing the objectives we have named for ourselves and our students in our curriculum guides; it might instead be in enriching the ways in which we address those objectives.

An example is in order. You're teaching a ninth-grade literature class, and your curriculum includes instruction in those elements of fictional narrative that so often occupy a first systematic course in literature: plot, character, setting, point of view, theme, and even—Lord help you—symbol, style, and figurative language. Conveniently, your literature anthology offers selections that highlight each of those elements: short stories by Poe and O. Henry, for example, and poems by Dickinson and Giovanni. You worry a bit about whether your students will enjoy Dickinson or, in the age of sensationalistic television talk shows and action movies with stunning special effects, still be surprised by O. Henry. But even more, you worry that by the time you've introduced each of those elements and read several illustrative examples of literature for each, Thanksgiving (or even year's end) will be upon you, and you'll already be racing toward the close of the first semester.

And so you head for the department storage room, looking for an alternative. On a shelf are several dozen copies of Paul Zindel's *The Pigman* (1968), a slim book of about 150 pages that you recall seeing listed in *English Journal* as one of the best young adult novels of all time (Hipple 1989, 79).

Rereading the book that night, you realize how it will serve perfectly as a model of most of what you had hoped to get students to notice about various literary elements, and even more than that, about how those elements work together to create effect and engage readers. You recall the book's vividly drawn characters, people like the sweet and tragic Mr. Angelo Pignati, the Pigman, who hides his grief over the death of his wife with visits to Bobo the baboon at the nearby zoo; like teenagers John Conlan and Lorraine Jensen, the book's two narrators, who befriend and are befriended by the Pigman; and like Zindel's fascinating minor characters: delinquents Dennis and Norton, overweight school librarian Miss Reillen (called "the Cricket" by John because of the scratching sound made by her nylons as she walks), and Lorraine's eccentric mother, a home-care nurse who specializes in dying cancer patients and who steals home-care products from their homes.

You also recall the vividness of the settings of *The Pigman*: the Staten Island neighborhood in which John, Lorraine, and the Pigman live; the Pigman's old, simple home, to which John and Lorraine retreat after school each day and through which they recklessly roller-skate; and the zoo at which the climactic events of the story occur. Certainly, the brief novel reveals much about how setting is used deftly in a good story.

Paging through the book, you observe how effectively it will serve to teach your ninth graders about the importance of point of view to a novel. The use of dual narrators by Zindel will illustrate how details emerge not only from events but also from the perspective of the storyteller. John's voice in the opening chapter, full of bravado and wisecracks, is followed by Lorraine's in Chapter Two, the first sentence of which already reveals the psychobabble she layers over everything: "I should never have let John write the first chapter because he always has to twist things subliminally" (6). The book will provide an excellent opportunity to show how truth in a novel often resides between narrators, not in any particular one.

Of course, you can't forget the thematic implications of this novel—the far from simple explorations of friendship and love; the connections of life to death; and the meaning of personal responsibility, elegantly reported by John at the end of the novel after the Pigman's tragic death:

> There was no one else to blame anymore. No Bores or Old Ladies or Nortons, or Assassins waiting at the bridge. And there was no place to hide . . .
>
> Our life would be what we made of it—nothing more, nothing less.
>
> Baboons.
>
> Baboons.
>
> They build their own cages, we could almost hear the Pigman whisper, as he took his children with him. (148–49)

You also recall Zindel's sequel to the novel, *The Pigman's Legacy* (1984), and the later nonfiction work *The Pigman and Me* (1991), and you realize how effective it might be to coax students into extra-credit projects about how the themes in *The Pigman* are extended and developed in those two works.

Finally, your brief rereading alerts you to examples of *The Pigman's* stylistic craftsmanship. In the prologue, for example, Zindel not only quickly introduces his main characters but also creates tension by having them swear to tell "the truth" about their experiences with the Pigman. What, readers are made to wonder, *is* the truth, and why do these narrators make such a point of sticking to it?

In Lorraine's first chapter, the effectiveness of stylistic repetition is illustrated when she muses about dropping off papers at her teacher Miss Stewart's house and seeing her ill mother in the living room:

> Miss Stewart kept her mother in this bed right in the middle of the living room, and it almost made me cry. She made a joke about it—how she kept her mother in the middle of the living room because she didn't want her to think she was missing anything when people came to visit. Can you imagine keeping your sick mother in a bed right smack in the middle of the living room? When I look at Miss Reillen [the librarian] I feel sorry. When I hear her walking I feel even more sorry for her because maybe she keeps her mother in a bed in the middle of the living room just like Miss Stewart. Who would want to marry a woman who keeps her sick mother in a bed right in the middle of the living room? (1968, 8)

This brief reminiscence about a classic young adult novel reminds you that many of your course objectives about literary elements and devices can be achieved quickly and coherently with a book that even your reticent ninth graders can read easily in several hours. Using a book like *The Pigman* first to engage students in shared discussions of their feelings about what they have read and then to illustrate various literary elements allows you to quickly dispense with a whole fistful of objectives and still leaves time for other readings that students themselves might choose. The literary terminology has been introduced and illustrated, and it's still only late September, not late December.

Other young adult novels might serve equally well for introducing students to what literature is and how it creates its impact and effect. Particularly useful might be those novels that have vivid characters and settings and illustrate the interdependence of character and place in creating dramatic situations. Katherine Paterson, for example, is a master at characterization, creating such vivid portraits that characters such as Jess Aarons and Leslie Burke in *Bridge to Terabithia* (1987); Gilly Hopkins, William Ernest Teague, and Maime Trotter in *The Great Gilly Hopkins* (1978); and Lyddie Worthen and her siblings in *Lyddie* (1991) remain in one's thoughts long after the books have been read. Sue Ellen Bridgers' characters are also vividly drawn: Stella Willis and her family in *Home Before Dark* (1985); Casey Flanagan and Dwayne Pickens in *All Together Now* (1987); Rob Dickson and his fatherly Uncle Fairlee and reclusive Aunt Coralee in *Permanent Connections* (1987); and Bethany Newell and Joel Calder in the heartbreaking *All We Know of Heaven* (1996). So are those in many of Virginia Hamilton's books: Junior Brown in *The Planet of Junior Brown* (1971), for example, and Teresa and Dabney Pratt in *Sweet Whispers, Brother Rush* (1982).

Settings are equally memorable in many young adult novels. Students might learn a great deal about how effective settings are used in fiction to influence characters and affect events by examining the Great Smoky Mountain setting of Vera and Bill Cleaver's *Where the Lilies Bloom* (1969); Kingcome Inlet on the Pacific coast of British Columbia in Margaret Craven's *I Heard the Owl Call My Name* (1973); the Chesapeake Bay area of Voigt's Tillerman family cycle and of Paterson's *Jacob Have I Loved* (1980); the Appalachian coal country of eastern Kentucky in Jenny Davis' *Good-bye and Keep Cold* (1987); the Grand Canyon of the Colorado River in Will Hobbs' *Downriver* (1991) and its sequel *River Thunder* (1997); and even the fantasy world of Pern in Anne McCaffrey's *Dragonsong* (1976) and other dragon books.

Theme is a literary concept that adolescents commonly struggle with, and many YA books depict basic human conflicts that easily carry thematic and symbolic elements. The nature of evil and our struggles against it are vividly explored, for example, in the works of Robert Cormier, including *The Chocolate War* (1974), *After the First Death* (1979), and the complex and disturbing *Tenderness* (1997). Lloyd Alexander's *Westmark* (1981) presents students with a story in which the complexity lies not in situation or event but in the moral values placed upon those events as Theo, in seeking both to survive and to do what is right, finds that the two impulses are sometimes in conflict. Symbolism is effectively used in such works as Natalie Babbitt's *Tuck Everlasting* (1975), which uses common symbols such as water and the circle or wheel that are easy for students to grasp, and M. E. Kerr's *Night Kites* (1986), which uses the kite as an accessible symbol for exploring freedom and identity.

Point of view can be introduced to students not only through Zindel's *Pigman* (1968) but also through books with multiple narrators such as Bridgers' *All We Know of Heaven* (1996) and Alice Childress' *A Hero Ain't Nothin' But a Sandwich* (1973). Point of view is also crucial to the impact of Bruce Brooks' *Moves Make the Man* (1987), a story that reveals at least as much about its narrator, black teenager Jerome Foxworthy, as it does about the person he is supposedly writing about, his white friend Bix Rivers. Finally, the use of various documents and accumulated bits of information presents an interesting lesson about point of view in works like

Sharon Draper's *Tears of a Tiger* (1994), Avi's *Nothing But the Truth* (1991), and Cormier's *I Am the Cheese* (1977).

Time, then, can be saved in the literature class by replacing works in the literature anthology or other classics with more easily accessible and appealing young adult novels, rather than by attempting to add those works to an already extensive reading list. Books that engage adolescents and employ the rich array of literary devices found in more extended adult works will serve well as introductions to literary conventions and terminology.

Another common means for organizing literature study in the secondary school is historically, and one of our most common teaching objectives is to use literature to give students, through their reading, a history of their own and others' cultures. By eleventh grade, history and chronology become a dominant means for organizing literary study. The eleventh-grade American literature class and the twelfth-grade study of English literature are as familiar to us teachers as they were to us as students.

It would seem that young adult literature has little place in such surveys, since young adult novels occupy only the most recent moments of our literary history and since none of them has yet attained the classic status of the masterpieces that fill most of the anthologies published today. Still, the range of subject matters of young adult books is so broad that there are titles that do fit nicely into such study.

Students reading through various periods of our literary history are often limited in their appreciation because they know so little of the cultural and political histories surrounding those works. Chaucer, for example, is challenging to teach not only because of the language differences but also because the political tensions between church and state during the medieval period and the customs and beliefs of the times are unknown to students and not likely to be appreciated on the basis of brief explanatory notes embedded in a text.

Karen Cushman's *Catherine, Called Birdy* (1994) or Malcolm Bosse's *Captives of Time* (1987), however, might make that era better known to students. Set in the fourteenth century, Bosse's novel tells the story of Anne Valens and her mute younger brother, Niklas, who return home to see their parents being tortured and then killed by marauding soldiers and the mill that has provided their family's livelihood being pillaged. For their survival, they set off to find their Uncle Albrecht in a distant town, and after an extraordinarily difficult journey, they locate him and arrange to stay with him.

Albrecht is an ironworker and armorer, but his real obsession is to build a reliable clock. As Anne first observes his efforts and then assists him, she slowly begins to realize that without a reliable means for measuring time, the people of her age are captives to it. She also comes to understand the struggle between church and state about the ownership and control of the clocks when and if they are made. Those who control the timepieces control time itself, and thus control all those who will be regulated by its measurements.

Captives of Time is a violent book, containing graphic depictions of rape and murder as well as a chilling portrayal of the effects of the plague on a fourteenth-century village. Yet it is a book of courage and determination as Anne overcomes one crisis after another to assert control over her own life. Most of all, *Captives of Time* is a memorable account of medieval life, one that dramatizes the period vividly for students.

An excellent source of information on the treatment of the Middle Ages in young adult literature is Rebecca Barnhouse's *Recasting the Past* (2000). Other historical periods, however, are equally well captured in young adult novels. Leon Garfield brings the eighteenth century to life in *Smith* (1987), a novel about a London street urchin. Puritan America is dramatized in Elizabeth George Speare's *Witch of Blackbird Pond* (1958) and Kathryn Lasky's *Beyond the Burning Time* (1994), and nineteenth-century America comes to life in Joan Blos' fictional *A Gathering of Days: A New England Girl's Journal 1830–1832* (1982). The conflicts between Native Americans and white settlers during America's westward expansion are depicted in Conrad Richter's *Light in the Forest* (1953) and Brian Burks' *Runs with Horses* (1995), and the evils of slavery become more fully understood upon reading Paula Fox's *Slave Dancer* (1975) or Gary Paulsen's *Nightjohn* (1993).

Many of the periods of literary history that we have students study, particularly those occupying the nineteenth and twentieth centuries, are periods marked by war, and the wars of our recent experience are dramatized amply in young adult novels. The American Revolution, for example, that period often associated in literature anthologies with the treatises of Franklin, Jefferson, and Thomas Paine, might be enriched with the reading of Esther Forbes' classic *Johnny Tremain* (1969) or with the more somber and perhaps more thought-provoking account Howard Fast gives of the beginning of the revolution in his novel *April Morning* (1962), about a young boy who loses his father on the green at Lexington.

Our Civil War, that struggle for national identity, brings to mind the anthologized works of Lincoln, Frederick Douglass, and even Twain and Sidney Lanier. It is a conflict often examined in the secondary literature class with Crane's classic *Red Badge of Courage*, a work that still achieves intensity, but because of its language seems to many adolescents as impenetrable as Shakespeare. Rather than reading literature of the Civil War period, perhaps students might be enriched by reading about the period in young adult novels such as Harold Keith's *Rifles for Watie* (1987), Gary Paulsen's *Soldier's Heart* (1998), or the 1987 Newbery

Award–winning *Lincoln: A Photobiography* by Russell Freedman, an easy-to-read but moving portrait of a president caught in the struggles and dilemmas of war.

An entire unit, either historical or thematic, might be devised around the young adult novels of the Second World War, perhaps with individual students or groups reading separate titles and using those readings to compile both information and impressions of that global struggle. Students might read James Forman's nearly forgotten but stunningly moving *Ceremony of Innocence* (1970), a novel based on historical accounts of a courageous but futile attempt by Munich students to publish an underground newspaper calling for the overthrow of Hitler's Third Reich. To extend students' understanding of the Holocaust beyond the instruction that might accompany the reading of Anne Frank's diary, students might read Aranka Siegal's autobiographical *Upon the Head of the Goat* (1983), a story of the experiences leading up to Siegal's family being taken to a concentration camp, or Marietta Moskin's *I Am Rosemarie* (1981) or Gerda Weissman Klein's *All But My Life* (1995), two other autobiographical accounts of life in a concentration camp.

Other facets of World War II are depicted in John Hersey's famous *Hiroshima* (1986), about the dropping of the first atomic bomb (the 1986 edition contains an account of Hersey returning to Japan forty years later to learn of the bomb's continuing effects); in Harry Mazer's autobiographical masterpiece *The Last Mission* (1979); in Theodore Taylor's *The Cay* (1969), a novel of racial acceptance that opens on the Caribbean island of Curacao in 1945 just after German submarines have crossed the Atlantic to cripple the oil refineries there; in Fred Uhlman's *Reunion* (1971), which tells how a childhood friendship between two German boys is destroyed by the war; in Jeanne Wakatsuki Huston and James D. Huston's *Farewell to Manzanar* (1973), about the government-ordered internment of Japanese Americans during the war, and Graham Salisbury's *Under the Blood-Red Sun* (1994), which also provides a Japanese American perspective; and in books about World War II veterans who still suffer from its effects, including Cynthia Rylant's *I Had Seen Castles* (1993), Gary Paulsen's *Foxman* (1977) and *Dancing Carl* (1983), and Robert Cormier's *Heroes* (1998).

A few young adult novels treat the wars of our own recent history. Walter Dean Myers' *Fallen Angels* (1988) examines the Vietnam War, and Gary Paulsen's *The Car* (1994) contains two prominent characters who are veterans of that war. Sue Ellen Bridgers' *All Together Now* (1980) tells the story of Casey Flanagan, who comes to a small southern town because her father is "off in Korea fighting his second war" (4), and M. E. Kerr uses the Gulf War as the context for her novel *Linger* (1993).

Certainly, then, there are young adult novels that fit the curricular patterns of many traditional literature classes—by illustrating various literary devices and elements, for example, or by extending students' awareness of various important periods in literary history, or by examining various themes commonly found in literature, as discussed in Ted Hipple's chapter in this book. Furthermore, young adult novels meet those needs in a way that may save the teacher time—both because the books are often relatively brief and because their closeness in experience and insight to teenagers today suggests that they might be read with less resistance and more efficiency.

Something more needs to be said about these advantages of economy and effectiveness, for if change is ever to come to our English classes, it must be built upon a reevaluation of our aims in the light of such benefits. Certainly an obvious advantage young adult novels have in secondary English classes is that, on the average, they are short enough to be read in a relatively brief time period. In this case length is both a function of the number of pages in a work—and young adult novels typically have fewer pages than adult works—and of difficulty, since the challenges of a text will influence greatly the time required to read it.

In his comments about reading instruction in general, Frank Smith discusses this factor of difficulty, suggesting that we have typically tried to coax students into becoming readers by giving them materials that are too difficult for them to comprehend. The result, says Smith, is that reading for them becomes "nonsense," and young readers deal with that nonsense by becoming bored or by giving up (1985, 90).

The same principle, certainly, applies to the reading of literature. If we are seeking to have students understand the elements of fiction, it makes no sense to use as a model of those elements a work so impenetrable or imposing that students aren't able to even perceive the model. Just as Smith says we help students learn to read by keeping reading simple and manageable, so we help students understand the way literature works by using selections that are accessible to them. And, because of their economy and relatively simple structures, young adult novels are accessible.

But there is a second reason that young adult novels might be particularly effective as a means of teaching about literature, and that reason has to do with the relationship between such texts and many adolescents. One of the problems that plague many literature classes is that of authority, in which students see themselves as subservient to, and controlled by, both the text being read and the teacher who chooses the text and directs the reading. Of course, the very nature of the teacher's role creates part of the problem, and teachers in all subjects struggle with the authority vested in their positions. In discussing the writing class, for example, James Moffett describes how authority eventually interferes with teaching:

Although younger children often want to write to a "significant adult," on whom they are willing to be frankly dependent, adolescents almost always find the teacher entirely too significant. He is at once a parental substitute, civic authority, and the wielder of marks. Any one of these roles would be potent enough to distort the writer-audience relationship; all together, they cause the student to misuse the feedback in ways that severely limit his learning to write. (1983, 193)

If we agree with Rosenblatt that "no one else can read a literary work for us" (1988, 278), or with Purves, Rogers, and Soter that "the mind as it meets the book . . . is the center of a curriculum in literature" (1990, 15), then it is easy to see why authority such as the kind described by Moffett can undermine the literature class. Certainly, as teachers, we inherently hold an authority that cannot be—and perhaps should not totally be—neutralized. Inevitably, teachers can and do inhibit student response by imposing their own readings upon the texts being studied.

Yet it isn't always teacher authority that causes the problem. Literary texts themselves also carry authority, particularly when they have been accepted into a recognized canon of great works. How many students would openly challenge Henry James as being tedious, even though many of them find his writing insufferable, or how many would argue with conviction that Melville is trivial because Ahab's obsession with the great white whale seems silly and illogical? It seemed silly to me when I first waded through *Moby Dick* as an eleventh grader, but I never dared to tell anyone that.

In discussing the authority of texts, Dennie Palmer Wolf refers to a student who once observed, "What is the point of analyzing the things in the anthology? They already made it into the book, so we know they are supposed to be good; so what are we taking them apart for?" "Deference . . . ," suggests Wolf herself, "deadens the senses. We cheat literature when we treat works as masterpieces rather than as experiences or questions" (1988, 52).

While young adult novels can be vested with as much authority as the classics, there is a chance, at least, that students will not so immediately defer to that authority because their experiences equip them with some knowledge they can use to talk back to those books. Since young adult novels are typically about young adults and their experiences, students inherently hold the authority to say, for example, "Yes, the relationships among the swimming teammates in Chris Crutcher's *Stotan!* [1986] are 'true' adolescent friendships. They are like friendships among teens that I know or imagine." Likewise, they might say, as one said to me, "The reaction of sixteen-year-old Anne Cameron to her mother's death in Zibby Oneal's *A Formal Feeling* [1982] doesn't ring true to me," even though it may ring true to many other adolescents in the class and to the teacher.

It remains to make some concluding comments about the methods we use in our literature classrooms, for method is closely related both to the issue of choice I have been discussing and to the matter of time that has initiated many of my claims about young adult novels. Louise Rosenblatt's comments about the importance of the reader to the literary transaction lead her eventually to a discussion of what ought to go on in a literature class. "In the *teaching* of literature, then," she suggests, "we are basically helping our students to learn to perform in response to a text" (1988, 279). If young adult novels lend themselves to student performances because of their closeness to adolescent understanding and experience, then what methods will help the teacher orchestrate student performances?

A number of methods being discussed today capture the spirit of Rosenblatt's performance metaphor. Dennie Palmer Wolf, for example, suggests that students be taught to "hold a conversation with a work" as they "make use of their experience to fill out the meaning of a work and to raise questions about it" (1988, 53). Virginia Monseau, in her essay in this book, suggests that the classroom become a "community of readers" whose individual conversations with works become shared openly.

In a previous essay, I have claimed that literature games, activities "in which students accept the constraints of an invented world" and interact with a book within that world, have promise for generating "performed" responses to literature (1987, 137). One such game, for example, might begin with the premise that a character students have read about has become a popular singer and has written an album of songs based on various experiences in the book—songs/poems that the students themselves will then write. Another might propose something as outrageous as characters from various books joining together to form a baseball team and then suggest that the students, as team promoters and managers, prepare a scouting report and baseball cards about the team players. Such gamelike scenarios are promising not because they are gimmicks but because they allow students to inquire about books within familiar contexts—to make connections between the new experiences of a book and elements of their own expertise and background. The juxtaposition of these new experiences with those things they have authority over can create stunning insights. If you're not convinced of this, try another game: ask students to transfer the key conflicts of a novel into a plan for a video game, which is nothing more than a visual representation of conflict. You may be surprised not only by their ingenuity in doing so but also by the insightful comments they are able to make afterward about conflict and plot structure in the novel.

Regardless of the specific methods we employ, our aim in teaching literature should be for students to avoid falling into the misconception Flannery O'Connor once described about her books: "The fact is, people don't know what they are expected to do with a novel, believing, as so many do, that art must be utilitarian, that it must do something, rather than be something" (quoted in Wolf 1988, 26–27). Young adult novels help achieve that aim by keeping our priorities straight. Because they are about adolescents and for adolescents, they put our students at the center of the learning experiences we devise. Because they illustrate for young readers what literature can be, moving them and revealing to them how literature builds knowledge and perspective, they use our time effectively. Time well spent with young adult novels may not eliminate our temptation to say "I'm late!" on occasion, but it will eliminate our anxiety about wasting time with literature that fails to speak to our students.

Works Cited

Alexander, Lloyd. 1981. *Westmark*. New York: Dell.

Avi. 1991. *Nothing But the Truth*. New York: Orchard Books.

Babbitt, Natalie. 1975. *Tuck Everlasting*. New York: Farrar, Straus & Giroux.

Barnhouse, Rebecca. 2000. *Recasting the Past: The Middle Ages in Young Adult Literature*. Portsmouth, NH: Boynton/Cook.

Blos, Joan. 1982. *A Gathering of Days: A New England Girl's Journal 1830–1832*. New York: Macmillan.

Bosse, Malcolm. 1987. *Captives of Time*. New York: Dell.

Bridgers, Sue Ellen. 1980. *All Together Now*. New York: Bantam.

———. 1985. *Home Before Dark*. New York: Bantam.

———. 1987. *Permanent Connections*. New York: Harper & Row.

———. 1996. *All We Know of Heaven*. Wilmington, NC: Banks Channel Books.

Brooks, Bruce. 1987. *The Moves Make the Man*. New York: Harper & Row.

Burks, Brian. 1995. *Runs with Horses*. San Diego: Harcourt Brace.

Carlsen, G. Robert. 1984. "Teaching Literature for the Adolescent: A Historical Perspective." *English Journal* 73.7: 28–30.

Childress, Alice. 1973. *A Hero Ain't Nothin' But a Sandwich*. New York: Avon.

Cleaver, Vera, and Bill Cleaver. 1969. *Where the Lilies Bloom*. New York: Signet.

———. 1979. *After the First Death*. New York: Pantheon.

Cormier, Robert. 1974. *The Chocolate War*. New York: Dell.

———. 1977. *I Am the Cheese*. New York: Dell.

———. 1997. *Tenderness*. New York: Delacorte.

———. 1998. *Heroes*. New York: Delacorte.

Craven, Margaret. 1973. *I Heard the Owl Call My Name*. New York: Dell.

Crutcher, Chris. 1986. *Stotan!* New York: Dell.

Cushman, Karen. 1994. *Catherine, Called Birdy*. New York: Clarion.

Davis, Jenny. 1987. *Good-Bye and Keep Cold*. New York: Dell.

Draper, Sharon. 1994. *Tears of a Tiger*. New York: Atheneum.

Fast, Howard. 1962. *April Morning*. New York: Bantam.

Forbes, Esther. 1969. *Johnny Tremain*. New York: Dell.

Forman, James. 1970. *Ceremony of Innocence*. New York: Dell.

Fox, Paula. 1975. *The Slave Dancer*. New York: Dell.

Freedman, Russell. 1989. *Lincoln: A Photobiography*. New York: Clarion Books.

Garfield, Leon. 1987. *Smith*. New York: Dell.

Hamilton, Virginia. 1971. *The Planet of Junior Brown*. New York: Macmillan.

———. 1982. *Sweet Whispers, Brother Rush*. New York: Avon.

Hersey, John. 1986. *Hiroshima*. New York: Knopf.

Hipple, Ted. 1989. "Have You Read . . . ?" *English Journal* 78.8: 79.

Hobbs, Will. 1991. *Downriver*. New York: Atheneum.

———. 1997. *River Thunder*. New York: Delacorte.

Huston, Jeanne Wakatsuki, and James D. Huston. 1973. *Farewell to Manzanar*. Boston: Houghton Mifflin.

Keith, Harold. 1987. *Rifles for Watie*. New York: Harper & Row.

Kerr, M. E. 1986. *Night Kites*. New York: HarperCollins.

———. 1993. *Linger*. New York: HarperCollins.

———. 1994. *Deliver Us from Evie*. New York: HarperCollins.

———. 1997. *"Hello," I Lied*. New York: HarperCollins.

Klein, Gerda Weissmann. 1995. *All But My Life*. New York: Hill and Wang.

Lasky, Kathryn. 1994. *Beyond the Burning Time*. New York: Blue Sky.

Mazer, Harry. 1979. *The Last Mission*. New York: Delacorte.

McCaffrey, Anne. 1976. *Dragonsong*. New York: Bantam.

Moffett, James. 1983. *Teaching the Universe of Discourse*. Boston: Houghton Mifflin.

Moskin, Marietta. 1981. *I Am Rosemarie*. New York: Dell.

Myers, Walter Dean. 1988. *Fallen Angels*. New York: Scholastic.

Oneal, Zibby. 1982. *A Formal Feeling*. New York: Fawcett Juniper.

Paterson, Katherine. 1978. *The Great Gilly Hopkins*. New York: Harper & Row.

———. 1980. *Jacob Have I Loved*. New York: Avon.

———. 1987. *Bridge to Terabithia*. New York: Harper & Row.

———. 1991. *Lyddie*. New York: Penguin.

Paulsen, Gary. 1977. *The Foxman*. New York: Puffin Books.

———. 1983. *Dancing Carl*. New York: Puffin Books.

———. 1993. *Nightjohn*. New York: Delacorte.

———. 1994. *The Car*. San Diego: Harcourt Brace.

———. 1998. *Soldier's Heart*. New York: Delacorte.

Purves, Alan C., Theresa Rogers, and Anna O. Soter. 1990. *How Porcupines Make Love II*. New York: Longman.

Richter, Conrad. 1953. *The Light in the Forest*. New York: Bantam.

Rosenblatt, Louise. 1988. *Literature as Exploration*. New York: Modern Language Association.

Rylant, Cynthia. 1993. *I Had Seen Castles*. San Diego: Harcourt Brace.

Salisbury, Graham. 1994. *Under the Blood-Red Sun*. New York: Delacorte.

Salvner, Gary M. 1987. "Readers as Performers: The Literature Game." *Children's Literature Quarterly* 12: 137–39.

Siegal, Aranka. 1983. *Upon the Head of the Goat*. New York: Signet.

Smith, Frank. 1985. *Reading Without Nonsense*. 2d ed. New York: Teachers College Press.

Speare, Elizabeth George. 1958. *The Witch of Blackbird Pond*. New York: Dell.

Taylor, Theodore. 1969. *The Cay*. New York: Avon.

"Teaching Literature in High School: 'The More Things Change . . .'" 1989. *Council-Grams* 52.2: 4–5.

Uhlman, Fred. 1971. *Reunion*. New York: Farrar, Straus & Giroux.

Voigt, Cynthia. 1981. *Homecoming*. New York: Fawcett Juniper.

Wolf, Dennie Palmer. 1988. *Reading Reconsidered: Literature and Literacy in the High School*. New York: College Entrance Examination Board.

Zindel, Paul. 1968. *The Pigman*. New York: Dell.

———. 1984. *The Pigman's Legacy*. New York: Bantam.

———. 1991. *The Pigman & Me*. New York: HarperCollins.

9

Who Am I? Who Are You?
Diversity and Identity in the Young Adult Novel

LOIS T. STOVER

More and more, "minority" populations are becoming the majority in the United States. Increasing numbers of young people are biracial, reflecting the growing numbers of mixed-race marriages and partnerships taking place. Our classrooms are becoming increasingly populated with recent immigrants from other cultures. Ever more students born in the United States find themselves living temporarily in other countries. In general, as barriers that formerly acted to keep peoples separated are broken, it becomes ever more important that teachers and their students search for means of understanding the co-inhabitants of our country—and this earth. We need to better understand diverse cultural perspectives, defined by Spradley and McCurdy as "the acquired knowledge that people use to interpret experience and to generate social behavior" (1975, 5), so that we are better able to appreciate why we behave in certain ways and why others may have different perceptions about various aspects of life, from whether wearing deodorant is desirable to how aging family members should be treated.

Waggoner notes, "In principle, the United States is a monolingual country where English is indisputably the language of all major institutions. In reality, it is a multilingual, multicultural country where one person in seven speaks a non-English language at home or lives with family members who do " (quoted in Gonzales 1990, 16). Multicultural education theorists such as Nieto define *pluralism* as meaning attention to "ethnic, linguistic, religious, economic, and gender [characteristics], among others" and go on to argue that students from pluralistic, diverse backgrounds who speak diverse languages need to be "acknowledged, valued, and used as important sources for their education" (1996, 8).

One method English teachers can employ to help students break down barriers of culture and ethnicity is to use young adult novels by and about individuals from various ethnic and cultural backgrounds, by and about recent immigrants to the United States, and even by authors from other countries who write literature about the adolescent experience in other lands. As Rudine Sims Bishop (1990) explains, multicultural literature is important because it provides "mirrors" in which students can see reflections of their own lives, as well as "windows" through which to examine the lives of others. Harte, in "Teaching and Learning Across Cultures" concurs, stating that

> the experience of reading is an interactive, dialectical process whereby readers transact with texts using their own lives and experiences as men and women in society to help them construct meaning and knowledge from the experiences of the texts. (1997, 84)

Banks adds to this argument by generalizing about the overall goal of multicultural/multiethnic education, which is to help students "develop the knowledge, attitudes, and skills to participate in a democratic and free society," skills they will not use if they feel marginalized or if they do not have an adequate knowledge base for understanding the diversity of that society (1994, 81).

For students who represent minority perspectives within the larger U.S. society, young adult novels about adolescents from those cultures and reflective of their ethnic backgrounds provide validation of their own experience. Romero and Zancanella state that students need "to know that authors and artists of substance and value come from their culture" (1990, 29). Hence, teachers and librarians need to be aware of new materials such as Harcourt Brace's recent *Mexican American Literature* anthology and should provide access for all students to young adult books by authors such as Yoshiko Uchida (*The Best Bad Thing* [1984]), who writes about the Japanese immigrant experience; Marie G. Lee (*Saying Goodbye* [1994]), whose characters reflect her own Korean American heritage; and Nicholasa Mohr (*Nilda* [1986]), whose characters are Puerto Ricans living in the United States. Maureen Crane Wartski (*A Boat to Nowhere* [1981]) provides a vivid picture of the Vietnamese refugee experience, while Rudolfo Anaya (*Bless Me, Ultima* [1972]), Gary Soto (*Jesse* [1994]), Victor Martinez (*Parrot in the Oven: Mi Vida* [1996]), and Sandra Cisneros (*The House on Mango Street* [1994]) depict some of the variations in Hispanic cultures within the United States. Virginia Hamilton (*Arilla Sun Down* [1997]), Mildred Taylor (*Roll of Thunder, Hear My Cry* [1976]), Walter Dean Myers (*The Glory Field* [1994]), Joyce Carol Thomas (*Water Girl* [1986]), Sharon Draper (*Tears of a Tiger* [1994]), Rita Williams-Garcia (*Like Sisters on the Homefront* [1995]), Jacqueline Woodson (*From the Notebooks of Melanin Sun*

[1995]), Rosa Guy (*The Friends* [1983]), Angela Johnson (*Toning the Sweep* [1993]), or Eleanora Tate (*The Secret of Gumbo Grove* [1988]), all detail the lives of black Americans in various periods of U.S. history. Laurence Yep (*Child of the Owl* [1977]) and Lensey Namioka (*April and the Dragon Lady* [1994]) describe the Chinese immigrant experience, and Kirin Narayan (*Love, Stars, and All That* [1994]) writes about being caught between the worlds of India and America. N. Scott Momaday (*House Made of Dawn* [1969]), Joseph Bruchac (*Flying with the Eagle, Racing the Great Bear: Stories from Native North America* [1993]), Michael Dorris (*Sees Behind Trees* [1996]), or Virginia Driving Hawk Sneve (*When Thunder Spoke* [1993]) provide books that describe life from the Native American perspective.

There are also many good young adult books about segments of the American population that are culturally and ethnically diverse but about whom students may have little knowledge. Jane Yolen (*The Devil's Arithmetic* [1988]), Fran Arrick (*Chernowitz!* [1981]), Chaim Potok (*The Chosen* [1978]), and Charlotte Herman (*What Happened to Heather Hopkowitz?* [1994]) have written novels about being Jewish. Normee Ekoomiak (*Arctic Memories* [1990]), Markoosie (*Harpoon of the Hunter* [1970]), and Pipaluk Freuchen (*Eskimo Boy* [1951]) develop characters who must come to terms with the Eskimo heritage. Graham Salisbury's *Jungle Dogs* (1998) is about a young man in Hawaii learning about courage and family connections, while *Blue Skin of the Sea* (1992) details the coming of age of Sonny Mendoza in the village of Kailua-Kona on the Big Island of Hawaii. Robert Newton Peck (*Arly* [1989]), Vera and Bill Cleaver (*Where the Lilies Bloom* [1969]), and Ruth White (*Weeping Willow* [1994]; *Belle Prater's Boy* [1996]) present daily life and its hardships for young adults growing up in very rural environments such as Florida and Appalachia, while George Ella Lyon, in *Borrowed Children* (1988), describes the differences between life in the coal-mining regions of Kentucky and life in the city of Memphis. Barbara Ann Porte (*Something Terrible Happened* [1994]) and Sharon Dennis Wyeth (*The World of Daughter McGuire* [1994]) chronicle the tensions faced by biracial adolescents. Carolyn Meyer contrasts the traditions of the orthodox Jewish religion with those of the Amish in *Gideon's People* (1996). Kathryn Lasky writes about an Amish father and daughter who experience the custom of shunning in *Beyond the Divide* (1995).

The point is that in our multicultural society and increasingly interconnected world, we need to emphasize certain goals of the literature program. Through their reading, students should be able to (1) explore issues of self-identification and ethnicity, (2) explore the relationships between themselves and others, and (3) explore the relationships between and among cultures. The inclusion of YA novels about adolescents from diverse cultural backgrounds in the literature curriculum should help accomplish these goals.

Selecting Young Adult Novels Representative of Cultural Diversity

As teachers seek to select young adult novels that represent the experiences of adolescents from culturally diverse backgrounds, they should consider several issues. Rudine Sims Bishop (1992) defines the differences among three types of books that deal with diversity. "Culturally neutral" books depict diversity only in an incidental way; the major themes are not identifiable as drawn from any one culture. "Culturally generic" books feature multicultural characters but are basically generically American in theme and plot. As an example, Patricia Baird Greene's *Sabbath Garden* (1992) is about Opie, a young African American teenage girl, and the friendship that develops between her and the elderly Solomon Leshko, a Jewish man who lives downstairs. The ethnic backgrounds of her characters are far less important to Baird's work than the urban setting and the intergenerational relationships. On the other hand, "culturally specific" works attempt to reflect the way members of a particular cultural group use language, develop their belief structures, or articulate their values. For example, in both Rita Williams-Garcia's *Like Sisters on the Homefront* (1995) and Martha Southgate's *Another Way to Dance* (1996), readers meet characters from at least two different African American communities who are struggling to overcome their prejudices against their peers who have different ways of looking at the world as a result of the environment in which they live.

Noll (1995) argues that it is also important to consider the perspective of the writer, stating that readers need to be aware of whether an author writes from an insider's perspective or from the outsider's experience. As Kaplan (1966) notes, just one inaccurate fact may be enough to cause members of the culture being portrayed to discount the book. Thus writers from the "outside," such as Paul Goble, who have "done their homework" by living with Native Americans, listening to them, and engaging in careful research, receive high critical acclaim. Readers must be aware that the experiences of Sandra Cisneros' Hispanic American characters from urban Chicago will be different from those of Gary Soto's Hispanic characters who live in Los Angeles.

Most important, when choosing young adult books for the classroom and the library, we need to avoid "tokenism." As Gonzales states, "Token representation of the histories and literatures of culturally different children are inadequate attempts at engaging and inspiring students' participation in the educational process. One piece of literature or one chapter in American history cannot counter the negative social perceptions that children of minority subcultures have of themselves or that society has of them. A significant proportion of the curriculum must be dedicated to positive ethnic histories and literature and the many contributions that all groups have made to American life" (1990, 18–19).

How can tokenism be avoided? Curriculum developers and librarians would have to first agree to accept as objectives for the literature program the three afore-mentioned literature goals. Organizing by themes representative of issues that cross cultural boundaries might better allow for these goals to be met than organizing the literature program by chronology or by genre. If the focus of the unit is on an issue, individuals from diverse cultural backgrounds can respond to that issue, sharing their own experiences as shaped by culture, as they also respond to the text and its presentation of the issue as shaped by the cultural background of the au-thor. By exploring themes such as "Courage," "The Nature of Childhood or Ado-lescence," "Peer Relations," "Who Am I?," "Death and Dying," "The Frontier Experience," or "Ways of Knowing" through young adult novels reflective of many diverse experiences, students could examine the nature of each theme in general and could investigate how various cultures approach each issue. For instance, the interrelated stories in Judith Ortiz Cofer's *An Island Like You* (1995) could be in-cluded in many of the aforementioned units. The twelve stories, all with different narrators but with characters who move in and out of the various plots, take place in the Puerto Rican barrio of contemporary New Jersey. Rita, of "Bad Influence," is sentenced to a summer with her grandparents in Puerto Rico after her parents discover her relationship with a young man, thus providing a good starting point for discussion about cultural differences in the way the roles of women and chil-dren are viewed. This discussion will be enhanced after reading about Sandi, in "Beauty Lessons," who despairs because of the differences between her own phys-ical appearance and Latino notions of beauty. Similarly, Arturo, of "Arturo's Flight," is ridiculed by his more macho classmates and so dreams of escape from the barrio into a world where his own gifts might be more appreciated.

The barrio could be discussed as an example of "frontier"; the barrio limits the world of Anita of "Home to El Building," who actually tries to run away from home, attempting to go beyond these limits into new, uncharted territory. On the other hand, the barrio is surrounded by a well-organized society, with many mem-bers who have a vested interest in keeping others locked within it. If the focus of the unit is on "frontier," the experiences of Cofer's characters and Daniel Boone could be compared and contrasted, and students could talk about the meaning of "frontier" on an individual basis and about the nature of "frontier" as experienced by members of various cultures; as a result, students and teachers might learn more about themselves and others by exploring this issue together. The last story in the collection, "White Balloons," describes the way in which the barrio serves—as Bruchac notes in an interview conducted by Zitlow, Sanders, and Beierle (1997)—as a set of boundaries that helps individuals define themselves in positive ways, both individually and collectively, leading to another fruitful topic for discussion.

Hoevler (1988) speaks of the need to look at literature for young people broadly, not just to regard books as useful if they deal with contemporary issues or attitudes and views but also to consider their literary worth. This, too, is a good caution. Otherwise, adults working with youth might jump on the bandwagon of issues and force didactic books "down the throats" of readers. Instead, these instructors, teachers, and librarians must search out the *best* of the books reflective of cultural diversity. Searching for such novels, and using them in genre-based units, is another possible way to avoid the problem of tokenism. For instance, in a unit focused on the discussion of the novel, students could compare and contrast novels such as *Letters from the Inside* by Australian John Marsden (1994) to Davida Hurwin's *Time for Dancing* (1995), since both effectively use alternating points of view in unfolding the plot line. At the same time, differences in character perspective due possibly to differences in cultural and ethnic background might be explored. In such a unit, the Marsden book would not just be a "token" work, thrown in to satisfy demands that the literature curriculum be expanded; rather, it would be viewed as an exemplar of the genre as a whole.

It might be wise, however, to reflect again on the implications of avoiding tokenism as they relate to the overall goals of the literature program. There are school districts in the United States serving students from more than thirty different cultural and ethnic groups. To provide novels reflective of each student's background would require that many different titles be available. We could allow one novel about an Asian culture to represent them all, but to do so would be more damaging than tokenism. In the current organization of schools, teachers and curriculum developers do have the power and authority to select certain books for all students to read. Whether teachers *should* have this authority is a question for another essay. However, given that we do, we need to select books that will help students understand diverse points of view and people from other times and places and will do so through stories to which they can realistically relate. Balance must be achieved—balance between students' need to feel validated through the experiences they read about and their need to learn about other worlds and perspectives; balance between teacher-made selections and student-made selections; and balance between novels selected because of the authors' excellent craftsmanship and those selected primarily because they appeal to students' interests.

Another set of criteria that may be useful in selection is found in *Through Indian Eyes: The Native Experience in Books for Children* by Slapin and Seale (1994). The editors advocate consideration of the following aspects of books when selecting titles in an effort to promote better human relations. They tell teachers, librarians, and parents to

1. Look for stereotypes—are members of other cultures portrayed as complex individual human beings? Are the cultural details included oversimplified?
2. Look for tokenism
3. Look for distortions of history—are historical events accurately portrayed from the perspective of individuals who may have different conceptions of the causes and reasons for those events? Are the contributions of members of other cultural groups to the history and culture of this country recognized and valued?
4. Look at the representation of the lifestyle—is it treated condescendingly or in a paternalistic fashion, or is it treated with respect? Are religions and traditions described accurately and in the context of the civilization?
5. Look at the dialogue—are multicultural characters allowed to speak with skill and to be articulate, or do they use stereotypical speech patterns?
6. Look at the standards of success—do members of the dominant European-American culture appear to know "what is best" for individuals from other cultural backgrounds, or are these individuals portrayed as mature and able to make their own decisions? Are such characters judged against the "norm" of white, middle-class suburban culture?
7. Look at the ways in which women and the culture's elders are portrayed
8. Look for any content that might embarrass a young adult or child from the cultural group being portrayed —are their positive role models provided?
9. Look for some indication that the author is qualified to write about the people in the work in an authentic, artful, and truthful way. (242–65)

Teachers and librarians might also do their best to find and stock young adult novels in which characters from diverse backgrounds interact realistically, reflecting both the prejudices of our society and the ability of individuals to overcome them by interacting in a more positive way and learning from each other. For instance, in Voigt's *Runner* (1985), Bullet Tillerman must face his prejudices against blacks head-on as he learns one of his best friends is of mixed racial heritage and as he comes to respect a new member of the school track team who happens to be black. Jerrie Oughton's *Music from a Place Called Half Moon* (1995) centers on the developing friendship, forged through a recognition of shared interest in the arts, between two teenagers, one white and one black, in the face of much concern on the part of the townspeople. In *The Shadow Brothers* (1992), by A. E. Cannon, Marcus and his foster brother, Henry, turn sixteen and then have to confront the realities of Henry's Navajo heritage and his attachment to a world in which Marcus will never belong. In *I Hadn't Meant to Tell You This* (1994) by Jacqueline Woodson, the author explores a variety of issues such as parent-child relationships, the nature of family, and friendship while describing the relationship between two young women, one white and one black. The same author, in *From the Notebooks of Melanin Sun* (1995), adds gay issues to the mix of relationship problems when a young black male has to cope with the fact that his mother's lover is a white female. Irina Strelkova's Russian novel *Playing the Game* (1983) describes the coming of age of a group of male friends who all represent various segments of the Soviet population and who must deal with their stereotypes about members of other cultures within the Soviet Union as they struggle to remain friends. Likewise, the female roommates, one African American and one Korean American, of Marie Lee's *Saying Goodbye* (1994) struggle to deal with their racial prejudices in the aftermath of the Rodney King incident. The characters in novels by Barbara Ann Porte, such as *Something Terrible Happened* (1994), have to confront the difficulties they face because of their biracial heritage.

These works are useful in promoting discussion about significant social issues because while the characters may not interact with others in ways free of prejudice, the authors present realistic individuals who must wrestle with their limitations—and who provide a mirror in which readers may examine their own behaviors. However, the effect of the books in their entirety should not serve to deprecate systematically any particular group or race. It is important that teachers selecting novels for use with students avoid choosing those that may either reinforce negative stereotypes or cause serious discomfort to some students because of any demeaning portrait of diverse characters. For example, Pat Frank's *Alas, Babylon* (1976), a novel written in the 1950s, may have been progressive in its treatment of relationships at that time, but in today's society, the patronage system described, the relationship of domestic to employer, is out of date. This novel is still often read because it deals with the timely topic of nuclear war, but there are more current novels that can provoke reader response and provide food for discussion of literary craftsmanship without reinforcing outmoded ways of interacting.

Obviously, much "classic" literature contains stereotyping reflective of the historical context in which it was written, and many contemporary figures in well-written young adult novels do interact with others based on their prejudices. For example, Hamilton's *A White Romance* (1987) often provokes anger in readers because of the stereotyping and prejudices the black characters have regarding some of their white peers. In *Kindred* by Octavia Butler (1981), the love Rufus feels for Alice, a freeborn black woman, is destroyed because of his inability to see her as an equal instead of through the eyes of a slave holder, and Lois Ruby's *Skin Deep* (1994) details the violent actions against minority groups taken by a group of white high school students. Julius Lester's *Othello: A Novel* (1995) provides an interesting examination of Shakespeare's plot and characters viewed through a lens that takes racial prejudices into account in explicit ways. Books that provide "an honest and authentic portrayal of the human condition" (Tway 1981, 6) will be full of characters who are condescending and deprecatory. Students need to be exposed to such characters who reflect current and historic realities, however uncomfortable those realities might be, and then they need to examine why those stereotypes exist and confront their own stereotyping behaviors as a result.

Those responsible for selecting novels for adolescent readers should be also aware that there is a growing body of young adult literature from other countries available. For instance, Pribic (1983) discusses the "blue jeans fiction of Yugoslavia," Osa (1986) describes "the new Nigerian youth literature," Jenkins and Austin (1987) discuss literature for young readers about Asians and Asian Americans, and Bello (1992) defines and describes Caribbean children's and young adult literature. Because many such works are now available in translation, teachers, parents, and librarians who are selecting books to which young adults will have access should make an effort to include them. Readers now have the opportunity to read books by Alvarez (*In the Time of the Butterflies* [1994]) from the Dominican Republic; Brainard (*When the Rainbow Goddess Wept* [1994]) from the Philippines; Danticat (*Breath, Eyes, Memory* [1994]) from Haiti; Gunesekera (*Reef* [1996]) from Sri Lanka; Hicyilmaz (*The Frozen Waterfall* [1993]) from Turkey; Huong (*Paradise of the Blind* [1994]) from Vietnam; Orlev (*The Man from the Other Side* [1995]) from Israel; Watkins (*My Brother, My Sister and I* [1994]) from Japan; and many others.

Students are often intrigued by the thought of living elsewhere and are interested in other countries, even when they may not be curious about the lives of their peers in the United States who come from diverse cultural and ethnic backgrounds. These novels provide insight for readers about both the commonalities of the adolescent experience and about how the cultural milieu in which a person acts affects decisions. Some of the common concerns of adolescents that seem to transcend cultural boundaries include the following:

- the need to define oneself outside the realm of the family
- the need to come to terms with new visions of one's parents as "less than perfect"
- the need to determine an individual set of moral, ethical, religious, or political principles
- the need to come to terms with a developing sexuality and with the physiological changes brought on by puberty
- the need to begin to develop positive relationships with the opposite sex
- the need to begin to think about the future, about career options and job possibilities, about whether to marry or remain single
- the need to forge a niche in the larger society

For instance, in *The Ink-Keeper's Apprentice* (1994), Alan Say tells the autobiographical story of Kiyoi, a thirteen-year-old boy living in Tokyo just after World War II. Kiyoi has to face family tensions and disapproval in order to pursue his apprenticeship to Noro, a famous cartoonist. Lesley Beake's *Song of Be* (1993) traces the life of Be, a young Bush woman caught in the chaos of Namibia's move toward independence. Readers of *The Boys from St. Petri* by Bjarne Reuter (1994) learn about wartime occupation from the point of view of young Danish men determined to risk everything in the fight for freedom from Nazi domination. And the German Janna of *Fall-Out* by Gudrun Paulsewang (1994) also must make difficult choices about her future and about the risks she is willing to take after she becomes the victim of a nuclear disaster.

Any student who has read and enjoyed Blume's *Are You There, God? It's Me, Margaret* (1972) and has related to Margaret as she tries to figure out what her twelve-year-old body is doing would also appreciate the Russian *Shadows Across the Sun* (Likhanov 1983). Fedya, the main character, is at that age when his body is growing and maturing, leaving him feeling gangly and awkward inside it. Also, he feels the first stirrings of sexuality as he becomes friends with Lena. She, too, is coping with the awkwardness inherent in puberty, but her situation is complicated by the fact that she is wheelchair-bound, a result of polio. Shell, in *Green Days by the River* by Michael Anthony (1989), is fifteen when he must contend with changes in his family situation compounded by his developing feelings of sexuality, which confuse and trouble him. His confusion in the face of awakening sensations of physical desire can easily be compared to those of the main character in British author Robert Westall's *Falling into Glory* (1995) or to those of the Syrian narrator in Rafik Schami's *A Hand Full of Stars* (1990). And Janine Boissard, in the French *A Matter of Feeling* (1977), beautifully captures the same feelings from the female point of view as she describes Pauline's experiences with first love.

It would seem that the questions "Who am I?" or "What is the meaning of my life?" are asked by young people all over the world. In Mori's *Shizuko's Daughter* (1993), Yuki is on a quest to determine who she is, a quest complicated by conflicts between her traditional Japanese family values and her sense of the world as colored by conflicts between her desire for others to tell her who to be and her frustration at not being allowed to determine this for herself. When her mother commits suicide and her father, always distant and reserved at best, remarries, bringing home a wife who replaces the rich colors of Shizuko's pottery and paintings with fragile store-bought items, Yuki retreats into bitter isolation. However, through her interactions with her grandparents, and through her own experiments with self-expression in art, Yuki gradually becomes an independent person poised to become involved in a relationship with a young man. *Shizuko's Daughter* is not easy to read; it is not easy to summarize. The characters and the setting in which they are growing and changing are complex, and the author does not, in the end, provide Yuki with any definite solutions. But the ending does provide a sense of hope. Although Yuki realizes that "everything and anything could bring on the sadness," she also realizes that she must learn to "look beyond . . . unhappiness" in order to become the person her mother wanted her to be, and she is able to step out of herself and move toward Isamu with genuine happiness (202). Mori, who left Japan as a young woman, provides an outstanding portrait of the confusion and search for answers experienced by young adults, and the book's setting in another country reminds us that this quest is common to emerging adolescents in many cultures.

Just as these novels from other countries point out the similarities of developmental tasks and issues that exist in many cultures, they can also be used as a springboard for discussing the role of one's cultural heritage in making decisions and for pointing out differences that exist among cultures. When young adult novels from the Soviet Union were used in a rural Maryland middle school, the students felt safe to explore topics such as racism, prejudice, the role of religion, and gender stereotyping because of the distance between them and the characters created by the differences in cultural backgrounds, and thus very free discussion of these issues occurred. These novels seemed to provide useful bridges to books by authors from the United States who wrestle with such concerns in settings more familiar and which are perhaps less comfortable for students to discuss. Possible topics for discussion include the following:

- differences in school systems and philosophies of education
- differences in the role of the state/government in the life of the individual
- differences in perception of "family"
- differences in the nature of the prevailing religious orientation
- differences in perceptions of history
- differences in the perception of the role of the adolescent in society
- differences in the routines of daily life
- differences in the perception of time
- differences in the nature of language use

For example, in *Imagining Isabel* by Casteneda (1994), the devaluation of women and their rights in Guatemala is heartbreakingly portrayed, as are the situations in South Africa under apartheid in Naidoo's *Chain of Fire* (1989) and in the Balkan Republics in Mead's *Adem's Cross* (1996). Lacey, the main character in *For the Life of Laetitia* by Merle Hodge (1993), struggles to fulfill her dream of graduating from a Caribbean secondary school in the face of prejudiced teachers and her own family's lack of support, and *Shizuko's Daughter* (Mori 1993) presents a very clear picture of the Japanese educational system. *So Loud a Silence* by Jenkins

(1996), set in Colombia, could be used to explore the nature of the relationship between the individual and the state, and the British *Handles* by Mark (1985) includes a wonderful glossary of British vocabulary that could be used to discuss differences in the use of language. Any novel from another country will convey something about the differences in the routines of daily life.

One final comment on selection: As Townsend writes, "any line which is drawn to confine children or their books to their own special corner is an artificial one. Whenever the line is drawn, children and adults and books will wander across it" (1979, 9). When selecting books for use in the classroom or for inclusion in the library collection, we must pay attention to what students tell us they want to read and find appropriate and stimulating. Thus novels such as *No Longer at Ease* by Chinua Achebe (1961), Gus Lee's *China Boy* (1994), or Dorothy West's *Wedding* (1995), or novels by "adult" authors such as Alice Walker, Toni Morrison, Leslie Marmon Silko, or Maxine Hong Kingston may be the books that students choose to read in order to explore issues related to differences in cultural and ethnic heritage. Donelson and Nilsen, writing about this point—that young adult literature includes, basically, whatever young adults can and will read—note that the selection process can be supplemented by the use of "current reviewing sources and annual lists of best books compiled by the Young Adult Library Services Association, the editors of *School Library Journal, Booklist, The ALAN Review*, the *New York Times, VOYA*, the *English Journal*, and other groups" (1980, xvi). *The ALAN Review* frequently publishes articles on young adult literature reflective of cultural diversity. Also, once a year, *Social Education* publishes a list of young adult novels useful for inclusion in the social studies classroom, many of which deal with issues of cultural diversity in a historical context.

In summary, teachers, librarians and others selecting novels for use in the classroom or guiding students' independent reading should consider the following selection principles:

1. Avoid tokenism.
2. Avoid dogmatism; choose books that are valuable in their own right for their literary merit.
3. Choose books that promote positive human relations.
4. Select books in which characters from diverse cultures interact in realistic ways.
5. Select books that deal with minority experiences, recent immigrant experience, and the experiences of young adults growing up in other countries in order to provide as much diversity as possible.
6. Listen to young adults as they describe books that stirred them and promoted their thinking.

Teachers, instructors, and librarians also have an obligation to make these works easily accessible to students. Students can't read what they can't find! If money is not available for class sets, individual copies can be purchased and the teacher can read them aloud, or an individualized reading program can be established that would allow students to read books of their own choosing and then come together in both small and large groups to share their new insights and perceptions. For example, Soto's *Canto Familiar* (1995, Hispanic), Adoff's *My Black Me: A Beginning Book of Black Poetry* (1994, African American), or Harjo's *Woman Who Fell from the Sky* (1994, Native American) can be read to provide an introduction to language cadences, imagery, and issues that are explored in the novel(s).

Conclusion

After reading the Russian novel *Shadows Across the Sun* (Likhanov 1983), one eighth grader said, "If Fedya and Lena were called Jack and Jill, I wouldn't have known this was a Russian book." In fact, that assessment is not quite true. The setting, the food, the clothing, the influence of the state on day-to-day life, the treatment of the handicapped within the society are all quite different from that which students from the majority culture in the United States experience. What this student seems to tell us as teachers is that he is willing to see the commonalities rather than the differences. These similarities of concern and experience among young adults from varied backgrounds can help our students as they read about their peers from other cultures to develop a tolerance and appreciation for diverse peoples. Through reading such novels, they may be exposed to the effects on society of prejudice, ethnocentricity, and cultural stereotyping and may begin to wrestle with their own values and related behaviors as a result. For instance, reading novels about the experiences of Native Americans may cause students to think about their own attitudes toward the environment. Even differences in language can provide insights. Choctaw poet Marilou Awiakta notes that when people use the term *Mother Earth*, "they take with love / and with love give back" in a way that does not happen when the individual's relationship with the Earth is not perceived as such a nurturing one, saying that if we call Earth *it*, we "use her/consume her strength" and then we die (1992, 68).

The hope is that by reading such literature we can help the "shadows across the sun" caused by a lack of understanding dissipate and so lay the foundation for a more tolerant and peaceful world. As Ronald Takaki, professor of ethnic studies, says, "The intellectual purpose of multiculturalism is a more accurate understanding of who we are as Americans. . . . Multiculturalism is an affirming of what this country stands for: opportunity, equality, and the realization of our dream" (Halford 1999, 11–13). But, perhaps Eloise Greenfield, author of *She Come Bringing Me*

That Little Baby Girl (1974a) and *Paul Robeson* (1975), best describes the goal of using young adult novels reflective of diverse cultural experiences and ethnic backgrounds in the classroom:

> I want to encourage children to develop positive attitudes toward themselves and their abilities, to love themselves . . . I want to write stories that will allow children to fall in love with genuine Black heroes and heroines who have proved themselves to be outstanding in ability and in dedication to the cause of Black freedom . . . I want to be one of those who can choose and order words that children will want to celebrate. I want to make them shout and laugh and blink back tears and care about themselves. They are our future. They are beautiful. They are for loving. (Tiedt and Tiedt 1979, 93)

Works Cited and Bibliography

Achebe, Chinua. 1961. *No Longer at Ease*. New York: I. Obolensky.

————. 1988. *Things Fall Apart*. Portsmouth, NH: Heinemann.

Adoff, Arnold. 1994. *My Black Me: A Beginning Book of Black Poetry*. New York: Puffin.

Alvarez, Julia. 1994. *In the Time of the Butterflies*. New York: NAL/Dutton.

Anaya, Rudolfo. 1972. *Bless Me, Ultima*. Berkeley, CA: Tonatuiuh-Quinto Sol International.

Anthony, Michael. 1989. *Green Days by the River*. Portsmouth, NH: Heinemann.

Arrick, Fran. 1981. *Chernowitz!* New York: Bradbury.

Atwell, Nancie. 1987. *In the Middle: Writing, Reading, and Learning with Adolescents*. Portsmouth, NH: Boynton/Cook.

Au, Kathryn H. 1993. *Literacy Instruction in Multicultural Settings*. Fort Worth, TX: Harcourt.

Awiakta, Marilou. 1992. "When Earth Becomes an 'It.'" In *Through Indian Eyes: The Native American Experience in Books for Children*, ed. Beverly Slapin and Doris Seale, 68. Philadelphia: New Society.

Baker, Houston, ed. 1982. *Three American Literatures: Essays in Chicano, Native American, and Asian American Literature for Teachers of American Literature*. New York: Modern Language Association.

Banks, James A. 1994. *An Introduction to Multicultural Education*. Needham Heights, MA: Allyn and Bacon.

Barrera, Rosalinda B., Olga Ligouri, and Loretta Salas. 1992. "Ideas a Literature Can Grow On: Key Ingredients for Enriching and Expanding Children's Literature About the Mexican American Experience." In *Teaching Multicultural Literature Grades K–8*, ed. Violet Harris, 203–31. Norwood, MA: Christopher Gordon.

Beake, Lesley. 1993. *Song of Be*. New York: Henry Holt.

Bello, Yahaya. 1992. "Caribbean Children's Literature." In *Teaching Multicultural Literature in Grades K–8*, ed. Violet Harris, 243–65. Norwood, MA: Christopher Gordon.

Bishop, Rudine Sims. 1990. "Mirrors, Windows and Sliding Glass Doors." *Perspectives* 6: ix–xi.

———. 1991. "African American Literature for Children: Anchor, Compass, and Sail." *Perspectives* 7: ix–xii.

———. 1992. "Multicultural Literature for Children: Making Informed Choices." In *Teaching Multicultural Literature in Grades K–8*, ed. Violet Harris, 37–54. Norwood, MA: Christopher Gordon.

Bishop, Rudine Sims, and the Multicultural Booklist Committee, eds. 1995. *Kaleidoscope.* Urbana, IL: National Council of Teachers of English.

Blume, Judy. 1972. *Are You There, God? It's Me, Margaret.* New York: Dell.

Boissard, Janine. 1977. *A Matter of Feeling.* Trans. Mary Feeley. Toronto: Little, Brown.

Brainard, Cecilia Manquerra. 1994. *When the Rainbow Goddess Wept.* New York: Dutton.

Brooks, Bruce. 1984. *The Moves Make the Man.* New York: Harper Junior.

Bruchac, Joseph. 1993. *Flying with the Eagle, Racing the Great Bear: Stories from Native North America.* Mahwah, NJ: Bridgewater.

Bruchac, Joseph, and Gayle Ross, eds. *The Girl Who Married the Moon.* Mahwah, NJ: Bridgewater.

Butler, Octavia. 1981. *Kindred.* New York: Pocket Books.

Cai, Mingshui. 1995. "Can We Fly Across Cultural Gaps on the Wings of Imagination? Ethnicity, Experience, and Cultural Authenticity." *New Advocate* 8.1: 1–16.

Cannon, A. E. 1992. *The Shadow Brothers.* New York: Dell/Laurel-Leaf.

Carlson, Lori, ed. 1994a. *American Eyes.* New York: Henry Holt.

———. 1994b. *Cool Salsa: Bilingual Poems on Growing Up Latino in the United States.* New York: Henry Holt.

Castaneda, Omar S. 1994. *Imagining Isabel.* New York: Lodestar.

Chall, J. S., E. Redwin, V. W. French, and C. R. Hall. 1985. "Blacks in the World of Children's Books." In *The Black American in Books for Children*, 2d ed., ed. Donnarae McCann and G. Woodard, 211–21. Metuchen, NJ: Scarecrow.

Cisneros, Sandra. 1994. *The House on Mango Street.* New York: Random House.

Cleaver, Vera, and Bill Cleaver. 1969. *Where the Lilies Bloom.* New York: Lippincott.

Cofer, Judith Ortiz. 1995. *An Island Like You.* New York: Orchard.

Cooperative Children's Book Center. 1991. *The Multicolored Mirror: Cultural Substance in Literature for Children and Young Adults*, ed. Merri V. Lindgren. Fort Atkinson, WI: Highsmith.

Cowan, Gregory, and Elizabeth Cowan. 1980. *Writing.* Glenview, IL: Scott, Foresman.

Curtis, Christopher Paul. 1995. *The Watsons Go to Birmingham—1963.* New York: Delacorte.

Danks, Carol, and Leatrice Rabinsky, eds. 1999. *Teaching for a Tolerant World, Grades 9–12: Essays and Resources.* Urbana, IL: National Council of Teachers of English.

Danticat, Edwidge. 1994. *Breath, Eyes, Memory.* New York: Vintage (Random House).

Day, Frances Ann. 1995. *Multicultural Voices in Contemporary Literature: A Resource for Teachers*. Portsmouth, NH: Heinemann.

Delpit, Lisa. 1988. "The Silenced Dialogue: Power and Pedagogy in Educating Other People's Children." *Harvard Educational Review* 58.3: 280–98.

de Vries, Anke. 1996. *Bruises*. Trans. Stacy Knecht. New York: Front Street/Lemniscaat.

Donelson, Kenneth, and Alleen P. Nilsen. 1980. *Literature for Today's Young Adults*. Glenview, IL: Scott, Foresman.

Dorris, Michael. 1994. "Why I'm Not Thankful for Thanksgiving." In *Through Indian Eyes: The Native Experience in Books for Children*, ed. Beverly Slapin and Doris Seale, 19–24. Philadelphia: New Society.

———. 1996. *Sees Behind Trees*. New York: Hyperion.

———. 1997. "Mixed Blood." In *Race: An Anthology in the First Person*, ed. Bart Schneider, 52–56. New York: Crown Trade.

Draper, Sharon. 1994. *Tears of a Tiger*. New York: Atheneum.

Ehle, Maryann. 1982. The Velveteen Rabbit, the Little Prince, and Friends: Postacculturation Through Literature. Paper presented at the annual meeting of the Professional Clinic of Association of Teacher Educators, 13–19 February, Phoenix, AZ. ERIC Document Ed 221 881.

Ekoomiak, Normee. 1990. *Arctic Memories*. New York: Holt.

Feder, Harriet K. 1995. *Mystery of the Kaifeng Scroll*. Minneapolis: Lerner.

Frank, Pat. 1976. *Alas, Babylon*. New York: Bantam.

Franklin, Paula. 1995. *Melting Pot or Not? Debating Cultural Identity*. Springfield, NJ: Enslow.

Frankson, Marie Stewart. 1990. "Chicano Literature for Young Adults: An Annotated Bibliography." *English Journal* 79.1: 30–35.

Freire, Paulo. 1970. *Pedagogy of the Oppressed*. New York: Seaburg.

Freuchen, Pipaluk. 1951. *Eskimo Boy*. New York: Lothrup, Lee.

Gay, Geneva, and William Baber, eds. 1987. *Expressively Black: The Cultural Basis of Ethnic Identity*. New York: Praeger.

George, Elizabeth. 1983. *Sign of the Beaver*. New York: Dell.

Goble, Paul. 1987. *Death of the Iron Horse*. Old Tappan, NJ: Bradbury (Simon and Schuster).

Gonzales, Roseann Duenas. 1990. "When Minority Becomes Majority: The Changing Face of the English Classroom." *English Journal* 79.1: 16–23.

Greene, Patricia Baird. 1992. *The Sabbath Garden*. New York: Lodestar/Dutton.

Greenfield, Eloise. 1974a. *She Come Bringing Me That Little Baby Girl*. Philadelphia: Lippincott.

———. 1974b. *Sister*. New York: Crowell.

———. 1975. *Paul Robeson*. New York: Crowell.

Gunesekera, Romesh. 1996. *Reef*. New York: Berkley.

Guy, Rosa. 1983. *The Friends*. New York: Bantam.

Halford, Joan Montgomery. 1999. "A Different Mirror: A Conversation with Ronald Takaki." *Educational Leadership* 56:7: 9–13.

Hamilton, Virginia. 1987. *A White Romance*. New York: Philomel.

———. 1997. *Arilla Sun Down*. New York: Scholastic.

Harjo, Joy. 1994. *The Woman Who Fell from the Sky*. Boston: Little, Brown.

Harris, Violet J. 1990. "African American Children's Literature: The First One Hundred Years." *Journal of Negro Education* 59: 540–55.

Harris, Violet J., ed. 1992. *Teaching Multicultural Literature in Grades K–8*. Norwood, MA: Christopher Gordon.

Harte, Joyce C. 1997. "Teaching and Learning Across Cultures: The Literature Classroom as a Site for Cultural Transactions." In *Rethinking American Literature*, ed. Lil Brannon and Brenda M. Greene, 81–96. Urbana, IL: National Council of Teachers of English.

Heath, Shirley Brice. 1983. *Ways with Words: Language, Life, and Work in Communities and Classrooms*. New York: Cambridge University Press.

Herman, Charlotte. 1994. *What Happened to Heather Hopkowitz?* Philadelphia: The Jewish Publication Society.

Hicyilmaz, Gayle. 1993. *The Frozen Waterfall*. New York: Farrar, Straus & Giroux.

Hodge, Merle. 1993. *For the Life of Laetitia*. New York: Farrar, Straus & Giroux.

Hoevler, Diane Long. 1988. "Text and Context: Teaching Native American Literature." *English Journal* 77.5: 20–24

Hudson, Jan. 1989. *Sweetgrass*. New York: Philomel.

Huong, Duong Thu. 1994. *Paradise of the Blind*. New York: Penguin.

Hurwin, Davida Wills. 1995. *A Time for Dancing*. Boston: Little, Brown.

Jenkins, E., and M. Austin. 1987. *Literature for Children About Asians and Asian Americans: Analysis and Annotated Bibliography with Additional Readings for Adults*. Westport, CT: Greenwood.

Jenkins, Lyll Becerra de. 1995. *Celebrating the Hero*. New York: Puffin.

———. 1996. *So Loud a Silence*. New York: Lodestar/Dutton.

Johnson, Angela. 1993. *Toning the Sweep*. New York: Orchard.

———. 1995. *Humming Whispers*. New York: Orchard.

Joseph, Stephen M. 1972. *The Me Nobody Knows*. New York: Avon.

Kaplan, Robert. 1966. "Cultural Thought Patterns in Inter-Cultural Education." *Language Learning* 16: 1–2, 15.

Krisher, Trudy. 1994. *Spite Fences*. New York: Delacorte.

Larrick, Nancy. 1965. "The All-White World of Children's Books." *Saturday Review* September 11: 63–65.

Lasky, Kathryn. 1995. *Beyond the Divide*. New York: Aladdin Paperbacks.

Lee, Gus. 1994. *China Boy*. New York: Penguin.

Lee, Marie G. 1994. *Saying Goodbye*. Boston: Houghton Mifflin.

Lester, Julius. 1995. *Othello: A Novel*. New York: Scholastic.

Likhanov, Albert. 1983. *Shadows Across the Sun*. New York: Harper and Row.

Lindgren, Merri V., ed. 1991. *The Multicolored Mirror: Cultural Substance in Literature for Children and Young Adults*. Fort Atkinson, WI: Cooperative Children's Book Center/Highsmith.

Longstreet, Wilma. 1978. *Aspects of Ethnicity: Understanding Differences in Pluralistic Classrooms*. New York: Teachers College Press.

Lynch, Chris. 1994. *Gypsy Davey*. New York: HarperCollins.

Lyon, George Ella. 1988. *Borrowed Children*. New York: Bantam.

Mark, Jan. 1985. *Handles*. New York: Atheneum.

Markoosie. 1970. *Harpoon of the Hunter*. Toronto: McGill-Queen's University Press.

Marsden, John. 1994. *Letters from the Inside*. Boston: Houghton Mifflin.

Martinez, Victor. 1996. *Parrot in the Oven*. New York: HarperCollins.

Maruki, Toshi. 1982. *Hiroshima No Pika*. New York: Lothrup.

Mead, Alice. 1996. *Adem's Cross*. New York: Farrar, Straus & Giroux.

Meyer, Carolyn. 1994. *Rio Grande Stories*. New York: Gulliver (Harcourt Brace).

———. 1996. *Gideon's People*. New York: Gulliver (Harcourt Brace).

Miller-Lachman, Lyn. 1992. *Our Family, Our Friends, Our World*. New Providence, NJ: R. R. Bowker.

Mitchell, Arlene Harris. 1988. "Black Adolescent Novels in the Curriculum." *English Journal* 77.5: 95–97.

Mohr, Nicholasa. 1986. *Nilda*. 2d ed. Houston: Arte Publico.

Momaday, N. Scott. 1969. *House Made of Dawn*. New York: Signet.

Monseau, Virginia R. 1996. *Responding to Young Adult Literature*. Portsmouth, NH: Boynton/Cook.

Mori, Kyoko. 1993. *Shizuko's Daughter*. New York: Henry Holt.

Morrison, Toni. 1970. *The Bluest Eye*. New York: Penguin.

Myers, Walter Dean. 1994. *The Glory Field*. New York: Scholastic.

Naidoo, Beverly. 1989. *Chain of Fire*. New York: Lippincott.

Namioka, Lensey. 1994. *April and the Dragon Lady*. New York: Browndeer (Harcourt Brace).

Narayan, Kirin. 1994. *Love, Stars, and All That*. New York: Pocket Books.

Naylor, Gloria. 1982. *The Women of Brewster Place*. New York: Viking.

Newman, Gerald, and Eleanor Newman Layfield. 1995. *Racism: Divided by Color*. Springfield, NJ: Enslow.

Nieto, Sonia, ed. 1983. "Puerto Ricans in Children's Literature and History Texts: A Ten-Year Update." *Bulletin of the Council on Interracial Books for Children* 14: 1–2.

———. 1996. *Affirming Diversity*. 2d ed. White Plains, NY: Longman.

Noll, Elizabeth. 1995. "Accuracy and Authenticity in American Indian Children's Literature: The Social Responsibility of Authors and Illustrators." *The New Advocate* 8.1: 29–43.

Okimoto, Jean Davies. 1995. *Talent Night*. New York: Scholastic.

Oliver, Eileen Iscoff. 1994. *Crossing the Mainstream: Multicultural Perspectives in Teaching Literature*. Urbana, IL: National Council of Teachers of English.

Orlev, Uri. 1995. *The Man from the Other Side*. Trans. Hillel Halkin. New York: Puffin/Penguin.

Osa, Osayimwense. 1986. "The New Nigerian Youth Literature." *Journal of Reading* 30.2: 100–104.

Oughton, Jerrie. 1995. *Music from a Place Called Half Moon*. Boston: Houghton Mifflin.

Paterson, Katherine. 1977. *Bridge to Terabithia*. New York: Avon.

Paulsewang, Gudrun. 1994. *Fall-Out*. New York: Viking.

Peck, Robert Newton. 1989. *Arly*. New York: Walker and Co.

Philip, Neil, ed. 1996. *Earth Always Endures: Native American Poems*. Photographs by Edward Curtis. New York: Viking.

Porte, Barbara A. 1994. *Something Terrible Happened*. New York: Orchard.

Potok, Chaim. 1978. *The Chosen*. New York: Fawcett.

Pribic, R. 1983. "Blue Jeans Fiction of Yugoslavia." *Journal of Reading* 26: 430–34.

Reuter, Bjarne. 1994. *The Boys from St. Petri*. New York: Dutton Children's.

Rief, Linda. 1991. *Seeking Diversity: Language Arts with Adolescents*. Portsmouth, NH: Heinemann.

Rochman, Hazel. 1993. *Against Borders: Promoting Books for a Multicultural World*. Chicago: American Library Association.

Rodriguez, Richard. 1982. *Hunger of Memory: The Education of Richard Rodriguez*. New York: Bantam.

Rollock, Barbara. 1984. *The Black Experience in Children's Books*. 2d ed. New York: New York Public Library.

Romero, Patricia Ann, and Dan Zancanella. 1990. "Expanding the Circle: Hispanic Voices in American Literature." *English Journal* 79.1: 24–29.

Ruby, Lois. 1994. *Skin Deep*. New York: Scholastic.

Rumbaut, Hendle. 1994. *Dove Dream*. Boston: Houghton Mifflin.

Rylant, Cynthia. 1994. *Something Permanent*. Photographs by Walker Evans. New York: Harcourt Brace.

Salisbury, Graham. 1992. *Blue Skin of the Sea*. New York: Delacorte.

———. 1994. *Under the Blood-Red Sun*. New York: Delacorte/Bantam/Doubleday/Dell.

———. 1998. *Jungle Dogs*. New York: Delacorte.

Say, Allen. 1994. *The Ink-Keeper's Apprentice*. Boston: Houghton Mifflin.

Schami, Rafik. 1990. *A Hand Full of Stars*. Trans. Rika Lesser. New York: Dutton.

Schon, Isabel. 1988. *An Hispanic Heritage: A Guide to Juvenile Books About Hispanic People and Culture*. 3d ed. Metuchen, NJ: Scarecrow.

Schon, Isabel, ed. 1994. *Contemporary Spanish-Speaking Writers and Illustrators for Children and Young Adults: A Biographical Dictionary*. Westport, CT: Greenwood.

Sinclair, April. 1994. *Coffee Will Make You Black*. New York: Avon/Hearst.

Slapin, Beverly, and Doris Seale, eds. 1994. *Through Indian Eyes: The Native Experience in Books for Children*. Philadelphia: New Society.

Smith, Karen Patricia, ed. 1994. *African-American Voices in Young Adult Literature: Tradition, Transition, Transformation*. Metuchen, NJ: Scarecrow.

Sneve, Virginia Driving Hawk. 1993. *When Thunder Spoke*. Lincoln: University of Nebraska Press.

Soto, Gary. 1994. *Jesse*. San Diego: Harcourt Brace.

———. 1995. *Canto Familiar*. Illus. Annika Nelson. New York: Harcourt Brace and Co.

Southgate, Martha. 1996. *Another Way to Dance*. New York: Delacorte.

Spradley, James P., and David W. McCurdy. 1975. *Anthropology: The Cultural Perspective*. New York: John Wiley and Sons.

Stover, Lois, and Rita Karr. 1990. "Glasnost in the Classroom." *English Journal* 79.8: 47–54.

Strelkova, Irina. 1983. *Playing the Game*. Trans. J. C. Butler. Moscow: Raduge Publisher.

Tate, Eleanora. 1988. *The Secret of Gumbo Grove*. New York: Bantam.

Tatum, Charles, ed. 1990. *Mexican American Literature*. Chicago: Harcourt Brace Jovanovich.

Taylor, Mildred. 1976. *Roll of Thunder, Hear My Cry*. New York: Dial.

Taylor, Theodore. 1995. *The Bomb*. San Diego: Harcourt Brace.

Temple, Charles, Miriam Martinez, Junko Yokota, and Alice Naylor. 1998. *Children's Books in Children's Hands*. Boston: Allyn and Bacon.

Thomas, Joyce Carol. 1986. *Water Girl*. New York: Avon.

Tiedt, Pamela L., and Iris M. Tiedt. 1979. *Multicultural Teaching: A Handbook of Activities, Information, and Resources*. Boston: Allyn and Bacon.

Townsend, John Rowe. 1979. *A Sounding of Storytellers*. New York: J. B. Lippincott.

Trimmer, Joseph, and Tilly Warnock. 1992. *Understanding Others: Cultural and Cross-Cultural Studies and the Teaching of Literature*. Urbana, IL: National Council of Teachers of English.

Tway, Eileen, ed. 1981. *Reading Ladders for Human Relations*. 6th ed. Urbana, IL: National Council of Teachers of English.

Uchida, Yoshiko. 1984. *The Best Bad Thing*. New York: Atheneum.

Velasques, Gloria. 1994. *Juanita Fights the School Board*. New York: Pinata Books.

Voigt, Cynthia. 1985. *The Runner*. New York: Atheneum.

Wartski, Maureen Crane. 1981. *A Boat to Nowhere*. New York: New American Library.

Watkins, Yoko Kawashima. 1994. *My Brother, My Sister and I*. New York: Bradbury.

West, Dorothy. 1995. *The Wedding*. New York: Doubleday.

Westall, Robert. 1995. *Falling into Glory*. New York: Farrar, Straus & Giroux.

White, Ruth. 1994. *Weeping Willow*. New York: Farrar, Straus & Giroux.

———. 1996. *Belle Prater's Boy*. New York: Farrar, Straus & Giroux.

Williams-Garcia, Rita. 1995. *Like Sisters on the Homefront*. New York: Lodestar/Dutton.

Woodson, Jacqueline. 1994. *I Hadn't Meant to Tell You This*. New York: Delacorte.

———. 1995. *From the Notebooks of Melanin Sun*. New York: Blue Sky (Scholastic).

Wyeth, Sharon Dennis. 1994. *The World of Daughter McGuire*. New York: Delacorte.

Yep, Laurence. 1977. *Child of the Owl*. New York: Harper Junior.

Yolen, Jane. 1988. *The Devil's Arithmetic*. New York: Viking/Kestral.

Zitlow, Connie, Toby Sanders, and Marlene Beierle. 1997. "Stories, Circles, People and Places: An Interview with Joseph Bruchac." *Ohio Journal of English Language Arts* 38.1: 36–52.

10

Gender Issues and the Young Adult Novel in the New Millennium

PAM B. COLE AND PATRICIA P. KELLY

If we believe that literature can make us reevaluate our ideas about others and ourselves, then the portrayal of male and female roles in young adult fiction is an important classroom consideration. If YA literature provides an environment for young adults to experience vicariously situations they may someday encounter, to see the results of decisions made by characters, and to evaluate their ideas and behaviors, then how males and females interact in those fictional situations can shape thinking by reinforcing stereotypes or by promoting alternative views. Because young adult novels are written by as many female as male writers and because the stories generally reflect a modern setting with male and female protagonists, they provide excellent opportunities to look at how gender roles are played out. Of course, any novel is much more than the gender issues embedded within the story line, but for that very reason it is an important consideration. Because readers get swept up into the story, they may not consciously note stereotyped behaviors yet they may unconsciously process the information.

Any consideration of gender during the act of reading is further complicated because it involves not only the gender of the characters but also the gender of the reader. In the early years of the young adult novel, Carlsen (1967) described the reading preferences of early adolescents. He said that by eighth grade, boys' and girls' reading interests differ sharply, and the difference continues even in mature adult readers. Boys want the main character to be male; girls will read books with either sex playing a major role. Boys prefer a large cast of characters in an action-packed plot, with subplots taking place over a long period of time and in many locales and lots of dialogue and description of action. On the contrary, according to Carlsen, girls like few characters in a more direct plot taking place in a specific locale, a school or a town, and covering a discrete period of time, a summer or a year, for example, with descriptions of inner thoughts and emotional reactions. Carlsen pointed out that it is not unusual for girls and women to read and enjoy a "masculine" story, but boys and men rarely enjoy a "feminine" one (23–24).

Other research of reading preferences and responses has generated similar findings. Beaven's study, for example, found that girls could identify with both male and female characters, though they listed more males than females, but boys identified with male characters only (1972, 60–61). To further complicate the process of looking at gender through literature, Symmonds found that as "male students get older, they seem less able to identify with characters that are not male. Conversely, as females get older they seem to relate equally if not better with male characters" (1990, 19). Muted-group theory, which assumes that "language and the norms for its use are controlled by the dominant group" (Crawford and Chaffin 1986, 21), may explain this occurrence. Specifically, in our male-dominated literary curriculum, females have grown up reading literature from the male perspective and in a male voice and, therefore, may have learned to value that literature more highly than the fiction that reflects their own experiences and feelings.

Preferences in reading and differing responses to characters make it difficult to select for classroom use literature that reflects a variety of gender relationships. The content of many young adult novels, however, makes it equally difficult to find good gender roles. This chapter first contains a discussion of gender issues of girls in selected young adult novels, then gender issues in romance novels, followed by gender issues related to boys in selected young adult novels, concluding with a description of one young adult novel particularly suited for gender study.

A Girl's Relationship with Her Own Body

Girls' acceptance of their own bodies as they grow and change is a theme of many novels and of particular importance when looking at young adult literature from a gender standpoint. Although there are occasional boys in young adult literature who are not as tall or athletic as others and who are labeled "geeks," male characters generally are more accepting of their bodies than are female characters. For boys, the visible characteristics of puberty are positive: they get taller, stronger, and hairier. Conversely, the visible signs of puberty for girls make them vulnerable: breasts are noticeable, and the entire body begins to change as it moves from an androgynous child's shape to a woman's form. This change, even when easy, is a distinct demarcation in a female's life, but when difficult, it can result in any number of behaviors, among them eating disorders and acute dissatisfaction with one's body.

In recent years a number of novels have been published about anorexia nervosa, a problem primarily of young females in affluent, industrialized countries. Sometimes the onset of puberty with the accompanying body changes triggers the initial diet, an effort to meet some ideal shape promulgated in the media. Then it becomes a matter of exercising control over one's life as a way to enhance self-esteem.

A particularly effective novel dealing with anorexia nervosa is Cathi Hanauer's *My Sister's Bones* (1996). Beautiful and smart, Cassie Weinstein attends Cornell University. Having been pushed by her authoritarian father to be the best at everything, Cassie develops anorexia and withdraws from her sister and her family. Having always turned to her sister for advice and guidance, sixteen-year-old Billie recognizes the severe physical and psychological changes in Cassie. She watches as Cassie wastes away to nothing but bones. Their parents, however, refuse to acknowledge Cassie's illness, leaving Billie, who struggles with her own esteem issues, to worry alone about her sister's health. Only when Cassie's weight drops to a dangerous level and she is hospitalized do her parents face the truth about Cassie's illness. Describing well the pathology of anorexia nervosa, this novel also looks closely at family relationships and how family dynamics can contribute to this eating disorder.

A different but related eating problem is bulimia. Primarily associated with females, bulimia stems from a need similar to that causing anorexia, the need to gain control over some element of one's life. With bulimia, the feeling of control comes through purging after binge eating. In Lesléa Newman's book *Fat Chance* (1994), thirteen-year-old Judi Liebowitz, dissatisfied with her weight, develops bulimia. Teased and taunted by boys at school and never having had a date, Judi comes to believe "guys like skinny girls, the skinnier the better" (3) and "fat girls don't deserve boys anyway" (134). Envying Nancy Pratt, the most gorgeous girl in eighth grade, Judi begins a cycle of crash dieting and bingeing. Her dieting efforts fail until she discovers Nancy's secret to weight control: purging after eating. Armed with her new secret weapon and a new friend, Judi begins losing weight.

Judi is an excellent role model for young girls who are concerned about their weight. Though Judi develops bulimia, she recognizes its danger when Nancy is placed in intensive care. Judi finds the courage to reveal all to Mrs. Roth, her overweight English teacher, despite the fact that Nancy threatens to reveal her secret. Judi discovers that Mrs. Roth was once bulimic but has learned to accept her body:

> "It's a perfectly good body. I [Mrs. Roth] just wish . . . people weren't mean to those of us who happen to be fat. . . . I'm very happy with my life, Judi. I have a job that means something to me, a husband who loves me, and a wonderful baby daughter. What more could I want? . . . There's more important things in life than a twenty-inch waist." (204)

Gaining courage from Mrs. Roth, Judi shares her journal with her mother, who helps Judi seek professional help.

Similarly, *Life in the Fat Lane* by Cherie Bennett (1998) is an excellent portrayal of the psychological ramifications of being overweight. Lara has everything: beauty, popularity, and a perfect family. However, when a rare disease causes her to gain excessive amounts of weight, she struggles with dieting to maintain her perfect shape. Lara loses to the disease but learns through the painful process that fat people do not choose to be fat and that beauty does in truth go beyond the surface. This latter point is driven home even more by the ending, in which her boyfriend sees beyond her physical self.

Girls' Relationships with Other Girls

Generally in young adult novels written for early middle school grades, the plots, regardless of the other twists, center on girls as friends. Novels appealing to girls in late middle school and early high school frequently include a female protagonist who knows a boy or dates a boy, thus making her female friends secondary characters. Even during the time the girls spend together, they tend to discuss boys. Ironically, the audience for these books is girls, yet the subtle message being communicated to them—however positive, humorous, or mysterious the rest of the plot may be—is that girls are second best, less significant. The underlying message in these novels for a female audience is that having a boyfriend is more important in a girl's life than having girlfriends. Girlfriends are there to listen, to plan, to console when the relationship goes awry, and to spend time with when a boy is not around. The importance of having a boyfriend is so central that girls are often depicted as jealous of other girls who are attractive and who win the attention of the male characters.

Nonetheless, positive examples of girlfriends in a middle school situation can be found in some young adult literature. In Paula Danziger and Ann Martin's *P.S. Longer Letter Later* (1998), for instance, Elizabeth and Tara*Starr are best friends whose worlds are vastly different. Tara*Starr is an only child whose parents are saving for a house; Elizabeth lives in a six hundred thousand dollar home where possessions take priority over feelings. When Tara*Starr and her family move away, the girls struggle to maintain their relationship through letter writing as their lives change. Tara*Starr's mother becomes pregnant, and Tara*Starr becomes jealous of her future sibling; Elizabeth's father loses his job, begins drinking too much, and leaves his family. Elizabeth moves with her mother and sister to an apartment where they begin a new life. Though Tara*Starr and Elizabeth have a long-distance friendship, they gain strength and insight into the problems in their lives through sharing their experiences with one another. As young girls often do in real life, Tara*Starr and Elizabeth use each other as sounding boards and barometers, measuring what is right, wrong, good, and bad in their lives. Though the two friends mention boys in their letters, boy talk is not a major focus of the story.

In *A Fate Totally Worse Than Death* (1995), Paul Fleischman has created a wonderful parody that looks at the vanities, quirks, and jealousies often found among teenage girls. Danielle, Tiffany, and Brooke, totally consumed by their appearances and obsessed with boys, plan an evil welcome to Cliffside High School for Helga, a stunning Norwegian exchange student who creates quite a stir among the male population. While plotting their evil schemes, the girls discover that they are aging rapidly. Though this novel is a cleverly crafted farce, it provides a wonderful opportunity for classroom discussion about relationships between girls, their beliefs about themselves, and their attitudes about girl-boy relationships.

Although early adolescent girls are depicted frequently as friends, one topic rarely portrayed in the young adult novel is a lesbian relationship. *Good Moon Rising* (1996) by Nancy Garden is a beautiful story about love between two teenage girls who meet during a school play, develop a relationship, and struggle with their feelings for one another. Problems arise, however, when Kent, the male lead in the school production of *The Crucible*, takes the lead in harassing the two girls. Despite his behavior, other students think the relationship is no one else's business. The novel contains no explicit sex scenes, no violence, and no foul language. Jan and Kerry experience feelings of love, hurt, and fear that are similar to those of girls in heterosexual relationships present both in the real world and in other young adult novels.

Girls and Their Mothers and Fathers

The teenager's world in young adult literature does not include parents to any great extent. At best, fathers are seen driving girls and their friends somewhere or commenting on various behaviors, such as grades, lateness, or clothing; although, occasionally, a father is portrayed as the nurturer. Marie's father in *I Hadn't Meant to Tell You This* by Jacqueline Woodson (1994) is a single parent and a loving father who plays basketball with his daughter. Marie's mother has abandoned her and her father, and Marie is lonely; she longs to be held and touched. Though the story begins with Marie feeling a bit alienated from her father, the two grow together as their wounds heal, and they begin living a satisfying life without Marie's mother.

Though young adult literature occasionally portrays a father in a positive relationship with his daughter, more often than not fathers are abusive, are mentally or physically ill, or abandon their daughters. In *Don't You Dare Read This, Mrs. Dunphrey* by Margaret Haddix (1996), sixteen-year-old Tish keeps a journal in English class in which she writes about her feelings and the events in her life.

Tish's father left Tish, her younger brother, Matt, and their mother two years earlier. Tish's mother is depressed and longs for his return. When Tish's father comes back into town, Tish's mother goes looking for him and finds him in a bar. Tish's father comes back into their lives, and their mother becomes happy once again. However, happiness does not last long; Tish's parents begin fighting, and Tish's father abuses both her and her mother. He has no true commitment to family, cares for neither of his two children, and soon checks out again, leaving Tish and her family to get by the best way they can.

Young adult literature reflects many variations of the ageless mother-daughter theme. Because this relationship is such a difficult one for a teenage girl, most books that include a mother and daughter have at least some reference to conflict, even in the best of circumstances. However, young adult literature often depicts young girls who have been abandoned by their mothers or who have mothers who are mentally ill. In *Don't You Dare Read This, Mrs. Dunphrey*, Tish's mother blames Tish for her father's leaving. Unable to cope with his loss again, Tish's mother abandons Tish and her younger brother, leaving them a small sum of money and a note saying she has gone to find their father. Tish fends for herself and her younger brother for a while but soon turns to her English teacher for help. The mother-daughter relationship in this book is a tough one. The behavior of Tish's mother is brought on by her depression and by her irrational way of thinking. Believing she cannot do better, believing she cannot create a life for herself without Tish's father, she leaves her children.

One conflict seldom addressed in young adult literature but present in the lives of many young girls is competition between girls and their mothers. In *Life in the Fat Lane* by Cherie Bennett (1998), Lara Ardeche's mother is as beautiful as Lara and takes great pleasure in knowing she looks ten years younger than her real age; nonetheless, she is jealous of Lara because Lara's father dotes on his daughter. Though Mrs. Ardeche tries helping Lara diet, she secretly is glad she does not have the weight problem and is repulsed by Lara's weight.

A more positive mother-daughter relationship is depicted in *Missing Pieces* by Norma Fox Mazer (1999). Fourteen-year-old Jessie is very close to her mother. They go for walks together, work together at the stables, and share in caring for Aunt Zis, who lives with them. Together they share everything, everything except the secrets surrounding the father Jessie has never met. When Jessie sets out on a journey to find her father, her relationship with her mother becomes strained, and Jessie feels some distance from her:

> I told myself to go to her, but something held me where I was. I wanted to do it—go and put my arms around her, the way I'd done so many times before. But I didn't. I couldn't. I couldn't move. (105)

Nonetheless, Jessie's mother remains a source of strength for her daughter, giving her the freedom to search for her father and reassuring her that she is loved when she feels despondent. Jessie's mother realizes that Jessie needs to know about her father; thus, she gives her the room to explore, to ask questions, and even to get angry. Knowing the ordeal will be a painful one for Jessie, she constantly reassures her of her love.

Gender Issues in the Romance Novel

The romance novel is not new, but the proliferation of adolescent romance novels that began in the '80s and continues today is somewhat disturbing. Young adult romances, such as those in the *Silhouette First Love* series (an '80s series) and those in *Love Stories* (a '90s series) have changed very little, if at all. These romance novels for young girls have many of the same characteristics as adult romance novels. The heroine is in some way vulnerable, a condition brought on by a move to a new environment, an illness, or some secret flaw; she meets a handsome hero, who is initially drawn to her; some type of conflict occurs that separates them or causes a misunderstanding; and in the final resolution they are happily together (Radway 1984, 134). In the teen versions, a great deal of description about clothes, hair, makeup, figures, long looks, and touching hands always exists. People are beautiful, houses are decorated, and love scenes are dramatic, as in Liesa Abrams' *Stolen Kisses*:

> Laura's breath caught, and the whole room seemed suspended in time. She looked into his eyes, her heart thumping a million beats a minute. And then he pressed his lips against hers. Laura let herself melt into the kiss, and it was . . . incredible. Explosive. She put her arms around Mark, holding him and shutting out everything but the delicious sensation of his mouth on hers. (1999, 39)

Similar scenes appear in every romance novel. Like the adult versions, the adolescent heroine's happiness depends on her having the love of a man. Her identity is tied to "coupleness."

Though characters in romance novels remain stereotypical, a new voice is developing as a response to these stereotypes. For example, Bruce Lansky has compiled a series titled *Girls to the Rescue* in which girls are "clever, courageous, and kind. They don't rely on their beauty. They don't rely on magic. They don't resort to violence. . . . Most of the stories are about helping families, friends, and country—not about getting married" (1995, x–xi). Those stories that do deal with marriage place the woman in more positive roles. Heroines, for example, must slay dragons and trolls prior to marriage. Such stories as these may empower girls to believe in their own capabilities and not believe that they must play submissive roles to boys.

Carlsen suggests that girls' interest in the romantic novel peaks around ninth or tenth grade (1967, 38). However, according to Symmonds' study, high school girls through twelfth grade prefer novels of love and romance (1990, 18). Although more studies may need to be done to substantiate that finding, it is clear that sales of these books indicate a substantial market. Ironically, at a time when teens should be reading to find direction for their lives, to develop personal values, and to picture themselves in an adult world, many female adolescents are receiving one message: a woman has value only if she is with a man.

Even books that are not strictly in the romance genre often send the same message. For example, a book like *All for the Love of That Boy* by Linda Lewis (1989) makes a good statement about peer pressure to drink, and the fifteen-year-old protagonist, Linda, is intelligent, attending a special high school for technology. However, her major interest in life is Lenny, who hangs out and drops out of school. She wants to graduate early, not to go to college but to marry Lenny, despite their on-again, off-again relationship. Linda sees herself as important only with Lenny: "I stood next to him the whole time, thinking how glad I was to be Lenny's girlfriend. He was so full of life and had so much personality" (45). Because this type of novel has realistic settings with characters who are less than beautiful and contains some type of social commentary, the gender messages may be more "dangerous." A romance novel sets itself forth as a fairy tale, making it easier perhaps to separate oneself from the stereotypical view of male-female relationships. When those same messages are conveyed in a more realistic format, teenage girls may have difficulty avoiding internalization of such views.

Other Boy-Girl Relationships

Even in novels other than romance, boy-girl relationships in books targeted toward female readers tend to be stereotyped. A girl's happiness depends on having a boyfriend. Books for boys have a different perspective; they fit girls into their other activities, where appropriate. They talk things over with girlfriends, party with them, and occasionally fall in love. Only occasionally does a broken relationship result in turning their lives upside down, and seldom does the relationship consume their thoughts throughout their waking hours. Often they are even ambivalent about their feelings, as Walker is in Chris Crutcher's *Stotan!* (1986). He dates Devnee, a prettily stereotyped, nurturing female, but he wants to break off with her because he likes Elaine, a nontraditional girl who is also a friend. Walker eventually decides to stop dating Devnee, even though Elaine has let him know that they will be friends only. Such decisions would be rare in a book written for a female audience.

Generally, fictional accounts of boys and girls as true, long-lasting friends are also rare. An excellent example of such a relationship, however, is in Julie Reece Deaver's *Say Goodnight, Gracie* (1988), in which Jimmy Woolf and Morgan Hackett have been like brother and sister since birth; they are friends almost to the exclusion of others. They share similar interests—Jimmy's is dancing and Morgan's is acting; they support each other emotionally; and they thoroughly enjoy each other's company. A more recent example of an endearing relationship between boys and girls can be found in Chris Crutcher's *Staying Fat for Sarah Byrnes* (1993). Eric (Moby), who is overweight, and Sarah, who has severe burn scars on her face and hands from an accident, are drawn together by their physical differences, which make them outcasts. Moby joins the swimming team and begins losing weight; Sarah becomes ill and is placed in a psychiatric hospital. Moby's weight loss and gain in popularity threaten his relationship with Sarah; however, he struggles to help her reveal the truth about her accident, about how her father deliberately pushed her against a hot stove when she was a small child, severely burning her. Sarah makes Moby promise to keep her childhood secret; however, when Moby realizes that her dad is getting more and more threatening, he must decide whether to break the secret. Moby thinks to himself: "I'd rather have her hate my guts and be safe than love me and be alone" (131). Moby cares deeply for Sarah and will protect her, even if the end result is losing her friendship. Crutcher creates an intense and moving friendship that is tested by fire over time.

Boys' Relationships with Other Boys

In realistic young adult fiction, boys may be high achievers or athletes, but just as frequently their characters are troubled or in trouble; are rebels or at least testing the boundaries of societal expectations; or appear to be without ambition or at least do not perform well in school. Although not all male characters fit this description, many do. And even though the culminating messages of the novels are usually appropriately positive, the image subtly conveyed to the male teenager is that of the man alone with his inner feelings, depending primarily on his own resources. Extremely popular with boys, these books do encourage them to read, but perhaps the stereotyped portrayal is as invasive of their self-perceptions as romance novels are of girls' self-perceptions.

A current issue of concern for parents, teachers, and teenagers is that of tension and competition between and among boys and how they deal with these issues. Perhaps more boys than girls find a strong piece of their identity through athleticism. Societal norms teach us that manliness is closely connected with athletic prowess; not only is a teenage boy cool, macho, and popular if he excels in sports, but being athletic is the way to get girls. If a teenage boy is not athletic or has little interest in sports, he becomes a geek or an outcast. Boys who are artistic, who like to write, who do not project an image of toughness, and who are smaller than their classmates are often humiliated by their peers and, in some cases, humiliated by their fathers, who feel their own manliness challenged when their sons are not athletic. Perhaps this issue is as powerful for boys as physical beauty is for girls. A number of writers narrate these conflicts realistically, among them Chris Lynch.

In Lynch's *Slot Machine* (1995), Elvin attends a summer camp where he tries to find his "slot" in sports. Overweight and having more in common with geeks than jocks, he fails miserably at football, baseball, wrestling, and golfing, does not fit in with the religious group, and becomes frustrated when he cannot find a place for himself in the arts. His size and his lack of athletic skill place him on the outer fringes in camp, where he is scorned by those who do fit. He is abused by some of the other boys and by the camp directors and experiences a great deal of humiliation. Though he covers his experiences with a wonderful sense of humor, inside Elvin is confused:

> Myself, I remained. Like the moment before, and the year before. Undecided. Unclear. Unmoved. Unattracted. Paralyzed with the depth of my own nothingness. I made my decision the way I made all my decisions. By sitting passively. (206)

The Slot Machine is an excellent example of how boys deal with being teased and taunted. Though Elvin appears to be a wimp, inside he is tough; he fights back with sarcasm and humor and comes to realize that he is okay just as he is. His friend Frank, however, lacks Elvin's strength. He needs to prove his manliness so much that he falls into a nasty hazing ceremony, during which he allows the older boys to abuse, torture, use, and humiliate him just so he can belong. Though he is ashamed of himself for allowing this abuse, his desire to be one of the crowd overpowers his feelings of disgrace.

Overall, the characters in *The Slot Machine* are well developed, providing an excellent story for talking about relationships and power struggles between and among boys. Elvin illustrates how boys can use wit and humor to deal with those who harass them; Frank represents the troubled boy, the boy who is willing to be tormented and abused just so he can become a part of the power group; and Mikie, a second friend, represents the mature boy who is comfortable with who he is.

Though many books for boys illustrate competitive relationships among boys, books do exist that show loyalty and close bonds. Rod Philbrick does a superb job with friendship in *Freak the Mighty* (1993). Max is a misfit. Extremely large for his age and learning-disabled, he shuns others; however, when Kevin, a crippled but ingenious dwarf, moves in next door, Max finds a true friend and begins breaking out of his shell. Together they become Freak the Mighty. Inspired by King Arthur tales, they perform deeds of bravery and become inseparable. As the story progresses, Max's heartbreaking past unfolds, revealing the tragic story of his mother's death at the hands of his father. At the same time, an illness that racks Kevin's body takes over and he dies. Though feeling deep loss, Max is left with warm memories of his friendship with Kevin and a stronger sense of his own self-worth. The characters of Max and Kevin are memorable and represent the strong bonds that often exist between boys.

Although there are more young adult novels dealing with homosexuality of males than females, relatively few still exist, with one of the earliest, *Sticks and Stones* by Lynn Hall (1972), only treating the subject obliquely. Many more recent books for adolescents address the issue more directly. Francesca Lia Block's *Baby Be-Bop* (1995), for example, focuses on a character by the name of Dirk McDonald. Sixteen-year-old Dirk struggles with his sexual identity; he meets and falls in love with Pup, who cannot handle the relationship and checks out. Dirk sinks into a deep well of self-hate. Teased and abused by others who call him "faggot," Dirk does not see a way out of his pain and misery until he is severely beaten. Through the use of surrealism, Block reveals Dirk's past and future, allowing him to discover truths about himself and his family and showing him a glimpse of the man who will be his mate. Dirk learns to love himself, learns how to deal with loneliness, and learns how to cope in a world that seems to loathe him. Young boys who are struggling with their sexual identities will readily identify with *Baby Be-Bop*.

Boys and Their Mothers and Fathers

In many young adult novels written for boys, mothers, if not totally absent, play minor roles. The limited interaction between mothers and sons makes it difficult to picture the women as characters. They say hello and good-bye, serve meals, and occasionally express an opinion, which the son often views as criticism. In many novels they are abusive or either physically or emotionally abandon their children, leaving them to deal with relationship and identity issues.

One such example can be found in *Gypsy Davey* by Chris Lynch (1994). Severely abused and neglected by his mother since birth, Davey is raised by Jo, his sister. As small children he and his sister care for themselves, often going without food, living in filth, watching their mother drink and hang out with men, and occasionally seeing their father storm in and out of their lives. Jo grows up as irresponsible as her mother and has her own baby, illustrating that relationships are learned behaviors. As Jo took care of Davey in his infancy, so does Davey take care of Jo's baby. Davey feels he owes Jo for taking care of him, so he spends time taking care of little Dennis. *Gypsy Davey* is a tough read but an excellent example of the story of a negligent mother and the impact her absence has on her children and on generations to come.

Of course, positive models, though few, do exist. An example is Mrs. Baggs in Will Weaver's *Striking Out* (1993). Mavis Baggs is an exceptionally strong female. As the story opens, she plays the typical farm wife role, performing chores around the farm and preparing meals for her husband, Abner, and her only son, Billy. Having lost her older son in a farming accident five years earlier, Mavis struggles to help her husband and her younger son work through their feelings of guilt and pain surrounding the accident. Abner has a distant relationship with his son and works Billy like a man on the farm, giving him no time to be a boy. Knowing that Billy lives a man's life, Mavis convinces Abner to let Billy occasionally play baseball in town.

Billy's first official game happens on his brother's birthday. Feeling proud and happy in his new baseball uniform, Billy is at first surprised when his mother begins to cry, but then he remembers his brother's birthday. Believing he does not deserve to feel any sense of happiness because of his brother's death, Billy begins removing his uniform. His mother, however, will not allow him to continue blaming himself for the loss of his brother:

> "No, Billy!" she said. She grabbed him by the shoulders so hard his head rattled. "You're playing ball today. You need this, don't you see? The timing is just bad luck—that's all. You're going to play and you're going to do fine and we're all going to do fine." (251)

Mavis' strength at the moment of her own pain creates a turning point for Billy. She gives him strength to believe in himself. He knows he needs his mother, and he feels safe letting her hold him for a while. He realizes at last that he has to release the guilt and that his mother does not blame him for the death of his brother. With his mother's help, Billy begins making peace with himself.

Father-son relationships in adolescent literature are also as varied as they are in real life: absent fathers, single-parent fathers, supportive fathers, physically and mentally ill fathers, and abusive and controlling fathers all have places in young adult literature. Chris Crutcher's *Ironman* (1995), for instance, is a classic power struggle between a controlling, abusive father and an enraged son. Bo Brewster and his father have been at war as long as Bo can remember. When Bo quits the football team to become a triathlete, Mr. Brewster becomes angry and sets out to teach Bo a lesson: quitters do not prosper. Mr. Brewster becomes so obsessed with proving his point that he buys an expensive bicycle for Bo's leading competitor, hoping the boy will beat Bo and prove him right. Though the story is tough, the reader is left believing hope exists in the relationship.

Yet a different father-son relationship is integral to the plot of *Rats Saw God* by Rob Thomas (1996). Once a model student, high school senior Steve York now uses drugs and is in danger of flunking English. When a high school counselor suggests a one hundred–page writing assignment to bring up his failing English grade, Steve acquiesces and finds himself narrating the events that plunged him into a downward spiral. From freshman year to his life as a senior, Steve details his high school years: his parents' divorce, his distant relationship with his famous astronaut father, his involvement with a dadaist group in school, falling in love for the first time, and having his heart broken.

Steve finds comfort in his dadaist friends at school, particularly with Dub, the girl with whom he falls in love. Steve shares his innermost feelings about his father with her:

> I can't stand the fact he's in better shape than me. I hate it that he buys American. He watches CNN nonstop. He drinks bottled water. He reads the entire newspaper, section by section, and he folds it back the way it was delivered. He thinks it's normal to work sixteen hours a day. (110)

Steve admits that these are little things and that his feelings are grounded deeper:

> I always feel like I'm disappointing him, like he's waiting for his share of the gene pool to kick in. I'm sure he thinks that one day I'm going to rush into a burning building and save an orphan's life or jump out of the stands at a football game and run back a punt for the winning touchdown, and then he'll finally know, "Yep, that's my boy." (110)

When Steve's relationship with Dub falls apart, he unravels and moves to San Diego to live with his mother, where he continues to feel bitter toward his father. Devastated over the breakup and feeling very alone, he becomes involved with drugs and his grades plummet. When Steve's father calls and asks Steve to attend his wedding and be his best man, Steve is shocked; he hardly expected to get a personal phone call. Steve decides to go and is surprised again when he finds that the wedding is a quiet, not public, event. At first he wonders why his dad wanted him there; there are no VIPs, no society columnists, no pomp, no one he needs to impress in attendance. While watching his father say his vows, reality hits Steve:

> I watched the astronaut [Steve's father] as he repeated the vows. His voice was so strong. I had seen weddings where the groom trembled and squeaked each pledge. Not the astronaut. He made it very clear he intended to marry this woman, to love, honor, and obey. He would too—of this I was certain. The astronaut didn't make

promises lightly. . . . I had spent four comfortable years blaming the astronaut; but, thinking about it, the astronaut would have never gotten a divorce of his own volition. Divorce is failure, and the astronaut simply couldn't stomach failure. (195)

The reader is left at the end believing that Steve is beginning to learn some truths about himself and that he is beginning to understand his father. Steve's future is brighter.

As exemplified in *Rats Saw God* (Thomas 1996), fathers generally play a conflicting or absent role in young adult literature for boys. Sometimes young boys and their fathers work through conflict, as in *Rats Saw God*, and other times they do not. Seldom do fathers play understanding and supportive roles, but the father in Rich Wallace's *Wrestling Sturbridge* (1996) is one such character. Ben is a high school senior who is on the school wrestling team and is growing up in a small town. Ben's close friend Al is the state wrestling star, and Ben must decide whether to compete with him or to remain in Al's shadows. Ben's father is proud of Ben and does not put pressure on him; in the end, when Ben beats Al, he thanks his dad for giving him strength and support.

Whole-Group Discussion of Gender Issues with *Tangerine*

Edward Bloor's *Tangerine* (1997) is one book that classroom teachers might use to generate a realistic discussion about gender roles and gender relationships. In this young adult novel, Paul Fischer and his family move to an affluent community in Tangerine, Florida, where Paul, a good soccer player, attends middle school and his older brother, Erik, a football star, attends high school. When Paul's school is condemned because of faulty construction, he chooses to attend a nearby middle school. Paul learns that the soccer team is coed and that the players, both boys and girls, are rough and tough. Fitting in becomes a challenge, and being partially blind and living in the shadows of his brother's stardom complicate his life.

Relationship issues abound in this book. Paul's parents, particularly well-developed characters, appear to be "average" parents; however, both are alienated in some way from their children. Paul's father lives and breathes football with Erik; he keeps computer records of Erik's college possibilities and does not want to believe that Erik has problems, even when Erik is involved in a neighborhood theft. When Mr. Fischer learns that Erik is involved, he convinces the neighbors not to press charges against his son.

Paul is an interesting character for classroom discussion on gender issues and gender relationships. Though his father's neglect hurts him, he uses good coping skills to deal with his feelings; he has a strong sense of self-worth. Paul develops friends through his involvement in soccer and learns that social status does not develop character. He accepts the fact that the girls on the team have earned positions ahead of him; he acknowledges that they are good and does not feel "less than" because the girls are star players.

It is difficult for any individual to live in the shadows of another. Paul, however, is perhaps saved somewhat by his mother. Though his mother stays busy with community service, she takes time for Paul; she takes him to school, senses when something is wrong with him, offers him a chance to talk, and takes Paul's side when she feels his father is neglecting him. Acknowledging Paul's father is obsessed with his older son becoming a hero, Mrs. Fischer asks, "What if Erik has no future in football?" (227). The question makes Mr. Fischer uncomfortable, and he responds as though her question is ridiculous.

When Erik is called down to the police station to be questioned about the death of Luiz Cruz, both Mr. and Mrs. Fischer are forced to recognize Erik's viciousness and amoral behavior. Mr. Fischer feels powerless and says Erik's fate is in the hands of justice; Mrs. Fischer, however, shows some concern over her older son. Both parents admit that they should have sought psychological help for Erik when, as a child, he purposely blinded Paul. Their responses to Erik throughout the story make for good classroom discussion questions: What motivates them to deny Erik's sociopathic behavior? Are they afraid of Erik? If so, why? Why does Paul's mother not take a stronger stand against her husband? These questions and others can spark an interesting classroom discussion about gender issues in *Tangerine*.

It is important that we continue considering gender as an issue when selecting books for class study and recommended independent reading, for a look at much young adult literature from a gender perspective shows that stereotypical trends continue: that girls are likely to be stereotyped as dependent in their relationships with boys, that mothers and fathers play fairly insignificant roles at best and detrimental roles at worst, and that boys are also frequently stereotyped as athletes or loners. There are, of course, notable exceptions, and those books can appeal to young people as they struggle with defining themselves in relation to others.

Works Cited

Abrams, Liesa. 1999. *Stolen Kisses*. New York: Bantam.

Beaven, Mary H. 1972. "Responses of Adolescents to Feminine Characters in Literature." *Research in the Teaching of English* 6: 48–68.

Bennett, Cherie. 1998. *Life in the Fat Lane*. New York: Delacorte.

Block, Francesca Lia. 1995. *Baby Be-Bop*. New York: HarperCollins.

Bloor, Edward. 1997. *Tangerine*. New York: Scholastic.

Carlsen, G. Robert. 1967. *Books and the Teen-Age Reader*. New York: Bantam.

Crawford, Mary, and Roger Chaffin. 1986. "The Reader's Construction of Meaning: Cognitive Research on Gender and Comprehension." In *Gender and Reading,* ed. Elizabeth A. Flynn and Patrocinio P. Schweickart, 3–30. Baltimore: Johns Hopkins University Press.

Crutcher, Chris. 1986. *Stotan!* New York: Dell.

———. 1993. *Staying Fat for Sarah Byrnes.* New York: Greenwillow.

———. 1995. *Ironman.* New York: Greenwillow.

Danziger, Paula, and Ann M. Martin. 1998. *P.S. Longer Letter Later.* New York: Scholastic.

Deaver, Julie Reece. 1988. *Say Goodnight, Gracie.* New York: Harper & Row.

Fleischman, Paul. 1995. *A Fate Totally Worse Than Death.* Cambridge, MA: Candlewick.

Garden, Nancy. 1996. *Good Moon Rising.* New York: Farrar, Straus & Giroux.

Haddix, Margaret Peterson. 1996. *Don't You Dare Read This, Mrs. Dunphrey.* New York: Simon & Schuster.

Hall, Lynn. 1972. *Sticks and Stones.* New York: Dell.

Hanauer, Cathi. 1996. *My Sister's Bones.* New York: Dell.

Lansky, Bruce. 1995. *Girls to the Rescue.* New York: Simon & Schuster.

Lewis, Linda. 1989. *All for the Love of That Boy.* New York: Pocket Books.

Lynch, Chris. 1994. *Gypsy Davey.* New York: HarperCollins.

———. 1995. *The Slot Machine.* New York: HarperCollins.

Mazer, Norma Fox. 1995. *Missing Pieces.* New York: Morrow.

Newman, Lesléa. 1994. *Fat Chance.* New York: G. P. Putnam's Sons.

Philbrick, Rod. 1993. *Freak the Mighty.* New York: Scholastic.

Radway, Janice A. 1984. *Reading the Romance.* Chapel Hill, NC: University of North Carolina Press.

Symmonds, Andrea. 1990. "High School Students, Gender Identification and Literature." *Idaho English Journal* 18–19.

Thomas, Rob. 1996. *Rats Saw God.* New York: Aladdin.

Wallace, Rich. 1996. *Wrestling Sturbridge.* New York: Alfred A. Knopf.

Weaver, Will. 1993. *Striking Out.* New York: HarperCollins.

Woodson, Jacqueline. 1994. *I Hadn't Meant to Tell You This.* New York: Dell.

11

Playing the Game
Young Adult Sports Novels

CHRIS CROWE

In an editorial from a recent issue of *Coach and Athletic Director*, Herman L. Masin laments the lack of respect given to sports in literature. "We have in front of us," he writes, "a list of the '100 Best Novels' of this century, compiled by the editorial board of the Modern Library, and not one of these novels contains as much as a sub-plot on anything having to do with sports. The shut-out is disconcerting" (1998, 10). Masin wonders how a nation so proud of its athletic heroes and its sports tradition can ignore sports in its "great literature."

What Masin may not understand is that in the minds of literary canon makers, literature about sports is usually shelved with other subliterature, written works that don't merit the title of "literature." Perhaps because young adult literature has long lurked on the lower shelves of literature, elements of sports in its fiction do not lessen its quality; though no sports story has ever won the coveted Newbery Medal, Bruce Brooks' story of basketball player Jerome Foxworthy and his friend Bix, *The Moves Make the Man* (1984), did receive Newbery Honor status in 1985. The Newbery shutout notwithstanding, various honor lists show that literature for teenagers has a long—and proud—history of sports stories.

In an article reviewing some of the best young adult novels written in the past 125 years, Ken Donelson (1997) includes ten sports novels in his honor list of almost 120 novels that begins with Alcott's *Little Women* (1868) and ends with James Bennett's basketball story, *The Squared Circle* (1995). The first sports story on Donelson's list is Ralph Henry Barbour's *The Crimson Sweater* (1908); his list includes nine more sports books: John Tunis' *All-American* (1942), *Yea! Wildcats!* (1944), and *Go, Team, Go!* (1954); Robert Lipsyte's *The Contender* (1967); Richard Blessing's *A Passing Season* (1982); Chris Crutcher's *Running Loose*

(1983); Brooks' *The Moves Make the Man*; Tessa Duder's *In Lane Three, Alex Archer* (1989); and Bennett's *The Squared Circle*.

Sports books also figure prominently in *Booklist*'s "Best of the Best Books for Young Adults." Of the seventy-nine novels appearing on *Booklist*'s roster of best books from 1967 to 1994, seven are sports stories: Brooks' *The Moves Make the Man*, Crutcher's *Athletic Shorts* (1991) and *Stotan!* (1986), Terry Davis' *Vision Quest* (1979), Carl Deuker's *On the Devil's Court* (1989), David Klass' *Wrestling with Honor* (1989), and Lipsyte's *The Contender*.

The most recent recommended list, the American Library Association's "Popular Paperbacks for Young Adults 1999," cited twenty-three sports books, seventeen of which were fiction: Edward Bloor's *Tangerine* (1997), Brooks' *The Moves Make the Man*, Crutcher's *Ironman* (1995) and *Staying Fat for Sarah Byrnes* (1993), Thomas Dygard's *Halfback Tough* (1986), Don Gallo's short-story collection titled *Ultimate Sports* (1995), Dan Gutman's *Honus and Me* (1997), Dayton O. Hyde's *The Major, the Poacher, and the Wonderful One-Trout River* (1985), W. P. Kinsella's *Shoeless Joe* (1982), Klass' *Danger Zone* (1996), Gordon Korman's *The Toilet Paper Tigers* (1995), Lipsyte's *The Contender*, Chris Lynch's *Iceman* (1994), Claire Murphy's *To the Summit* (1992), Walter Dean Myers' *Hoops* (1981) and *Slam!* (1996), and Rich Wallace's *Wrestling Sturbridge* (1996).

The number and variety of sports titles mentioned above clearly show that unlike "great" adult fiction, quality young adult literature certainly has not ignored sports stories. This is not to say that all sports stories are great young adult novels. Of course, the field has had its share of strikeouts to go with the home runs, but when it comes time for the fat lady to sing about great young adult novels, a significant number of sports stories will always be included.

Sports stories endure because sports have become an integral part of modern American society. For the last century, Americans' passion for sports has reached levels that would have been unthinkable one hundred years ago. Just a few decades ago, fans knew and cared little about the personal lives of athletes. Back then, the press focused on sports heroes' performances on the field but largely ignored their off-field exploits. Because today's TV programs, magazines, and newspapers often give as much or more time to athletes' personal lives as they do to their athletic accomplishments, modern sports fans know star athletes—as players *and* as celebrities—more intimately than ever before.

But Americans, and especially American teenagers, are not only reading about and watching sports; the personal involvement of teenagers in sport is now higher that it has ever been. Title IX essentially doubled athletic opportunities by mandating in 1972 that schools offer as many sports programs for women as they do for men. The trickle-down effect of Title IX triggered the unprecedented growth of junior and recreational sports leagues for girls along with the wider acceptance of women as athletes. Add to this growth the near-universal school requirement for physical education, and it's guaranteed that more teenagers than ever have had some personal involvement with competitive athletics. This personal involvement, combined with the media popularity of sports, has prepared young adult readers and writers to accept—and perhaps even to expect—that sports will play an important role in the books they read.

Finally, sports doesn't merely mirror contemporary life, it pervades it. Most American teenagers are more familiar with sports than with any other single aspect of society. They hear and use sports metaphors in their language. They can attend or view a sports event every day of the year. Their style of dress is influenced by sports. Much of the food they eat and the beverages they drink have a sports connection, and even nonsports products are promoted by celebrity athletes in commercials.

Considering the overwhelming presence of sports in today's society, it's not surprising that publishers continue to look for ways to incorporate sports into the books they produce for teenagers. America has a long tradition of sports books for teenagers, and an article in *Publishers Weekly* suggests that the tradition is growing stronger. Hoping to cash in on the popularity of sports in general and sports books in particular, the National Basketball Association, the National Football League, and the National Hockey League have joined with a variety of publishers in joint ventures and licensing agreements to produce sports books for young readers (Raugust 1997, 34). This recent growth in young adult sports books reflects a trend that began more than one hundred years ago.

A Brief History of Sports Novels for Teenagers

For more than a century, publishing and sports have been important American activities even though, in terms of revenue, the publishing business far outstripped sports for years. Many American publishers enjoyed robust years in the nineteenth century, while sports remained almost exclusively an amateur venture; however, as sports became more popular and more professional, publishers started paying attention. Christian K. Messenger suggests that the notion of boys' sports stories originated from the success of Thomas Hughes' *Tom Brown's School Days* (1857) and *Tom Brown at Oxford* (1861). "Here," says Messenger, "was the classic fictional portrayal of youth's initiation into traditions of school life in which athletic skill defined and singled out the leadership boys more than any other activity" (1981, 159). Publishers took note, and in 1882, publishing and sports began their long relationship with the publication of the first piece of baseball fiction. While a junior at Brown University, Charles Munroe Sheldon, who would later become the author of the best-selling *In His Steps*, published "The Captain of the Orient Nine," a baseball morality tale about a player named Gleason who knows that his team won an important game because of a missed call by an umpire. "There wasn't too much sport in the story," says Robert Cantwell, "but Sheldon worked on Gleason's moral dilemma until he looked like a character in *Pilgrim's Progress*, chasing a fly ball into the Slough of Despond" (1962, 69). Didactic though it may be, Gleason's story staked out new territory for publishers: fiction primarily about sports.

The second work of baseball fiction and the first baseball novel, Edward Wheeler's *High Hat Harry, the Baseball Detective; or The Sunken Treasure* (1885), appeared fairly early in the pulp fiction era (about 1870 to 1930), when many books, mostly Westerns and adventure stories, were being published for mostly male "juvenile" readers. The popular and critical reception of *High Hat Harry* disappointed its author and his dime novel publisher, Beadle and Adams, but it helped establish sports fiction as an important market for the teenage audience (Cantwell 1962, 70). Despite the failure of Wheeler's baseball novel, publishers believed that sports stories might appeal to teenage readers. By the turn of the century, many writers were producing sports novels for teenagers, most of which were baseball and football stories; basketball, which wasn't invented until 1891, became a topic for teenage sports fiction later. An army of writers, hacks and artists alike, tried their hands at sports stories, including Zane Grey, Gilbert Patten, Edward Stratemeyer, Ralph Henry Barbour, and William Heyliger, and the market flourished. Though Patten, with his Frank Merriwell books, may have been the most prolific of the bunch, Cantwell claims that the best writers of juvenile baseball fiction were Ralph Henry Barbour and William Heyliger, each of whom published more than 150 novels in the early part of the twentieth century (70–71).

In the early days, sports novels for teenagers were well-defined, almost formulaic stories about white male athletes in high school or college. The hero, often a prep school student, was an athletic, clean-cut, handsome, and unflinchingly honest young lad who excelled in several sports, especially football and baseball. Coaches, though minor characters, typically were portrayed as noble dispensers of wisdom and ethics. Parents and other adults also played minor roles, and the stories' conflicts usually arose from the unethical or immoral conduct of a rival athlete. Naturally the novel's hero played an essential role in resolving the conflict through his courage, honesty, and superior athletic skill. This type of young adult sports novel has disappeared, and some readers and writers like Cantwell miss them:

> A handful of good writers of boys' books still write about baseball, but their product is of a different sort. For one thing, there is only a handful where there were once a hundred or more. For another, they write relatively few books, where the giants in the field produced hundreds. At best the new breed resembles careful handicraft operators, trying—but failing—to keep alive a vanished art form that everybody once appreciated. Millions of future Little Leaguers are going to play ball without a deep

source of solace and inspiration; the romance of the diamond, in which the young
star walloped a bully, was disgraced by a false accusation, usually of theft (something
was planted in his locker), but was cleared in time to play in the big game and often
wound up saving the town from destruction by fire or flood as well. (1962, 68)

Though the kinds of sports novels that Cantwell loved are no longer being written, the field of sports fiction for teenagers has continued to expand since the
1930s, providing a wide variety of good books that appeal to a wide variety of
teenage readers.

Game Novels

The next generation of sports novels for teenagers began appearing in the 1940s.
Authors like Clair Bee, who published more than twenty sports novels for teens in
his Chip Hilton series from 1948 into the 1960s, and Matt Christopher, who published more than 120 series and single-title sports novels from 1954 to 1997, carried on in the tradition of the earlier sports novels. Though their characters
remained clean-cut all-American males, their books tended to focus more on game
action than on moral issues. Game novelists did not avoid moral lessons about
such subjects as making ethical decisions, being a good friend, dealing with fear, or
overcoming obstacles, but they did so much more subtly than the previous era's
sports books while working diligently to make certain that their stories took place
primarily on football and baseball fields or on basketball courts. Readers of these
novels could experience vicariously nearly unadulterated game action, whether it
be attempting the last-second free throw, making the game-saving tackle, or wind-
ing up for the crucial 3–2 pitch with two outs in the ninth inning. Sports novels
by Bee, Christopher, and other writers still have appeal for readers who want to re-
live play-by-play game action.[1]

In recent years, the game novels have changed in several notable ways. First,
since the advent of Title IX, publishers and their authors have—perhaps too
slowly—expanded the world of game novels to include female athletes. Second,
since the 1970s, game novels have reflected the increased offering of sports beyond
the major games of football, basketball, and baseball. It is no longer impossible to
find young adult game novels about soccer, tennis, swimming, track, and other so-
called minor sports. A third change is the direction of marketing for game novels.
While they were once targeted predominantly for teenage readers, more and more

---

1. Because of sustained interest in game novels for teenagers, many of Clair Bee's Chip Hilton sports novels have
been recently reissued, and several of Matt Christopher's game novels will be published posthumously.

game novels are being written for and marketed to preteen readers. Dean Hughes' multiple-sport *Angel Park* series and his later *Scrappers* baseball series are good examples of this trend. Hughes' *Scrappers* series also suggests a final departure from the earlier game novels, a departure that has been too long in coming. In nearly all the game novels prior to the 1970s, the important characters were white males. The *Scrapper* books and most other recent game novels feature male and female athletes from a variety of ethnic groups.

More-Than-a-Game Novels

As the field of young adult sports novels matured, authors and readers were prepared for more sophisticated stories, tales that went beyond the playing fields and locker rooms, narratives that would develop characters more fully and allow them to wrestle with challenges on and off the field. Rebecca J. Lukens' characterization of sports fiction shows both how sports novels were once regarded by critics and how the genre has improved:

> Once a kind of formula fiction, sports stories have become increasingly individualized, with well-developed characters struggling with personal issues and discovering the forces and choices they must confront. . . . Once a genre of undistinguished stories, sports fiction is much improved. (1990, 17–18)

The leader in this improvement was John R. Tunis, a World War I veteran and graduate of Boston University law school whose love of sports turned him into a newspaper sportswriter. After several years of work in various sports journalist positions, Tunis wrote his first novel, *Iron Duke*, in 1938. He continued to write quality sports novels for teenagers at the rate of almost one per year for the next twenty years. Nearly all his books earned praise from readers and critics, and Tunis' high-quality fiction did more than perhaps the work of any other young adult writer to elevate sports fiction from its pulp fiction beginnings up the rungs of literature.

Tunis was most adept at blending important issues of life or society with sports, and many of the issues he tackled were only rarely dealt with by his contemporaries. For example, in *All-American* ([1942] 1989), talented football player Ronald Perry chooses to leave the snobbish class society of his prep school to attend a local public school. While at his new school, he helps his teammates and the community at large learn a valuable lesson about racial discrimination. *All-American* contains plenty of game action, but Tunis artfully expands the scope of the novel by integrating issues he considered important for young readers.

In his introduction to the 1989 reissue of *All-American*, Bruce Brooks praises the strengths of the novel:

As in Tunis's other novels, the athletic theme of the novel represents only one part—and a fairly superficial one—of the characters' lives. And as in his earlier books, Tunis darts back and forth from sports to tougher issues. In *All-American*, we find some of the old enemies of decent living (racism, capitalistic conservatism) and some new (snobbery, reverse snobbery, academic laziness), but as usual the challenge is met by defiant self-reliance, whereby young people take responsibility for the decency of a community by taking responsibility for themselves. (vii)

One of the most important figures in the study and promotion of young adult literature, G. Robert Carlsen, also had high praise for Tunis' novels. In writing about *Go, Team, Go!* (1954), Carlsen points out the qualities of Tunis' work that separate him from his predecessors:

[*Go, Team, Go!*] not only presents the actual excitement of the physical contest, but shows the distortion of values that can occur in an American community as the result of this adulation of young high school players. It is a critical book but not a didactic one. Each incident arises out of the characters of the people involved and the nature of the social values under which they live. It leaves the reader to make his own decisions of right and wrong for himself. More and more stories like *Go, Team, Go!* explore the fundamental problems of human relationships and goals. These are, therefore, quite different from the series books centering on sports that many of us read in junior high school, books in which the main concern was the contest itself and the struggle to win the game. (1967, 50–51)

The sports novels of John R. Tunis have had a lasting impact on young adult literature.[2] His work cleared the way for authors with an interest in sports to incorporate important adolescent themes with one of the most pervasive social influences of the last few decades of the twentieth century: sports.

Another sportswriter turned young adult sports fiction author, Thomas J. Dygard, followed the path established by Tunis. Play-by-play action is an important feature in all of his novels, but, like Tunis', his novels also include important issues for the protagonists to confront and grow from. In *Outside Shooter* (1979), a high school basketball player must learn to cope with personality problems that affect him and his teammates. *Infield Hit* (1995) is the story of Hal Stevens, the son of a well-known major league baseball player. In addition to dealing with the pressures of being the son of a famous athlete, Hal must also cope with his parents' divorce and fitting into a new school. Dygard published more than fifteen sports novels for

---

2. Tunis' final novel, *Grand National*, appeared in 1973, two years before his death, but many of his best novels have been reissued and are currently available to readers interested in stories that deal with sports and the people who play them.

teenagers from 1977 until his death in 1996, and all of them combine character issues and sports in the manner established by Tunis.

Sportlerroman

Since the 1980s, a handful of young adult authors has continued in the development of sports fiction by taking sports novels a step further from those of Tunis and Dygard. These young adult novels are a kind of sports novel I call a *sportlerroman*—a form of the traditional bildungsroman apprenticeship novel—in which the protagonist is an athlete struggling to maturity. Like the kunstlerroman, in which the protagonist is an artist, the sportlerroman is a coming-of-age story. Sports figure prominently in the main character's story, but the central conflicts of the sportlerroman lie beyond athletics. As Brooks points out, the sportlerroman differs from the more-than-a-game novels in that play-by-play game action fades to the background of the story. "Back then," he writes, "a book wouldn't qualify [as a sports book] if it contained more than a smidgen of 'real life' blurring the focus on pure sports; now, a book is wedged into the classification if it has an athlete as a character or a little sports action to cut the 'real life' themes" (1986, 20).

The sportlerroman combines modern America's preoccupation with sports and its fascination with youth. This combination allows young adult authors to create conflicts that integrate the agonies of adolescence with the potential agonies of athletic competition. In some sportlerroman, conflict begins in a sporting event and eventually works its way into other aspects of a character's life. In others, sports provides an outlet—and often a mentor—to help a protagonist deal with off-the-field troubles. Still other sportlerroman provide the central character with problems in and out of sport that are in some way related. In any case, by including sports in the narrative, authors are able to expand a character's conflict and create more opportunities to confront that conflict in different and interesting ways.

The sportlerroman recognizes the pervasiveness of sports among teenagers and plays to their view of sports as a part of life, a natural part of adolescence, and hence a part of growing up. Sports also offers authors an effective hook into modern trends and themes. One of the newer authors of sportlerroman, Chris Lynch, likes what sports add to his novels:

> The truth is, you can find almost any parable you want in sports. . . . So when a writer is in need of a handy metaphor, a microcosm of society, a model of right and wrong ways to do things, it's simply hard not to find it in the sports world. And the fact that the contemporary culture insists on making athletes our children's most recognizable icons of success . . . more through advertisements and peripheral endorsements than through game broadcasts, the opportunity for us to exploit the exploitation is tremendous. In short, we, through sports, have got their attention. (1996, 25)

And once authors like Lynch have their readers' attention, they can put their characters smack in the middle of real-life conflicts. For some characters, sports provides the means to maturity. For others, it provides an outlet essential for survival when adolescent life is too intense, too dangerous. Sports furnishes mentors, friends, physical release and stress reduction, time for introspection, opportunities for growth and goal setting, a chance to compare oneself to another. Whether sports contributes the conflict or the solution, it's integral to modern adolescence and logically a natural fixture in the contemporary coming-of-age novel.

The field has grown substantially in the last twenty years, with Chris Crutcher emerging as perhaps the most successful practitioner of the sportlerroman. Crutcher denies he is a writer of "sports fiction" and explains why sports plays a central role in his novels:

> I love that human beings of any sex, color, sexual preference, size, or religious belief can find a challenge in athletics. I love that the full range of human emotion can be touched within the structure of agreed-upon rules . . .
>
> Athletics provides a rich background for my fiction because all of the elements of good storytelling exist in a given contest. An exciting athletic encounter snatches me straightaway from the clutches of writer's block, breathes life into dying characters, tests the limits of their will, and mine. But I will be sad if I'm remembered only as a writer of sports fiction, because I hope that contests in the real world are as evident as those in the arena in my stories. (1993, 176)

Real-world contests are indeed the focus of Crutcher's young adult novels. He uses sports as a staging area, a vehicle, or a catalyst for presenting young men or women with conflicts that ultimately lead them closer to maturity. Because of that, his books aren't "sports novels" as much as they are sportlerroman, which, like the bildungsroman, deal "with the development of a young person, usually from adolescence to maturity" (Harmon and Holman 1996, 59).

There are many fine sportlerroman to choose from. In addition to all of Chris Crutcher's young adult novels, some great ones include Duder's *In Lane Three, Alex Archer*, Will Weaver's *Striking Out* (1993), Brooks' *The Moves Make the Man*, Thomas Cochran's *Roughnecks* (1997), Randy Powell's *Dean Duffy* (1995), Myers' *Slam!*, Klass' *Danger Zone*, Berlie Doherty's *The Snake-Stone* (1996), Deuker's *Heart of a Champion* (1993), Jim Naughton's *My Brother Stealing Second* (1989), Lynch's *Shadow Boxer* (1993), and Wallace's *Wrestling Sturbridge*.

Sports Novels for Young Women

For most of the history of young adults sports fiction, female characters have been ignored, relegated to the sidelines, or treated as oddities in a male world. In the early years of sports fiction, publishers and authors saw sports books as boys' books.

A century ago, the athletic opportunities for girls were almost nonexistent; women might play tennis, or maybe golf, but few women were considered—or considered themselves—athletes. As athletic opportunities for women increased, sports novels lagged far behind. Girls began to appear in some sports novels, but as cheerleaders or statisticians or girlfriends of the heroes, not as athletes. Finally, sports novels began to present girls as athletes, but they were usually portrayed as women in a man's world. Klass' *A Different Season* (1988), Dygard's *Forward Pass*, and Jerry Spinelli's *There's a Girl in My Hammerlock* (1991) are good examples. These stories and others like them don't necessarily denigrate women as athletes, but they do limit the role female athletes may play.

Given that Title IX has finally changed the nature of school sports and that female athletes are finally receiving credibility, it's important that sports fiction for women and about women present female athletes in legitimate roles. Joli Sandoz, editor of *A Whole Other Ball Game* (1997), an anthology of fiction, essays, and poetry written by women about women's sporting experiences, stresses just how important good sports fiction for women can be:

> As long as an athlete is without her own authentic story, she remains vulnerable to scenarios written by others. So do those who oppose or belittle her, though in a different way. This individual and collective vulnerability is one consequence of ignoring women's actual experiences in sport, of choosing not to incorporate them into our definitions of "female." Lack of engagement with sportswomen's truths, accessible in part through their own expressive writings, simply helps to perpetuate the inequitable, and universally damaging, sports status quo.
>
> When women tell their stories, though, and are heard, by themselves and others, the story line changes. The new generations of female athletes ushered in by Title IX have begun challenging sexist athletics tradition. (1999, B8)

Fortunately, sports novels have begun to catch up with the times. R. R. Knudson broke new ground in the 1970s with her young adult game novels, *Zanballer* (1972), *Zanbanger*, (1977), *Zanboomer* (1978), and *Fox Running* (1975), which presented young women as serious athletes. Linnea A. Due took the young adult female sports novel a step closer to the sportlerroman with *High and Outside* (1980), the story of a brilliant student and star softball player who is battling a severe drinking problem. Rosemary Wells' *When No One Was Looking* (1980), the story of a star tennis player who must deal with her overbearing parents and coach—and the mysterious death of a rival player—is also a fine more-than-a-game novel.

While sports novels featuring male protagonists still dominate the field, a handful of good sportlerroman with female protagonists have been published, and I hope more are on their way. Here are some worth reading and recommending: Duder's story of a New Zealand swimmer working to qualify for the Olympics, *In Lane Three, Alex Acher*, and its sequel, *Alex in Rome* (1991); Michael Cadnum's *Heat* (1998), the story of a terrific young platform diver who must simultaneously deal with a potentially career-ending injury and the unraveling of her father's personal and professional life; Virginia Euwer Wolff's story of two girls softball teams and the challenges they face after World War II, *Bat 6* (1998); and *Finding My Voice* (1992), Marie G. Lee's story of a Korean American high school gymnast who must deal with pressure from her parents and prejudice from some of her classmates.

Sports Novels and Reluctant Readers

Male protagonists dominate young adult sports novels because publishers, teachers, parents, and perhaps even writers believe that most reluctant readers are male. Many of these same people also believe that sports stories are more likely to appeal to reluctant male readers than other kinds of books. Tradition, experience, and research tend to support this belief. In "Cool Books for Tough Guys," Lawrence Baines says that the most popular young adult novels among his reluctant readers include the sports novels *Running Loose*, *Vision Quest*, and *The Contender* (1994, 43–44); Sam D. Gill's article "Young Adult Literature for Young Adult Males" also recommends *The Contender* along with *Ironman*, *Striking Out*, and *Hoops* as books that will appeal to students who avoid reading (1999, 61). Her experience working with reluctant readers in an alternative school convinced Lindy Purdy Carter of the power of sports novels in overcoming the reluctance to read:

> I have found that sports literature provides an effective means for combating negative attitudes toward reading. Furthermore, the study of sports writing and fiction provides an excellent opportunity for a teacher to engage informally in bibliotherapy, as students are encouraged to re-evaluate their attitudes and ambitions in light of their reading experiences. (1998, 309)

Authors of young adults sports novels share similar beliefs about the potential effects of their books on teenager readers. In discussing his young adult sports books, Robert Lipsyte suggests that boys tend to be reluctant readers for the following reasons:

> I think that boys don't read as much as we'd like them to because (1) current books tend not to deal with the real problems and fears of boys, and (2) there is a tendency to treat boys as a group . . . which is where males are at their absolute worst . . . instead of as individuals who have to be led into reading secretly and one at a time. (1997, 259)

Because Lipsyte's novels and many other sports novels deal with real problems of boys—and girls—and because of the unique appeal of stories about sports, young adult sports novels can indeed be useful in leading reluctant students into books "secretly and one at a time."

Other authors of sports fiction understand the appeal of stories of athletics and the power of those stories to reach readers. Walter Dean Myers has published a number of acclaimed young adult sports novels. Naturally he hopes his novels reach his audience in meaningful ways, but he also hopes that his books will reveal some of the complexity of sports:

> Sports books can be more than just a game or series of games, just as sport is most often more than just a ball bouncing off a backboard or a set of statistics. I want to bring an understanding to sports that I've developed in the streets of Harlem and on basketball courts across the country. . . . I have an absolute need to bring meaning to the acts which attract so many young boys and, in increasing numbers, young girls. (1996, 21)

It is Myers' attention to sporting detail that often engages reluctant readers in his novels. But in addition to the appeal of the game, good sports fiction can effectively accomplish what was attempted by juvenile sports novels a century ago: teaching important lessons about life. Carter reports that after reading aloud a passage from Myers' *Slam!*, her students joined in a lively discussion that "confirmed my belief that sports literature provides invaluable life lessons for adolescents who find it difficult to function academically or socially in traditional high school settings" (1998, 309). Of course, young adult sports novels are not intended solely for boys or for reluctant readers; the field is full of talented writers producing a wide range of sports stories that will please good students and bad, males and females, tennis players and football players.

Conclusion

Although athletics and great young adult literature once held each other at arm's length, they now embrace each other in an unbreakable full Nelson. In the past one hundred years or so, young adult sports novels have earned the respect of publishers, critics, teachers, and most important, readers. They've outgrown their preachy pulp novel beginnings by building over time upon the best qualities of the best sports books of the past, and now sports novels figure prominently in nearly any list of great young adult novels. With American society's passion for sports, it is certain that sports will continue to play central or background roles in many novels for young adults, not just because teenagers like sports but because sports can reveal the best and worst of society and human nature, and it is those revelations that make any story worth reading and writing.

Works Cited

Baines, Lawrence. 1994. "Cool Books for Tough Guys: 50 Books Out of the Mainstream of Adolescent Literature That Will Appeal to Males Who Do Not Enjoy Reading." *The ALAN Review* 22.1 (Fall): 43–46.

Brooks, Bruce. 1986. "Playing Fields of Fiction." *New York Times Book Review* 6 April: 20.

———. 1989. Introduction to *All-American* by John R. Tunis. San Diego: Harcourt Brace Jovanovich.

Cantwell, Robert. 1962. "A Sneering Laugh with the Bases Loaded." *Sports Illustrated* 23 April: 67–76.

Carlsen, G. Robert. 1967. *Books and the Teenage Reader*. New York: Bantam.

Carter, Linda Purdy. 1998. "Addressing the Needs of Reluctant Readers Through Sports Literature." *The Clearing House* 71.5 (May/June): 309–11.

Crutcher, Chris. 1993. "Chris Crutcher on Writing Sports Fiction." In *Literature for Today's Young Adults*, 4th ed., ed. Alleen Pace Nilsen and Ken Donelson, 176. New York: HarperCollins.

Donelson, Ken. 1997. "Honoring the Best YA Books of the Year: 1964–1995." *English Journal* 86.3 (March): 41–47.

Gill, Sam D. 1999. "Young Adult Literature for Young Adult Males." *The ALAN Review* 26.2 (Winter): 61–63.

Harmon, William, and C. Hugh Holman. 1996. *A Handbook to Literature*. 7th ed. Upper Saddle River, NJ: Prentice Hall.

Lipsyte, Robert. 1997. "Robert Lipsyte on Books for Boys." In *Literature for Today's Young Adults*, 5th ed, ed. Ken Donelson and Alleen Pace Nilsen, 259. New York: Longman.

Lukens, Rebecca J. 1990. *A Critical Handbook of Children's Literature*. 4th ed. Glenview, IL: Scott Foresman/Little, Brown.

Lynch, Chris. 1996. "The Reluctant Sportswriter." *SIGNAL Journal* 21.1 (Fall): 23–26.

Masin, Herman L. 1998. "Novel-ties." *Coach and Athletic Director* 68.3 (October): 10.

Messenger, Christian K. 1981. *Sport and the Spirit of Play in American Fiction: Hawthorne to Faulkner*. New York: Columbia University Press.

Myers, Walter Dean. 1996. "Of Games and Men." *SIGNAL Journal* 21.1 (Fall): 19–22.

Raugust, Karen. 1997. "Sports Leagues Target Young Fans with Books." *Publishers Weekly* 244.8 (24 February): 34–35.

Sandoz, Joli. 1999. "Women as Athletes: Creating a Literature of Vindication." *The Chronicle of Higher Education* 45.37 (21 May): B7–B8.

"Top One Hundred Countdown: Best of the Best Books for Young Adults." 1994. *Booklist* 91.4 (14 October): 412–16.

Young Adult Sports Novels Mentioned in This Chapter

Barbour, Ralph Henry. *The Crimson Sweater*

Bennett, James. *The Squared Circle*

Blessing, Richard. *A Passing Season*

Brooks, Bruce. *The Moves Make the Man*

Cadnum, Michael. *Heat*

Cochran, Thomas. *Roughnecks*

Crutcher, Chris. *Athletic Shorts*

    Ironman

    Running Loose

    Staying Fat for Sarah Byrnes

    Stotan!

Davis, Terry. *Vision Quest*

Deuker, Carl. *Heart of a Champion*

    On the Devil's Court

Doherty, Berlie. *The Snake-Stone*

Duder, Tessa. *Alex in Rome*

    In Lane Three, Alex Archer

Due, Linnea A. *High and Outside*

Dygard, Thomas. *Forward Pass*

    Halfback Tough

    Infield Hit

    Outside Shooter

Gallo, Donald R., ed. *Ultimate Sports*

Gutman, Dan. *Honus and Me*

Hyde, Dayton O. *The Major, the Poacher, and the Wonderful One-Trout River*

Kinsella, W. P. *Shoeless Joe*

Klass, David. *Danger Zone*

    A Different Season

    Wrestling with Honor

Knudson, R. R. *Fox Running*

    Zanballer

    Zanbanger

    Zanboomer

Korman, Gordon. *The Toilet Paper Tigers*

Lee, Marie G. *Finding My Voice*

Lipsyte, Robert. *The Contender*

Lynch, Chris. *Iceman*

    Shadow Boxer

Murphy, Claire. *To the Summit*

Myers, Walter Dean. *Hoops*

    Slam!

Naughton, Jim. *My Brother Stealing Second*

Powell, Randy. *Dean Duffy*

Sandoz, Joli. *A Whole Other Ball Game*

Spinelli, Jerry. *There's a Girl in My Hammerlock*

Tunis, John R. *All-American*

    Go, Team, Go!

    Iron Duke

    Yea! Wildcats!

Wallace, Rich. *Wrestling Sturbridge*

Weaver, Will. *Striking Out*

Wells, Rosemary. *When No One Was Looking*

Wheeler, Edward. *High Hat Harry, the Baseball Detective; or The Sunken Treasure*

Wolff, Virginia Euwer. *Bat 6*

12

Reading Their Television World

ALAN B. TEASLEY AND ANN WILDER

As any teacher or parent can attest, students are influenced by a constant barrage of media messages. They watch television, listen to the radio, go to movies, watch videos, read magazines and newspapers, play video games, and surf the Internet. Some days it must seem that the only respite from this information overload is the time they spend in school!

We take the position that it is important for students to be aware of their own participation in the various mass media, to understand how these media operate to shape the messages that they convey, to analyze both the content and the context of the messages, to craft a personal and creative response to media messages, and to express themselves powerfully within the various media of interest to them. In short, we advocate for media literacy—being able to read and compose various messages in our media-saturated world. We contend that it is not enough for our students to be able to read, understand, and respond to a wide variety of literature. We agree with the authors of *Standards for the English Language Arts* (National Council of Teachers of English and International Reading Association 1996):

> Being literate in contemporary society means being active, critical, and creative users not only of print and spoken language but also of the visual language of film and television, commercial and political advertising, photography, and more. Teaching students how to interpret and create visual texts such as illustrations, charts, graphs, electronic displays, photographs, film, and video is another essential component of the English language arts curriculum. (5–6)

In advocating for studying a "broad range of texts," the authors of these standards include among their list of such texts:

mass media and other visual texts, including films, selected television programs, magazines, and newspapers; socially significant oral and written texts, such as speeches, radio and television broadcasts, political documents, editorials, and advertisements . . . (15)

In this chapter we discuss some of the issues surrounding the study of television, propose methods of incorporating television into the secondary language arts classroom, and offer suggestions as to how teachers might connect television to the study of YA novels. We know that some educators see television as an enemy of literacy. Certainly if students are using all of their leisure time watching television and videos *instead* of reading, they are not likely to become lifelong readers. Our experience, however, has been that students will in fact do both—and sometimes even choose reading over television—if they are introduced to compelling books and given strategies for thinking critically about both literature and television. At the end of the chapter, we will present a list of YA novels set in the world of television production, television tie-ins, and "novelizations," as well as some books related by theme or situation to several of the most popular current shows.

In our book *Reel Conversations: Reading Films with Young Adults* (1997), we address specific methods for teaching students about film, for integrating film study with literature and composition, and for connecting specific films and young adult novels through thematic units. We provide a number of strategies for the close reading of films by analyzing their literary, dramatic, and cinematic (visual and auditory) aspects. Although this type of analysis would be appropriate for studying individual television shows, in this chapter we address how "teaching television" is different from teaching both literature and film. Also, we are confident that any literature teacher reading this book would be able to devise strategies for teaching the content of individual programs.

One problem with television is that the content changes constantly. At the time we're writing this, *Dawson's Creek* is a popular series with teenagers, but it may have been canceled by the time the book is published. Increasingly, television shows are released on video, such as the episodes of *My So-Called Life* from 1994–95, and there's always the possibility of the shows reappearing in syndication. However, the fact remains that television is often ephemeral, and there is no guarantee that a particular series or show will be available when a teacher wants to include it in the curriculum. A second characteristic of television that renders its study problematic is that the content of one program is seldom the whole story.

Reading Television

Teaching students to "read" any mass medium—and in particular television—is both similar to and different from teaching literature. We adopt a "viewer-response" stance that, like the reader-response approach to literature, acknowledges that individuals will have different interpretations of and responses to a visual text based on their prior knowledge and experience, their purposes in viewing, and their ability to think critically about such texts. As with literature, reading/ viewing for a book or television show's plot and characters usually comes easily, but when teachers prompt students to notice images, symbols, and patterns and then speculate on their meaning, students develop more sophisticated readings— reading for theme, attitude, rhetorical arguments, political stance, and so forth. With a mass medium like television, we have found that additional levels of reading are not only possible but necessary.

For the study of television and other mass media, we propose that teachers consider five distinct types, or levels, of reading:

1. *Reading for Basic Comprehension:* This type of reading involves understanding the initial message—the plot, setting, and character development in a fictional show, such as a drama, sitcom, soap opera, or miniseries, or the basic facts and opinions of a nonfiction show, such as a news report, investigative journalism, sports coverage, and so on.

2. *Reading for Interpretation:* At this level of reading, the reader goes beyond the surface, analyzing meanings and creating interpretations. We could think of these as secondary messages created through the collaboration of the viewer and the "authors" of the media text—the writers, directors, editors, actors, correspondents, and others. Readers can create these interpretations alone or in dialogue with other readers or by comparing and contrasting the current text with other texts. For example, after showing an episode of the situation comedy *Mad About You* from the 1990s, a teacher could show an episode of *The Honeymooners* or *I Love Lucy* from the 1950s and ask students to compare the relationships and social mores of the two series. The comparison will likely reveal aspects of the relationships in *Mad About You* that were invisible to the students until they noticed how different things were in the television marriages of the 1950s.

3. *Reading for Ownership:* Readers demonstrate that they have achieved this level of reading when they express a sophisticated response to a text. In literature study, we see this kind of ownership when students fashion a response such as readers theater adaptations, book reviews, film treatments, advertisements, book jackets, missing chapters, sequels, prequels, "discovered journals" of a main character, and so forth. Similarly, with individual

television shows or series, teachers could have students write critical reviews or missing scenes, invent a lost episode, write a parody, write the
first episode of the next season, "novelize" a scene or episode (rendering a
teleplay into a short story, for example), or invent a spin-off of the series,
telling which characters will form the nucleus of the new show, giving the
basic situation, and writing the first episode.

4. *Reading to Analyze the Context:* This type of analysis requires the student
   to "step back" from the content of the show itself to examine the show's
   packaging, to describe how it comes to us. When does the show air—daytime, prime time, late night? On what network—broadcast, cable, pay-
   per-view? Who are its target audiences, and how do we know that? What
   is the rating of the show? What products are advertised during the show?
   What products are "placed" prominently in the show? Who is making
   money from the viewers' attention?

   There really is little equivalent to this level of reading in the world of
   literature. We suppose you could talk about what gets published and what
   doesn't, whether a book's first appearance is in hardcover or paperback,
   whether it is "positioned" for the YA market or a general adult market, or
   how well the cover design represents the book, but for the most part, these
   questions don't reveal much of interest about the literature. However,
   with regard to television, these questions are essential to understanding
   the total effect of the program on the viewer.

5. *Reading for Evaluation and Reflection:* This type of reading involves not
   only the critical evaluation of an individual work but also the awareness
   of the general role of literature or media in one's life. In the study of television, this might take the form of such questions as these: Has television
   desensitized me to violence? What stereotypical messages about men and
   women are reinforced in the television I watch? To what extent do I mod-
   ify my behavior and purchases based on my TV viewing?

Because the strategies for teaching the first three types of reading television are
not that different from teaching literature, we have focused in this chapter on
strategies to develop the level four and five reading skills, that is, developing students' ability to read both the context and content of television and to reflect on
their viewing.

Classroom Strategies for Teaching Television

In working with students in a study of television, we used Ann's mass communications class. This class is an elective offered through the English department at

her high school and is composed primarily of juniors and seniors, although a few sophomores and freshmen are enrolled. The class described here had studied the history of television, viewed and discussed different types of shows, and analyzed different television networks, but the techniques described could be used in any English or language arts class without the background material or previous study.

The sequence of lessons on television begins with heightening the students' awareness of themselves as television viewers. Ann typically begins by asking students to analyze their viewing habits using a media log (see Figure 12–1), which

Mass Communications   **Name:** _____

Media Log/Reflection   **Entry #** _____

In the middle column in the chart below, record any contact you have with mass media for the days of the week given. Include newspapers, radio, television, records, CDs, tapes, magazines, cartoons, news, movies, or videotapes. In the right-hand column, write your reactions to **at least three** of the entries.

Week of _____

Day	Brief Description of Media	Reflections/Reactions to Media
Monday _____		
Tuesday _____		
Wednesday _____		
Thursday _____		

Figure 12–1. Media Log/Reflection Form

asks students to keep a record of their contacts with various forms of mass media during a four-day period and to write reflections on three of their entries. Class discussion includes informal conversations about the shows class members have watched during the week.

Another method of having students gauge their viewing habits is to have them keep a record of the number of hours they watch television in a given week. Ann uses a chart (Figure 12–2) that helps students record the number of hours they spend each day on the following activities: watching television; attending school, doing homework, or reading; socializing with friends; and other activities such as working or participating in sports. After a week of keeping the chart, students calculate the percentage of their waking hours spent watching television.

Weekly Television Chart

Name: _____

Entry # _____

This assignment will help you become more aware of television's impact on your life. Please keep track of how you spend your waking hours for the next week. I recommend that you fill in the graphs at the end of each day. Each square should indicate the total number of hours spent on an activity during a given day.

	Mon.	Tues.	Wed.	Thurs.	Fri.	Sat.	Sun.	TOTAL
TV Viewing								
Study/School/ Reading								
Social Time								
Sports/Work/ Other								

At the end of the week, calculate the percentage of time you spent on television by completing the following equation:

$$\frac{\text{Your total \# of television hours for the week}}{\text{total waking hours for the week}} \times 100 = \underline{\quad} \%$$

Television takes up _____ % of my waking life

Figure 12–2. Weekly Television Chart

The results are wide-ranging: some of these teenagers watch four or five hours of television a day; some watch almost no television at all. The final step in drawing attention to the students' own viewing habits is a written reflection in which they describe themselves as television viewers and make conclusions about the types of shows they prefer and why they prefer these shows.

Once students have evaluated and reflected on their viewing habits, the next step extends their inquiry as they investigate the viewing habits of a large number of teenage viewers. Our primary goal is for the students to determine which shows are the most popular among their peers. We also want the students to discuss why these shows are popular and what the target audience for each show is; moreover, we want students to analyze these shows to discover ways in which the networks and advertisers are marketing various shows and products to teenagers.

Since we want to have students examine the TV shows most often watched by teenagers, our first task is to develop a preliminary list of shows that teenagers like. We begin by holding a conversation with the class about the TV shows they and their friends watch. As they brainstorm, we write the list on overhead transparencies. The first time we did this, twenty-one students produced a list of more than sixty shows in less than ten minutes. To narrow the list, we ask each student to vote for ten shows that are personal favorites. From their votes, we come up with a shorter list. For example, we narrowed this first list of sixty to thirty shows that had received at least five votes. We were surprised by the variety of the shows on the list. We were not surprised to find *Dawson's Creek* or *Moesha* or *SportsCenter* there; we were surprised to find *20/20* and something called *The Tom Green Show*, which we had never even heard of.

The next activity is to determine the popularity of the thirty shows with a larger group of teenagers, so we give the class an assignment: each student must survey twenty of his or her friends to determine which of the thirty shows they watch most frequently. The ballots ask respondents to give their race, gender, and age because these could be important variables affecting the popularity of certain shows. (Figure 12–3 shows the ballot we used with this first class; the ballot will of course be different for each class.) The shows on the ballot are listed alphabetically, and respondents are asked to indicate for each show whether they watch the show "never," "occasionally," "frequently," or "almost every week/day." We give each student twenty ballots and send the students out to conduct the surveys. To prevent duplication, the student asks each respondent if he or she has filled out a ballot previously. If so, the student moves on to another respondent.

With this first class, we received a total of 285 responses: 42 percent male, 58 percent female, 62 percent African American, 38 percent white, and 10 percent Hispanic and "other," which approximates the racial demographics of our school. Class members tallied the scores for each show, noting the number of votes in each

Mass Communications Television Survey

Age: _____   Race/Ethnicity: _____   Gender: _____

How often do you watch the following shows?
1 = Never; 2 = Occasionally; 3 = Frequently; 4 = Almost Every Week/Day

Name of Show	1	2	3	4
20/20				
America's Most Wanted				
Baywatch				
Beverly Hills 90210				
Buffy, the Vampire Slayer				
Celebrity Death Match				
Comic View (BET)				
Dawson's Creek				
Family Guy				
Guiding Light				
Guinness Prime Time				
Jamie Foxx Show				
Jerry Springer Show				
Martin				
Moesha				
Monday Night Raw				
Oprah Winfrey Show				
Rap City				
Real TV				
Sabrina, the Teenage Witch				
Sanford and Son				
Simpsons				
Smart Guy				
South Park				
Spider-Man				
SportsCenter				
Tom Green Show				
Wayans Brothers				
X-Files				
Young and the Restless				

List other shows here:	1	2	3	4

Figure 12–3. Television Survey

category. Using a spreadsheet program, we weighted the scores—"never" got a 1, "every week/day" got a 4, and so forth—and ranked the shows from highest to lowest total score. We also determined a "loyalty" rating for each show by ranking the shows only by the number of votes they received in the every week/day column to see if there were any differences in the rankings. Figure 12–4 shows the rankings of our first class. Incidentally, our conclusions about this particular group of teenagers are that they have a fondness for sitcoms about teenagers or young people like themselves, for sensational talk shows, and for shows that spotlight professional wrestling, but since we wanted the students to come up with their own conclusions about the results, we asked them to draw conclusions for themselves.

After the students have determined their own TV preferences and those of a large group of their peers, we ask them to respond to three questions, first individually in writing, and then in class discussion: What do you notice about the rankings? What surprises you about the rankings? What doesn't surprise you about the rankings? We also give them a listing of a recent week's top thirty shows according to the Nielsen ratings, as reported by *Entertainment Weekly*, so that they can compare the rankings of their peer group to a nationwide sample from all age groups. Sample responses to the three questions among our first group included the following individual comments.

What do you notice about the rankings?
- "Shows that are watched by more females than males are more towards the bottom of the list."
- "Most comedy shows are ranked highly."
- "Comedy and violent shows are tops."
- "The top 'every week/day' shows were mostly comedy and ethnic."

What surprises you about the rankings?
- "I was surprised to see that no matter how many people are watching a certain show like *Guiding Light*, those shows have loyal viewers that watch every day."
- "How many people watch cartoons."
- "I was surprised that informative shows about what goes on in America were so low."
- "It also surprises me that the Wayans Brothers were ranked as the 'every week/day' for the highest. It beat out some better shows."

What doesn't surprise you about the rankings?
- "Most soap operas are toward the bottom of the list."
- "That *Jerry Springer* was going to be in the top five because a lot of people like to see the fighting and arguing."

TV Ratings Survey
April 1999

[Highest Average Score to Lowest]

TV Show	[1]	[2]	[3]	[4]	Total Points	Total Votes	Average
1 Comic View (BET)	69	53	76	96	787	294	2.677
2 Wayans Brothers	74	50	46	106	736	276	2.667
3 Jerry Springer Show	51	93	51	85	730	280	2.607
4 Jamie Foxx Show	82	64	51	91	727	288	2.524
5 Martin	86	53	57	86	707	282	2.507
6 Rap City	78	65	45	81	667	269	2.480
7 South Park	97	73	44	65	635	279	2.276
8 Smart Guy	91	88	59	54	660	292	2.260
9 Moesha	105	57	51	60	612	273	2.242
10 Celebrity Death Match	104	81	64	44	634	293	2.164
11 Simpsons	107	74	50	50	605	281	2.153
12 Monday Night Raw	138	51	24	59	548	272	2.015
13 Guinness Prime Time	139	51	55	37	554	282	1.965
14 Dawson's Creek	149	62	44	40	565	295	1.915
15 SportsCenter	161	47	30	45	525	283	1.855
16 Real TV	127	81	45	19	500	272	1.838
17 Sanford and Son	152	69	32	29	502	282	1.780
18 Buffy, the Vampire Slayer	140	73	35	21	475	269	1.766
19 Tom Green Show	174	38	27	39	487	278	1.752
20 Baywatch	147	91	29	21	500	288	1.736
21 Sabrina, the Teenage Witch	145	78	26	21	463	270	1.715
22 X-Files	165	51	29	28	466	273	1.707
23 Oprah Winfrey Show	158	79	21	21	463	279	1.659
24 Young and the Restless	199	25	19	38	458	281	1.630
25 20/20	154	99	22	11	462	286	1.615
26 Family Guy	191	42	23	29	460	285	1.614
27 America's Most Wanted	143	87	24	8	421	262	1.607
28 Spider-Man	188	43	19	27	439	277	1.585
29 Beverly Hills 90210	189	60	18	16	427	283	1.509
30 Guiding Light	218	29	8	34	436	289	1.509

Key: [1] = Never; [2] = Occasionally; [3] = Frequently; [4] = Every Week or Day

Figure 12–4. TV Ratings Survey, April 1999

- "It doesn't surprise me that the entertaining or comedy shows beat out the ones that are informational."

When these students met in groups to discuss their opinions and draw conclusions based on their study of the rankings, they made comments such as these:

- "Most teens seem not to like NBC and CBS because the content of the shows is not interesting and is on a more adult level."
- "Teen shows are not that big on the Nielsen ratings."
- "We knew that a lot of people would vote for *Jerry Springer* because a lot of people like violence, especially teenagers."

Once we have had students reflect on their own viewing habits and the viewing preferences of their peers, and with the list of most popular shows in hand, we shift the focus to studying individual TV shows.

The first assignment asks students to watch a thirty-minute episode of a sitcom and time everything during that thirty minutes: titles, narrative, commercials, credits, news breaks, and previews of later shows. They list each part including each commercial and estimate the time it takes. They then add up how much of the thirty minutes is taken up with the actual show and how much of the time is filled with advertisements. They typically discover that during a thirty-minute time period, about twenty-two minutes is actually devoted to the show, and the other eight minutes is filled with fifteen-second or thirty-second commercials. Almost one-third of the time allocated for a show such as this is spent exposing viewers to ads for everything from snack foods and cosmetics to floor wax and prefabricated homes. Some of the students are quite indignant about this ratio of commercials to show, but others seem to take it in stride and just use the mute button on their remotes.

As far as the content of the show is concerned, we ask them to summarize the plot of the episode, describe the main conflict driving the plot, list the regular main and supporting characters (this presumes some prior knowledge of the show), note whether the show is filmed or on videotape, and whether it is taped before a live audience. When they bring their data back to class, our discussion focuses first on the characteristics of the sitcom formula: static characters, simple conflicts always resolved at the last minute, and reliance on one or two comic leads with several one-dimensional supporting characters. We also ask them to speculate on the connection between the products advertised and the target audience of the particular show. They usually see this connection immediately, noting that shows aimed at teenagers are often sponsored by soft drinks, snack foods, athletic shoes, and other such products.

A final activity in the television unit is to have the students conduct an in-depth analysis of one of the thirty most popular shows identified in the survey assignment. We give students charts to use in viewing and analyzing the shows (see Figure 12–5) and assign each student two shows to watch. Students note a show's

TV Show Analysis

Name of show:	Rating:	Regular day/time of show:
Content. Describe the plot of this episode in one or two sentences:		
Advertising/Product Placement		
List below the products advertised during the show (include here any music being "plugged"):	List below the named products "placed" within the show (for example, soft drinks, snack foods):	List below any prominent use of products such as beepers, cell phone, wine, etc.
Describe any use of drugs, tobacco, or alcohol in this episode:		
Describe any instances of violence or death in this episode:		

Based on your viewing of this show, what do you find kids are being exposed to on television?

Do you think this exposure from television is a problem? Explain.

Figure 12–5. TV Show Analysis

rating and time slot and summarize the content of the show. They also pay particular attention to commercials and to products placed in the show, that is, products used by characters in the show. One reason we want to bring these product placements to students' attention is that this form of advertisement is insidious. In explicit commercials, the advertiser is acknowledging, "We are selling you this now," and students' response can be to watch, get something to eat, press the mute button, or fast forward the tape. When the product is promoted during the story, the students have no choice about the matter. On the analysis chart, we also ask them to note any use of alcohol or drugs or instances of violence in the show. Two final questions ask the students to state, based on their viewing of the show, what kids are being exposed to on television and whether they feel that this exposure is a problem.

Our original group of students found that many of their favorite shows do contain violence and some have characters using drugs, tobacco, and alcohol, particularly beer. In addition to all of the products they noted in the commercials, the students also discovered a number of brand-name products placed within shows they watch. The most conspicuous example was Coke, which they found being used by characters on *Buffy, the Vampire Slayer*, *The Wayans Brothers*, and *Beverly Hills 90210*. *Beverly Hills 90210* also featured M&Ms and Reese's products. In *Dawson's Creek* and *Just Shoot Me*, characters used Apple iMac computers. Students also noted that the characters in these shows used beepers, pagers, cell phones, compact discs, and computers. An interesting question for the students to discuss then: Are these shows *promoting* the use of these products among teenagers or merely *reflecting* reality?

Students came up with interesting answers to the two summary questions on the viewing guide.

Based on your viewing of this show, what do you find kids are being exposed to on television?

- "violence, cussing, yelling"
- "action heroes"
- "violence, vulgar language, and vulgar content that is not meant for children"
- "Overall, kids are exposed to a lot on television."
- "Kids are exposed to real life situations that are faced in today's society. Society is much more dangerous and it lets you know you have someone to go to if you are in a difficult situation. Although Kelly (in *Beverly Hills 90210*) did purchase a gun to protect herself, I believe the future episodes will show her consequences for not being careful with it."
- "Drugs, violence, comedy . . . everything we as Americans value in entertainment." (*The Simpsons*)
- "jokes about drugs, crime, sex, and disabilities" (*Comic View*)

- "... their lives ... what most kids go through" (*Dawson's Creek*)
- "extreme cartoon violence" (*Celebrity Death Match*)

In general, students do not think that exposure to these things is a problem, as their answers to the second question reveal.

Do you think this exposure from television is a problem?

- "Not as long as kids learn it's all fake."
- "Sometimes, because Bart is a kid and he uses lots of profanity. Some stupid person may think they can too." (*The Simpsons*)
- "It depends on how it is interpreted and how it is presented. If a child is watching the show, then yes, it is bad. But if a teen or adult watches only for entertainment, it's okay." (*Buffy, the Vampire Slayer*)
- "No, as long as people know the difference between what is real and what is fake, then everything is OK." (*The Jerry Springer Show*)
- "No, because it shows you how to make decisions in different types of situations." (*Beverly Hills 90210*)
- "No, because children know real from make-believe today and it is a very interesting show to watch." (*Sabrina, the Teenage Witch*)
- "No, because it shows that the consequences of things you do are dangerous." (*Real TV*)
- "No they really don't do much violence or drugs ... only sometimes, but they learn from their mistakes." (*Dawson's Creek*)
- "Not really, because this is what goes on in the world, and the kids will learn about it if not from these shows, then definitely from other kids and even the news." (*Guiding Light*)

Clearly, these high school students do not see a problem with what *they* are watching. They may have some reservations about shows for *children*, but they see themselves as mature enough to handle their media messages. Even though we may disagree with them, we try not to push our views on them. There are numerous articles about the effect of television on behavior and attitudes. An appropriate follow-up activity would be to have them read such an article and respond to it. We think it's sufficient at this point to have them reflect on what they're watching and to introduce a note of skepticism. We are confident that if they continue this sort of reflection, they will be able to read television at a more sophisticated level.

Strategies for Bridging Television and the YA Novel

We see three main opportunities for connecting the study of television with the reading of YA novels. First, there are some YA novels with protagonists that become involved in the "behind-the-scenes" world of television. Second, numerous TV series have resulted in novelizations and book tie-ins. Finally, literature teachers can use a student's fondness for a particular television show as an opportunity to recommend YA novels related in theme or situation to the show.

Books Set in the Television World

For a medium that is so pervasive in the lives of adolescents, there are few novels that actually deal with kids and television and the effect of television on teens. Barbara Morgenroth's *In Real Life I'm Just Kate* (1981) gives young adult readers a sense of what happens backstage on a soap opera as sixteen-year-old Kate lands a job on the daytime drama *Life to the Fullest*. In *Adorable Sunday* (Shyer 1983), Sunday Donaldson discovers the dark underside of television when she pursues a career as a TV model. *Confessions of a Prime Time Kid* by Mark Jonathan Harris (1985) is the "autobiography" of Meg Muldar, a thirteen-year-old television star who writes to tell the truth about kids in television. Another novel that takes readers behind the scenes in television production is Julie Reece Deaver's *You Bet Your Life* (1993). In this novel, while Bess is an after-school intern for a popular comedy show, the main conflict centers around the depression and eventual suicide of Bess' mother.

In *Satellite Down* by Rob Thomas (1998), Patrick Sheridan, a journalism student from a small Texas town, is selected as an on-air anchor on Classroom Direct, a Channel One–type news show viewed in high schools across the country. Patrick leaves his staunchly religious parents to live in an apartment in Los Angeles and discovers that the world of television news is not necessarily a world inhabited by people of principles. *Satellite Down* gives readers a close look at the job of a news anchor as well as at the way the television news is packaged.

Two series feature teens and media. Judy Baer's series *Live from Brentwood High* features seven teens in a student-run journalism and broadcast class. In each book in the series, the seven young reporters investigate and report on an issue. In *Double Danger* (1994a), for example, the focus is on gang warfare; in *Price of Silence* (1994b), the team exposes an instance of discrimination in the workplace. Another series—Cherie Bennett's *Trash*—has six teenagers who, out of the thousands who apply, win spots as interns on a hip TV show. While the setting of the show is a television set, other issues predominate. For instance, in *Trash* (1997b), the first book of the series, Chelsea has a deep, dark secret she hopes the other interns will not uncover. Other books in the series include *Good Girls, Bad Boys* (1997a) and *Truth or Scare* (1998).

Television Novelizations and Tie-Ins

Other series currently popular with teens are tie-ins with television shows. For instance, *Dawson's Creek* has spawned several companion books. Jennifer Baker's *Beginning of Everything Else* (1998a) is a novelization of the first two episodes of the series. Other books based on *Dawson's Creek* feature original plots not previously seen on television. Some of these include K. S. Rodriguez's *Long, Hot Summer* (1998) and Jennifer Baker's *Calm Before the Storm* (1998b).

Buffy, the Vampire Slayer has provided numerous opportunities for book tie-ins. Richie Tankersley Cusick, author of such popular vampire books as *The Mall* (1992) and *Silent Stalker* (1993), has written several novelizations of episodes from the television show, including *The Harvest* (1997) and *The Angel Chronicles* (1999). In fact, writing Buffy books seems to have become a cottage industry. In our research we found at least eight other authors who have contributed to the Buffy oeuvre.

Mel Gilden has written several books based on *Beverly Hills 90210*. In *No Secrets* (1992), a novelization of early episodes of the series, the Walsh family moves to Beverly Hills, and the family's teenage children begin to make friends at school. Another television show, *Moesha*, has generated a popular series of books: Stefanie Scott's *Everybody Say Moesha!* (1997a), *Keeping It Real* (1997b), and *Hollywood Hookup* (1998).

Judging from the reported sales on the Amazon.com website, these books based on television shows are doing quite well. We are not entirely sure of the reason for the appeal of these books, but we speculate that a familiarity with the setting and the characters of the series gives tentative readers an entry into these novels and eases some of the intimidation that books engender in readers who lack confidence. We do, however, find some irony in the fact that—in this case, at least—television is leading teens to, not away from, books.

Using Television Shows as a Link to YA Novels

Although we cannot imagine teaching any of the novelizations or tie-ins mentioned above as class novels in an English or language arts class, we can imagine teachers seizing the opportunity to direct students to other young adult books with similar characters, conflicts, and themes. Students who have read, loved, and exhausted all of the *Dawson's Creek* books, for instance, could be led to books by Chris Crutcher, M. E. Kerr, or Lurlene McDaniel. Similarly, teens who follow the Buffy show and read the Buffy books might be ready for the magical realism of Francesca Lia Block or for the more adult vampire books of Anne Rice. African

American teens who have read all the Moesha books might enjoy novels by Walter Dean Myers, Angela Johnson, and Jacqueline Woodson.

Conclusion

When teachers incorporate television and other media into the study of literature and composition, they provide students with an opportunity to learn how to read their world more fully.

Note

As of this writing, network television shows use a rating system designed to advise parents of the appropriateness of the show for children. For example, "TV-G" indicates a program for general audiences with almost no violence, sexual content, or objectionable language. The strongest rating, "TV-MA," is given to shows designed for adults only and considered unsuitable for children under seventeen because of violence, language, or sexual content.

Works Cited

Baer, Judy. 1994a. *Double Danger*. Live from Brentwood High, no. 3. New York: Bethany House.

———. 1994b. *Price of Silence*. Live from Brentwood High, no. 2. New York: Bethany House.

Baker, Jennifer. 1998a. *The Beginning of Everything Else*. New York: Archway.

———. 1998b. *Calm Before the Storm*. New York: Archway.

Bennett, Cherie. 1997a. *Good Girls, Bad Boys*. Trash, no. 3. New York: Berkley.

———. 1997b. *Trash*. Trash, no. 1. New York: Berkley.

———. 1998. *Truth or Scare*. Trash, no. 6. New York: Berkley.

Cusick, Ritchie Tankersley. 1992. *The Mall*. New York: Archway.

———. 1993. *Silent Stalker*. New York: Archway.

———. 1997. *The Harvest*. New York: Archway.

———. 1999. *The Angel Chronicles*. New York: Pocket Books.

Deaver, Julie Reece. 1993. *You Bet Your Life*. New York: HarperCollins.

Gilden, Mel. 1992. *No Secrets*. New York: Harper Paperbacks.

Harris. Mark Jonathan. 1985. *Confessions of a Prime Time Kid*. New York: Lothrop, Lee & Shepard Books.

Morgenroth, Barbara. 1981. *In Real Life I'm Just Kate*. New York: Atheneum.

National Council of Teachers of English & International Reading Association. 1996. *Standards for the English Language Arts*. Urbana, IL, and Newark, DE: National Council of Teachers of English & International Reading Association.

Rodriguez, K. S. 1998. *Long, Hot Summer*. New York: Archway.

Scott, Stefanie. 1997a. *Everybody Say Moesha!* New York: Archway.

———. 1997b. *Keep It Real*. New York: Archway.

———. 1998. *Hollywood Hookup*. New York: Archway.

Shyer, Marlene Fanta. 1983. *Adorable Sunday*. New York: Charles Scribner's Sons.

Teasley, Alan B., and Ann Wilder. 1997. *Reel Conversations: Reading Films with Young Adults*. Portsmouth, NH: Boynton/Cook.

Thomas, Rob. 1998. *Satellite Down*. New York: Simon & Schuster.

13

The Young Adult Novel Under Fire

GLORIA T. PIPKIN

A funny thing happened on the way to the twenty-first century. Challenges to literature in schools and libraries, which had increased steadily and often dramatically for the previous fifteen years, began to decline in the latter half of the 1990s. As Charles Suhor, a field representative of the National Council of Teachers of English (NCTE), noted in 1999, all of the major organizations tracking censorship complaints—the American Library Association, the National Coalition Against Censorship, People for the American Way, and NCTE—reported decreases in incident reports over the previous two or three years.

At the American Library Association, the numbers declined from an all-time high of 740 complaints in 1995, to 664 in 1996, to 595 in 1997. Significant decreases were also seen at NCTE, which compiles semiannual tallies. In comparable six-month periods from 1996–98, the NCTE count went from fifty-two in 1996 to just eleven in 1998 (Suhor 1999, 1). People for the American Way no longer maintains comprehensive annual data, but the number of incidents declined by nearly 10 percent from 1995 to 1996. It should be noted that these data include challenges to children's literature as well as to young adult novels, but the tallies do serve as a barometer of the censorship climate around the country.

Although the drop in censorship incidents may be temporary, there is no shortage of theories about what accounts for the declining numbers. As Suhor reported, various observers and activists have their own interpretations of the data:

ALA's Richard Matthews interprets the decrease as a shift in emphasis. He speculates that "Censors energies are refocusing on the use of the Internet in libraries." High school teacher Carol Jago, editor of *California English*, holds similarly that organized right-wing forces are going after "bigger fish," concentrating on election of sympathetic candidates to office at all levels and on hot button issues like bilingual education and abortion.

Mary Sheehy Moe, a censorship expert at Helena, Montana's Vocational-Technical College, points to the fact that states adopting English standards have often "frozen the curriculum." Lists of approved or suggested works for study serve both to limit teachers' choices and to act as a buffer against protesters, who find themselves challenging materials that have quasi-official status from the outset. (1999, 2)

Jerry Weiss, chair of NCTE's Standing Committee Against Censorship, attributes the decline, at least in part, to self-censorship that leads teachers to choose the least controversial materials in an effort to avoid community conflict (Suhor 1999, 2). Although it is difficult to obtain reliable figures on the frequency of self-censorship, anecdotal evidence abounds, such as a recent post to one of NCTE's e-mail lists in which a teacher asked for recommendations for "safe" books, because, she said, "I don't have time to defend books that kids can read later on their own."

Another disturbing trend I've noted in high schools in my district is a de-emphasis on literature altogether as a result of the imposition of high-stakes testing. Rather than studying young adult novels, students grind out five-paragraph essays on assigned topics or plod through test preparation booklets, answering questions about contrived passages. At our largest high school, the dean of curriculum recently convened the English department to talk about how to raise reading scores on standardized tests. When one teacher made the obvious suggestion—infuse the curriculum and fill classroom libraries with young adult literature—the response from the administrator was, "We have to focus on technical writing because that's what the tests ask students to read." This perception is reinforced by school critics and consultants who view literature as an expendable frill.

What Books Are Being Challenged and Why

Despite the decline in the overall number of challenges to literature in use in schools, teachers all over the country still face the prospect and too often the actuality of hearing the dreaded words, "We've had a complaint about one of your books." The same qualities that account for the young adult novel's appeal to adolescents and its richness as a classroom resource—realism and relevance in plot, themes, and language—also make it a frequent target of censors. Most parents' school experience with literature was limited to safely sanitized anthologies and a few hoary classics, so they aren't familiar with the genre that began to emerge as a distinctive form little more than thirty years ago. Names of authors like Robert Cormier and Jacqueline Woodson carry no cultural weight for most people;

consequently, works by such authors are more vulnerable to attack than those of the stalwarts of the British and American canon. Even among many teachers there persists a strong belief that only "classics" are worthy of school study.

The American Library Association's Office for Intellectual Freedom (ALAOIF) maintains one of the most extensive listings of challenges to materials in schools and libraries. Between 1990 and 1998 ALAOIF recorded 5,246 challenges, although its annual listing suggests that for every incident reported, as many as four or five go unreported. Nearly 70 percent of the formal complaints involved materials in schools or school libraries. In the nineties, the largest category of complaints involved references to sex. The second most common objection, in nearly 22 percent of the cases, was to material containing what the complainants considered to be offensive language. Another fifth contended that the material was inappropriate for the age group for which it was made available.

The last decade has seen a significant rise in the number of complaints alleging occult or "satanic" elements in literature available in schools and libraries. R. L. Stine's *Fear Street* series, for example, has often come under fire for containing demonic motifs. Accusations that materials promote homosexuality and objections to the presence of homosexual characters or themes made up another complaint category that experienced growth in the nineties. Other complaints involved allegations of racism, presence of nudity, and sexuality education (ALA 1999).

A report in NCTE's *SLATE* (Support for the Learning and Teaching of English) *Newsletter* for September 1998 (Suhor) includes challenges to *Always Running* by Luis Rodriguez, for alleged "pornographic" elements; *Deathwatch* by Robb White, for "nudity" resulting when a character takes off underwear to protect burning feet; *Go Ask Alice* by an anonymous author, for profanity; *The Drowning of Stephan Jones* by Bette Greene, for sympathetic portrayal of homosexuality; *Wolf Rider* by Avi; and *A Yellow Raft in Blue Waters* by Michael Dorris.

In People for the American Way's (PFAW) 1996 annual report on school censorship, *Attacks on the Freedom to Learn*, twelve literary works are listed as the "Most Frequently Challenged Books" for that year. Half of those were young adult novels. The challenged YA books included the following:

The Giver, Lois Lowry
The Chocolate War, Robert Cormier
Go Ask Alice, Anonymous
A Day No Pigs Would Die, Robert Newton Peck
My Brother Sam Is Dead, Christopher and James Lincoln Collier
Bridge to Terabithia, Katherine Paterson

As this list suggests, even the best young adult literature can trigger the urge to suppress. A closer look at some of the challenges to *The Giver*, winner of the

1994 Newbery Medal, provides insight into the censors' mindset and shows a variety of outcomes:

- A parent in Franklin County, Kansas, filed a formal complaint against Lowry's novel on the grounds that it is "concerned with murder, suicide, and the degradation of motherhood and adolescence." The book was removed from elementary libraries but remains available for classroom use at teachers' discretion.
- In Wrenshall, Minnesota, a school board member and two parents objected to the inclusion of *The Giver* on a list of books to be purchased for a high school, on the grounds of offensive language and objectionable themes (PFAW's characterization of the complaints). The school board approved the book but stipulated that parents would receive a list of books to be studied during the year.
- Johnson County, Missouri, complainants charged *The Giver* with desensitizing children to euthanasia and asked that the book "not be read in class to children under high school age." The book remains in the high school section of the K–12 library.
- A parent in Sidney, New York, publicly objected to the novel's "usage of mind control, selective breeding, and the elimination of the old and young alike when they are weak, feeble and of no more use . . ." but did not file a formal complaint.
- Somewhere in Oklahoma (no city given), a parent objected to the novel's use of terms such as *clairvoyance, transcendent,* and *guided imagery,* because these are "all occult New Age practices the Bible tells us to avoid." The review committee voted unanimously to retain the book but prohibited it from being read aloud in fourth grade. The committee also recommended that immature readers be discouraged from trying it and that the librarian should make fewer copies available.
- In the absence of a formal review policy, language arts teachers in Medford, Oregon, decided not to use the book in seventh-grade classrooms after a parent complained of graphic descriptions of euthanasia. (PFAW 1996)

Who Are the Censors?

In the eighties, censorship efforts were often spearheaded by local groups, some of which were affiliated with, inspired by, or represented by national organizations such as the Christian Coalition, Concerned Women for America, the Eagle Forum, and Citizens for Excellence in Education. In contrast, most challengers in the nineties are individuals who either have no ties to such groups or who don't openly acknowledge them. Unfortunately, the number of teachers and school officials who seek to remove books is on the rise.

One of the most sophisticated attacks of the last decade was launched in 1998 by a group in Richland, Washington, calling itself Citizens for Academic Responsibility. When English departments at the two Richland high schools decided to expand their literature curriculum by adding sets of books for small-group reading in literature circles, they submitted a list of more than eighty books for approval by the school board. A few parents objected to some of the titles, prompting two conservative board members to push for the creation of citizens review committees.

After the Richland school board considered the citizens' reviews and approved all the books, Citizens for Academic Responsibility (CAR) created a website on which they critiqued the literature curriculum of the two high schools in the district. The CAR home page designated the site as "a community effort to keep parents in touch with their public school . . ." offering "mini reviews for the books used as well as discussion questions for home use." They also made clear their perspective: "If your family assumes a Biblical worldview, these questions should help you and your student to draw some of the truths out of this reading material and be able to dismiss some of the falsehoods that flow through it" (CAR 1998).

CAR also wrote a letter to all the youth pastors in town telling them that the books were required reading and that "God will use our stand to call His People to fulfill their Christian roles and take charge of their children's education."

Late in 1998, CAR filed formal complaints against seven of the books, including Sandra Cisneros' *House on Mango Street*, and *Jay's Journal*, and posted their objections on their website. The review committee recommended that all of the challenged books remain available for use, although two teachers on the committee voted to remove *Jay's Journal*. The complainants have indicated they will appeal the committee's recommendations, which will take the controversy into its second year.

We often hear that censorship stems from the left end of the political spectrum as well as from the right, but I have found little evidence of this regarding attacks on young adult literature. Although Ann Rinaldi's novel *My Heart Is on the Ground*, one of the fictionalized diaries published by Scholastic in its *Dear America* series, has received scathing criticism from Native Americans—and others—who object to its portrayal of the experiences of native children who attended government-run boarding schools in the latter part of the nineteenth century, the book's critics have thus far stopped short of advocating censorship. Some of its critics have made clear their opinion that the book should never be selected by culturally sensitive teachers and librarians, and others have indicated that it should be placed on a "high shelf," but I have been unable to document any actual challenges to the book's presence in schools or libraries. For a fascinating discussion of the book's flaws as well as a response from the publisher, see the archives of the children's literature e-mail discussion list maintained at Rutgers University (Joseph 1999).

Professional Preparation: The Best Defense Against Censorship

One of the most effective tools teachers who use young adult literature in the classroom have for defusing controversy and defending their books against censorship is a carefully prepared professional rationale. Basically, a rationale is a statement explaining why teachers chose a particular work and how they plan to use it in the classroom. SLATE, the intellectual freedom network of NCTE, offers guidelines for teachers to use in developing professional perspectives on curriculum, which I have adapted slightly.

Guidelines for Writing a Rationale

1. **The bibliographic citation:** A rationale should begin with a complete bibliographic citation including author's name, complete book title, publisher, publication date, edition, and number of pages.
2. **The intended audience:** The rationale should articulate the type of class and the range of grade levels at which the book will be used. It should indicate whether the book is going to be used for individual study, small-group work such as literature circles, or whole-class study.
3. **A brief summary of the work:** The summary provides a context for the rationale as well as an overview of the book for anyone who chooses to read it. It can also reflect aspects of the work that the teacher considers most important and aspects that relate to its educational significance.
4. **The relationship of the work to the program:** The rationale should state the curricular goals, objectives, themes, units, and so on that the work addresses and how will it be used to meet them.
5. **The impact of the work:** The rationale should discuss the potential impact on readers' perspectives, behavior, and attitudes.
6. **Potential problems with the work:** The reflective process of developing a rationale is an opportunity for anticipating uses of language, actions, and situations that might be the source of challenges to the work. The rationale should also include a plan for addressing potential problems.
7. **Critical support for the work:** Critical reviews, published rationales, professional book lists, and other professional selection tools that address or include the work should be listed in the rationale or physically attached to it.
8. **Related works:** The rationale should include a list of works for supplemental reading or for consideration as alternative selections when students

or families opt out of reading the assigned work. (Brown and Stephens 1994, 2)

Sample Rationale for Robert Cormier's *Tenderness*

The rationale that follows is slightly amended from a version published in "Rationales for Challenged Material," a themed issue of *Statement*, the journal of the Colorado Language Arts Society edited by Louann Reid.

Bibliographic Information

Cormier, Robert. *Tenderness*. New York: Delacorte. 1997.

Intended Audience

This work can be read and studied profitably by students in grades 9–12, depending on the maturity, interest, and ability of the readers themselves. Such decisions are best made by teachers who know both the students and the novel well.

Summary

Fifteen-year-old Lori Cranston decides to leave home to avoid the growing chemistry between her and her mother's boyfriend. A nomadic existence with her well-intentioned but alcoholic single mother has forced Lori into a self-reliance that sometimes involves using her sexuality to get what she needs, although she has thus far managed to remain a virgin. Her latest hitchhiking odyssey takes her to a small town in Massachusetts, where she sees a televised news story about Eric Poole, an eighteen-year-old being released from a juvenile facility after serving three years for killing his mother and stepfather. Lori recognizes Eric from a brief encounter a few years back in which he rescued her from a group of bikers, and she becomes obsessed with seeing him again. What Lori doesn't know (and what the reader knows almost from the beginning) is that Eric has also murdered and sexually assaulted three girls. The story moves inexorably toward the fateful meeting of two young people seeking their own forms of tenderness.

Relationship of the Work to the Program

The novel is an excellent vehicle for addressing two overarching goals of any English program: social imagination and critical literacy. Through the study of this novel, learners will read and experience literature as a record of human experience. The novel offers unique opportunities to understand unfamiliar people and events by exploring the motives and actions of the novel's protagonist and antagonist. Students will develop critical literacy as they use literary terminology (including theme, irony, diction, style, characterization, point of view, and epigraph) accurately, examine and extend personal responses to literature, compare and contrast the novel with other works of American literature (Faulkner's *Light in August* is one with many parallels), and analyze and form judgments about the characters' action as well as the literary quality of the novel.

The novel is suitable for whole-class study or for use in small groups such as literature circles. Teaching strategies may include (but are not limited to) silent and oral reading, response logs, graphic organizers, Socratic discussion, oral interpretation, readers theatre, and formal writing on self-selected aspects of the novel. Assessment methods may include examination of response logs, teacher monitoring of discussions, essay examination, or independent projects.

Impact of the Work on Readers

This novel provides readers with a haunting perspective on two interrelated and deeply troubling issues of contemporary American society: personal violence suffered by children and adolescents and its complex relationship to violent juvenile crime. The novel can also serve as the impetus for exploring factors that foster resilience in children, that is, the qualities that enable many youth—even those with multiple and severe risks in their lives—to develop into confident, competent, caring adults.

Potential Problems and Ways to Address Them

The novel's antagonist is a juvenile serial killer, and although his crimes are not presented in a sensational manner, the basic premise of the novel may trouble some readers. Students understand fairly readily that to read about crimes is not to condone them, and parents, too, can be helped to achieve this understanding. *Tenderness* no more promotes serial killing than *Romeo and Juliet* glorifies teenage suicide. There are also a few passages that depict sexual activity, but these are neither gratuitous nor unnecessarily explicit. For those who find the novel objectionable despite efforts to inform and enlighten them, alternative selections are available.

References

Robert Cormier is widely recognized as one of the preeminent authors writing for adolescents today. An overview of his work and critical views of his earlier novels are available in *Presenting Robert Cormier* by Patricia Campbell.

Booklist (February 1, 1997) called "Cormier's latest . . . a mesmerizing plunge into the mind of a psychopathic teen killer that is both deeply disturbing and utterly compelling." *School Library Journal*'s March 1997 reviewer noted that "The ugliness of the story contrasts with the beauty of the language. . . . Where other writers would have screamed the story in full-blown tabloid prose, Cormier is the model of decorum." *The Horn Book Magazine* (March/April 1997) review characterized Cormier as "a master of irony" and this novel as "suspenseful and chilling."

Related Works

Nathan's Run by John Gilstrap
Hard Time: A Real Look at Juvenile Crime by Janet Bode and Stan Mack
Light in August by William Faulkner
Run, Shelley, Run by Gertrude Samuels
Oliver Twist by Charles Dickens
Letters from the Inside by John Marsden (Pipkin 1997)

Although I strongly advise teachers to develop their own rationales, tailored to their particular students, curriculum, and communities, it can be helpful to use others' rationales in establishing a work's use in widespread professional practice. In addition to the Colorado journal referenced above, Louann Reid has published another collection of rationales with Calendar Islands Press. NCTE sells a CD-ROM (*Rationales for Challenged Books*), prepared in cooperation with the International Reading Association, that contains more than two hundred rationales. The American Library Association has published *Hit List*, and Karolides, Burress, and Kean have two collections.

Instructional Materials Selection and Review Policies

Many school districts have adopted policies that spell out how new materials must be approved for use in the schools (the "selection" part of the process) and what happens if they are challenged (the review process). Organizations that monitor school censorship incidents, including the National Coalition Against Censorship and People for the American Way, report that districts with such policies in place are generally more successful in resisting censorship. All English departments and all language arts teachers should make it a priority to find out if their district has adopted a policy and to familiarize themselves with its requirements.

Although selection and review policies sometimes protect instructional materials from illegal removal, they also have their drawbacks. In my school district, for example, the local policy is a lengthy, cumbersome, formidable document. In its current form, it is more than fifteen pages long. The approval process—the sections of the policy that deal with getting new materials into the system—requires that any new book go through several levels of examination, ending at the school board. The policy is so byzantine that even school officials who are charged with administering it misinterpret and misrepresent it.

In my view, in the best of all possible policies, the approval process would consist of two sentences: Teachers or departments using non-state-adopted materials as primary instructional tools will submit a rationale to the principal. Lists of these materials and the accompanying rationales will be kept on file within each school, available for public review.

Although there are many problems with cumbersome approval processes as they are embedded in typical school board policies for selection of instructional materials, graver dangers lie with the provisions for review of challenged material. By spelling out in detail what procedures must be followed during review, we deliver a blueprint for the legal removal of books. When we set up review committees, establish time lines, specify appellate rights, and so on, in effect, we are saying to would-be censors, "Follow these steps, and you can censor with impunity."

In light of the pitfalls of such policies, teachers and departments should study them carefully and make sure they understand their provisions. Favorable amendments are much more easily accomplished when they are addressed calmly and routinely rather than in the midst of controversy stemming from challenges. Several years ago my colleague Alyne Farrell and I studied policies from around our state and made some recommendations regarding what we considered to be critical provisions:

- **Clear definitions of categories of instructional materials and processes for approval.** State-adopted textbooks, classroom library books, and supplemental novels used for whole-class study should all be addressed.
- **Specific and reasonable timelines for both approval and review processes.**
- **Specific provisions for challenged materials to remain in use while under review.** Any other arrangement constitutes prior review (assuming material to be guilty until proven innocent) and could conceivably be used to paralyze a school system through simultaneous challenges to multiple works.
- **Non-cumbersome approval procedures and exemptions for certain types of materials.** Teachers should not be burdened with delays that interfere with "the teachable moment."
- **Equitable review process.** Review meetings should be open to the public and allow advocacy by all parties.
- **Provision for subject-area expertise on all selection and review committees.** (Pipkin and Farrell 1986, 25)

179

Teaching About Censorship

Some teachers choose to educate themselves and their students about censorship by developing units around the theme of "Freedom to Read" or other aspects of the First Amendment. A number of young adult novels, including the following, address intellectual freedom issues.

- *The Last Safe Place on Earth* by Richard Peck
- *Memoirs of a Bookbat* by Kathryn Lasky
- *Nothing But the Truth* by Avi
- *The Day They Came to Arrest the Book* by Nat Hentoff

Lois Lowry's *The Giver*, with its themes of sacrificing freedom for the illusion of safety, also provides rich possibilities for inquiry and discussion of intellectual freedom issues.

Teachers may also encourage students to consider censorship-related topics for research papers and other projects. In helping students consider the underlying issues from a variety of perspectives, teachers develop a cadre of informed citizens who will be much more likely to help defend the right to read when the occasion arises.

Teaching resources on the First Amendment are available from the organizations below:

First Amendment Congress
University of Colorado at Denver
Graduate School of Public Affairs
1445 Market St., Suite 320
Denver, CO 80202
303-820-5688

The Freedom Forum
1101 Wilson Blvd.
Arlington, VA 22209
703-528-0800
http://www.freedomforum.org

At the Freedom Forum website, the Youth Guide to the First Amendment (*http://www.freedomforum.org/FreedomForumTextonly/resources/hs_and_coll/Youth_Guide_to_1A.html*) includes background information on the First Amendment; summaries of key U.S. Supreme Court rulings; discussions of current controversial issues including newspaper censorship, dress codes, school prayer, book banning, hate speech, "gangsta" rap, warning labels, and flag burning; suggestions for papers and projects; and pertinent quotes related to the First Amendment.

Other Resources

A wide variety of information about school censorship is available from the following organizations and websites:

National Council of Teachers of English
1111 Kenyon Road
Urbana, IL 61801–1096
800-369-6283; FAX 217-328-9645
http://www.ncte.org/

Among the materials and services available from NCTE are the following:

The Students' Right to Read—includes information on developing policies for material selection and review (free; available on-line at *http://ncte.org/positions/right.html*)
Guidelines for Dealing with Censorship of Nonprint Materials—addresses TV, film, software, and so on (available on-line at *http://ncte.org/positions/nonprint.html*)
Guidelines for Selection of Materials in English Language Arts (free)
Selection and Retention of Instructional Material—*What the Courts Have Said*
Common Ground—joint NCTE/IRA statement on intellectual freedom (free; available on-line at *http://ncte.org/positions/common.html*)
Preserving Intellectual Freedom: Fighting Censorship in Our Schools by Jean Brown

American Library Association
Office for Intellectual Freedom
50 E. Huron St.
Chicago, IL 60611
800-545-2433, ext. 4223; FAX 312-280-4227
http://www.ala.org/oif.html

ALA's Office for Intellectual Freedom has the following materials available:

Censorship and Selection: Issues and Answers for Schools
Censorship in the Schools (brochure)
Newsletter on Intellectual Freedom (bimonthly)
Workbook for Selection Policy Writing

National Coalition Against Censorship
275 7th Ave.
New York, NY 10001
212-807-6222; FAX 212-807-6245
ncac@netcom.com
http://www.ncac.org/

NCAC, an umbrella organization of more than forty national groups, provides support and assistance to those resisting censorship.

> American Civil Liberties Union
> ACLU Freedom Network: *http:www/aclu.org*

In addition to free speech, the ACLU website addresses students' rights, church and state issues, lesbian and gay rights, and much more. An on-line library provides complete texts of many relevant articles. There's also a section featuring first-person accounts of people, including students, who have taken stands on First Amendment issues (*http://www.aclu.org/court/clients/whoclient.html*).

The national office of the ACLU doesn't deal with individual cases of censorship; those must be reported through state ACLU offices. Contact information for each state organization is available at the website.

> People for the American Way
> 200 M St., NW
> Suite 400
> Washington, DC 20036
> 202-467-2388; FAX 202-293-2672
> *pfaw@pfaw.org*
> *http://www.pfaw.org*

From 1982 to 1996, PFAW published an annual report on school censorship called *Attacks on the Freedom to Learn*, which documented challenges to school materials and methods on a state-by-state basis. Copies of most of these reports are still available from PFAW. The annual report has since been replaced with a bimonthly newsletter of the same name. E-mail subscriptions to the newsletter are available on-line. An on-line form also invites reports of censorship incidents. PFAW occasionally provides legal support in important cases.

Materials available from PFAW include these items:

> *An Activist's Guide to Protecting the Freedom to Learn* (kit)—provides information and tools for organizing pro–public education advocates to combat censorship efforts and participate in school board races
> *Redondo Beach: A Stand Against Censorship* (1990)—a videotaped documentary of one community's successful resistance to school censorship

Response to Challenges

If, despite highly professional preparation, young adult novels come under attack, there is much teachers and departments can do. Teachers should make every effort to talk personally with parents, and with the department head, grade-group chair, principal, or some other ally present. Many parental concerns can be successfully addressed by school personnel who listen respectfully, provide copies of rationales, and make it clear that they're willing to work with the parent in choosing a mutually acceptable alternative and procedures for study. A good review policy should require complainants to start at the school level, with the teacher, before filing a formal complaint. Many grievances can be resolved at this level if cool heads prevail.

Teachers should be scrupulous about taking detailed notes during or after every conference or incident remotely connected with censorship. If the case goes to court, contemporaneous notes are invaluable. If it doesn't, these notes can serve as the basis for articles or even a book. Archives should also include dated news clippings and other artifacts such as memos, letters, relevant policies, the formal complaint, the teacher or department's response, and the rationale for the book. A portable file box makes the collection more accessible and useful.

Once a formal complaint is filed, I strongly recommend that teachers respond to it in writing and make copies of the defense available to all members of the review committee as well as to the press. If student responses to the work are available, those should also be included. Offering copies of the book to the review committee generates goodwill, but it is important to make it clear that they must be returned. In states with open government laws, the review committee meetings are open to the public, and teachers should be allowed to speak as advocates. Of course, so will the complainant(s).

For other assistance in defending young adult novels, teachers should contact NCTE and PFAW, their state affiliate of NCTE and NCAC, and the state ACLU office. After gathering the facts, these organizations will provide help that includes letters of support, organizing advice, moral support, and other technical assistance. Incidents can also be reported at the PFAW website, and NCTE will soon have a similar feature available on its website. Teachers who subscribe to professional e-mail discussion lists can post notices there and ask for advice, encouragement, or specific help.

Once a formal complaint is filed, calling attention to the challenge, the teacher should consider contacting local media, who are natural allies in censorship battles. Local talk shows (preferably on an NPR station) are another means of educating the public if the host is sympathetic; otherwise, there's danger of an ambush. Spokespersons should learn to speak in sound bites.

Teachers unions can be helpful when contractual violations are involved in the censorship. Some unions have strong intellectual freedom clauses that can be invoked. In major cases with egregious violations, the unions occasionally provide legal representation.

Public meetings provide another venue for informing and organizing natural allies such as supportive parents, colleagues, librarians, booksellers, civil libertarians, personal friends, professional organizations, and groups connected with the arts, theatre, music, and so on. These meetings can also be used to arrange guest appearances at local civic clubs and to organize letter-writing campaigns aimed at the local media and school officials and school board members. Special events such as "Banned Books Readings" at local coffeehouses, bookstores, libraries, community events, and so on also call attention to censorship and attract allies.

Resisting censorship is often an exhausting and disheartening enterprise as attacks on the freedom to learn take new forms and as we realize that the victories are never final. In her 1993 Nobel lecture, Toni Morrison used that august forum to sound a clarion call to all who value the right to read:

> Be it grand or slender, burrowing, blasting, or refusing to sanctify, whether it laughs out loud or is a cry without an alphabet, the choice word or the chosen silence, unmolested language surges toward knowledge, not its destruction. But who does not know of literature that is banned because it is interrogative; discredited because it is critical; erased because alternative? And how many are outraged by the thought of a self-ravaged tongue?
>
> . . . We die. That may be the meaning of life. But we do language. That may be the measure of our lives. (1994, 21–22)

How effectively we resist the efforts of those who would limit what we may read and learn in school may well be the most important measure of our own lives.

Works Cited

American Library Association. 1999. "The Most Frequently Challenged Books of 1998." *http://www.ala.org/bbooks/challeng.html#mfcb*, 1 July.

American Library Association's Young Adult Services Division's Intellectual Freedom Committee. 1989. *Hit List: Frequently Challenged Young Adult Titles: References to Defend Them.* Chicago: ALA.

Brown, Jean E., and Elaine C. Stephens. 1994. "Rationales for Teaching Challenged Books." SLATE Starter Sheet, April.

Citizens for Academic Responsibility. 1998. *http://www.televar.com/~crbatish*, 28 October.

Joseph, Michael. 1999. "Archives of child_lit." *http://www.scils.rutgers.edu/childlit/april99/0157.html*, 1 July.

Karolides, Nicholas J., Lee Burress, and John M. Kean, eds. 1993. *Censored Books: Critical Viewpoints.* Lanham, MD: Scarecrow.

Morrison, Toni. 1994. *Lecture and Speech of Acceptance, upon the Award of the Nobel Prize for Literature, Delivered in Stockholm on the Seventh of December.* New York: Alfred A. Knopf.

People for the American Way. 1996. *Attacks on the Freedom to Learn 1996 Report.* Washington, D.C.: People for the American Way.

Pipkin, Gloria. 1997. "Tenderness." *Statement: Rationales for Challenged Material* 33.3: 37–38.

Pipkin, Gloria Treadwell, and Alyne Farrell. 1986. "Instructional Materials Selection and Review: A Report of a Survey." *Florida English Journal* 22.2: 22–25.

Reid, Louann. 1999. *Rationales for Teaching Young Adult Literature.* Portland, ME: Calendar Islands.

Suhor, Charles. 1998. "From the Front Line: Update on Help from SLATE." *SLATE Newsletter* 23.2: 1–3.

———. 1999. "Censorship Cases Down, Various Organizations Report." *SLATE Newsletter* 24.2: 1–2.

Recommended Reading

Christenbury, Leila, ed. 1997. *English Journal.* 86.2 (February). Themed issue on censorship includes an important article challenging "the myth of appropriateness" and accounts of teaching about censorship.

DelFattore, Joan. 1992. *What Johnny Shouldn't Read: Textbook Censorship in America.* New Haven: Yale University Press.

Foerstel, Herbert N. 1994. *Banned in the U.S.A.: A Reference Guide to Book Censorship in Schools and Public Libraries.* Westport, CT: Greenwood.

Moffett, James. 1988. *Storm in the Mountains: A Case Study of Censorship, Conflict, and Consciousness.* Carbondale, IL: Southern Illinois University Press. Moffett's involvement in the violent 1975 Kanahwa County, West Virginia, censorship case led him to return eight years later and explore the roots and effects of censorship by interviewing many of the principals. His analysis is the best I've found.

Moshman, David. 1993. "Adolescent Reasoning, Adolescent Rights." *Human Development* 36: 27–40. Moshman is an educational psychologist whose work on the intellectual abilities of adolescents can help us in making the case for their intellectual freedom. From his conclusion: "Nothing about this process [of socializing each new generation] requires restriction on what adolescents may believe, express, or encounter."

Pipkin, Gloria T. 1993. "Challenging the Conventional Wisdom on Censorship." *The ALAN Review* 20.2 (Winter): 35–37. A critical look at instructional material selection and review policies.

———. "Confessions of an Accused Pornographer." 1994. *Arizona English Bulletin* 37.1 (Spring):13–18. Summarizes my own epic (five-year) battle with censors in Northwest Florida.

Contributors

Sue Ellen Bridgers' books include *Home Before Dark*, *All Together Now*, *Notes for Another Life*, *Sara Will*, *Permanent Connections*, *Keeping Christina*, and *All We Know of Heaven*. She lives in the Great Smoky Mountains of North Carolina.

Leila Christenbury is a former high school English teacher and is currently a professor of English education at Virginia Commonwealth University, Richmond. A past coeditor of *The ALAN Review* and a past editor of the *English Journal*, she was recently given the Rewey Belle Inglis Award for Outstanding Woman in English Education. Christenbury has published numerous articles and chapters on teaching and is the author of *Making the Journey* (Heinemann, 2000), which has been newly revised. She is currently the president-elect of NCTE.

Pam B. Cole is assistant professor of middle grades English education at Kennesaw State University, Kennesaw, Georgia. She teaches language arts methods, reading, interdisciplinary teaching, and adolescent literature for middle grades teachers. Vice president of the Georgia Council of Teachers of English, NCTE's state affiliate, she serves as ALAN (Assembly on Literature for Adolescents of NCTE) representative for the state of Georgia and is a member of the executive board for SIGNAL.

Chris Crowe is a professor of English at Brigham Young University, where he teaches courses in young adult literature, English education, and creative writing. He is editor of the Young Adult Literature column for the *English Journal* and the author of *Presenting Mildred D. Taylor* (Twayne, 1999). A former high school English teacher and coach, he has long had an interest in YA literature and sports.

Ted Hipple, one of the founders and a former president of ALAN and currently its executive secretary, is a professor of teacher education at the University of

Tennessee, Knoxville. He is editor of *Writers for Young Adults*, a four-volume reference series published by Charles Scribner's Sons, which offers 170 biocritical essays about writers who are widely read by young adults.

Will Hobbs is the award-winning author of eleven novels for middle school and young adult readers as well as two picture book stories. Six of his novels—*Bearstone, Downriver, The Big Wander, Beardance, Far North,* and *The Maze*—were named Best Books for Young Adults by the American Library Association, which also named *Downriver* one of the "100 Best of the Best Young Adult Books from the past 25 years." *Far North* was selected by the ALA as one of the "Top Ten" young adult books of 1996, and *Ghost Canoe* received the Edgar Allan Poe award in 1998 for Best Young Adult Mystery. A graduate of Stanford University and a former reading and language arts teacher, Hobbs lives with his wife, Jean, in Durango, Colorado.

Patricia P. Kelly, a former English teacher and department head, is professor of English education and director of the Center for Teacher Education at Virginia Tech. She has also been the director of the Southwest Virginia Writing Project for twenty years. She is a past president of the Assembly on Literature for Adolescents, NCTE, a former coeditor of *The ALAN Review*, and a former editor of *SIGNAL*, the journal of the International Reading Association (IRA) special-interest group on adolescent literature. She has been published in *English Journal, Journal of Reading,* and *Journal of Youth Services in Libraries*, among others, and has written critical analyses of young adult writers for the series *Writers for Young Adults*.

M. E. Kerr is a pseudonym for Marijane Meaker. Another of her pseudonyms when she writes for young people is Mary James. Kerr was born in Auburn, New York, and educated at Stuart Hall in Staunton, Virginia, and at the University of Missouri. She was given the Margaret E. Edwards Award in 1993 and an honorary doctorate in English literature from Long Island University in 1996. She lives in East Hampton, New York.

Virginia R. Monseau is professor of English at Youngstown State University, Youngstown, Ohio, where she teaches graduate and undergraduate courses in young adult literature, children's literature, English methods, and composition. Named Ohio's Outstanding College English Teacher in 1996, she is active in NCTE, serving on several commissions and committees, and is a past president of the Western Reserve of Ohio Teachers of English. Her publications include *Missing Chapters: Ten Pioneering Women in NCTE and English Education* (NCTE, 1991); *Presenting Ouida Sebestyen* (Twayne, 1995); and *Responding to Young Adult*

Literature (Boynton/Cook, 1996), as well as numerous articles, book chapters, and book reviews. With Gary Salvner, she has coedited a CD-ROM: *A Complete Guide to Young Adult Literature: Over 1000 Critiques and Synopses from* The ALAN Review (Boynton/Cook, 1997). A past president of ALAN, she is currently the editor of *English Journal*.

John Noell Moore is assistant professor of English education at The College of William and Mary, where he directs the program in secondary school certification (English) and teaches courses in young adult literature and secondary methods. The author of *Interpreting Young Adult Literature: Literary Theory in the Secondary Classroom* (Boynton/Cook, 1998), he has published articles in *The ALAN Review*, *Theory into Practice*, and other journals. He is editor of the "Talk About Books" column for the *English Journal* and of "The Library Connection" for *The ALAN Review*. He has taught secondary English in both public and private schools.

Gloria Pipkin taught English in Florida public schools for more than twenty years. When her junior high department's use of young adult literature came under fire during the 1980s, she led the defense that included a federal lawsuit against the school district. For her anticensorship efforts, Pipkin received the 1989 Courage Foundation Award, with C. Everett Koop, Paul Volcker, and Rudy Guiliani as co-recipients. She has written widely about intellectual freedom.

Gary M. Salvner, a former elementary and secondary teacher, is professor and chair of the English department at Youngstown State University, Ohio, where he teaches courses in English methods and young adult and children's literature. A former president of NCTE's Assembly on Literature for Adolescents and Ohio College English Teacher of the Year, he is the author of *Presenting Gary Paulsen* (Twayne, 1996) and *Literature Festival* (Interaction Publishers, 1991), a book of writing games designed to evoke student response to literature.

Lois Stover is chair of the educational studies department at St. Mary's College of Maryland, where she teaches courses in educational psychology, secondary school teaching methods, and children's and young adult literature. A former English and drama teacher at the high school and middle grade levels, she received her doctorate in curriculum and instruction from the University of Virginia. She has written about young adult literature throughout her career in higher education and has published titles including *Presenting Phyllis Reynolds Naylor* (Twayne, 1997) and *Young Adult Literature: The Heart of the Middle School Curriculum* (Boynton/Cook, 1996). With Stephanie Zenker, she coedited *Books for You* (1997), NCTE's annotated reading list for high school students. She has edited the Adolescent

Literature column for *English Journal* and has served as president of the Assembly on Literature for Adolescents of NCTE.

Alan B. Teasley currently serves as executive director for grants administration in the Durham, North Carolina, public schools and holds an adjunct faculty appointment at Duke University. He has taught English at the high school and college levels, including courses in composition, mass communications, filmmaking, and film criticism. His articles have appeared in *English Journal, The Iowa English Bulletin, Media and Methods, Telemedium,* and *The ALAN Review.* He is the coauthor of *Reel Conversations: Reading Films with Young Adults* (Boynton/Cook, 1997), a book for middle and high school English teachers on incorporating the study of film into the teaching of literature and composition.

Ann Wilder teaches English, mass communications, and young adult literature at Southern High School in Durham, North Carolina. She frequently conducts workshops and writes articles on using film and young adult literature in the English classroom. She is the coauthor, with Alan Teasley, of *Reel Conversations: Reading Films with Young Adults* (Boynton/Cook, 1997).

About the CD

The enclosed CD-ROM is designed to provide you with easy access to information about the best of young adult literature from the past twenty years. Here you will find nearly 2,000 critiques and synopsis of books for young adults—information that was originally published in The ALAN Review, the NCTE's journal for Young Adult Literature.

Searchable by title, author, appropriate grade level, theme, and genre, this CD is an invaluable teaching tool that will help you both plan your instruction and familiarize yourself with this rich and diverse body of literature. It will also lend your students a hand in finding and selecting books to read on the topics and themes that interest theme most.

Publication information for each book is provided on the CD-ROM.